○ ○ ● ● ●

BEYOND THE FORMALIST-REALIST DIVIDE

● ● ● ○ ○

BEYOND THE FORMALIST-REALIST DIVIDE

○ ○ ● ● ●

The Role of Politics in Judging

Brian Z. Tamanaha

Princeton University Press
Princeton and Oxford

Published by Princeton University Press,
41 William Street, Princeton, New Jersey 08540

In the United Kingdom: Princeton University Press,
6 Oxford Street, Woodstock, Oxfordshire OX20 1TW

Tamanaha, Brian Z.
Beyond the formalist-realist divide : the role of politics
in judging / Brian Z. Tamanaha.
p.   cm.
Includes bibliographical references and index.
ISBN 978-0-691-14279-1 (hardcover : alk. paper) —
ISBN 978-0-691-14280-7 (pbk. : alk. paper)
1. Judges—United States. 2. Judicial process—United States.
3. Law—Political aspects—United States. 4. Law—
United States—Philosophy. I. Title.
KF8775.T36 2009
347.73′14—dc22   2009019801

British Library Cataloging-in-Publication Data is available

This book has been composed in Palatino and Copperplate Gothic

Printed on acid-free paper. ∞

press.princeton.edu

Printed in the United States of America

3   5   7   9   10   8   6   4   2

For my little Sava

CONTENTS

○ ○ ● ● ●

ACKNOWLEDGMENTS

○ ○ ● ● ●

THIS BOOK WAS WRITTEN at the Institute for Advanced Study, where I had the privilege of being a Member of the School of Social Sciences in 2007–8. I am deeply grateful to the Institute for inviting me to spend a year in this unmatched setting. I also thank St. John's University School of Law for supporting my stay at the Institute with a research leave.

Many individuals offered helpful critical feedback on earlier drafts of the book. I owe special thanks to two reviewers for Princeton University Press. They helped me refine the argument and trim some of its excesses. I owe double thanks to Sandy Levinson, once for his comments on the manuscript and a second time for writing a letter that helped me gain an invitation to the IAS. I am indebted beyond repayment to Sandy for his generosity and support for my work over the years.

I thank Lawrence Friedman and Robert Gordon for their detailed feedback at an early stage in the project, when I was struggling to make sense of the situation. Bob pushed me to clarify the meaning of formalism in a way that helped crystallize the argument. I thank Ed Purcell for his patient and detailed responses to the argument about the formalists and Mark Fenster for a series of exchanges on the argument about the realists. I thank Frederick Schauer for responding to my argument about his position on the "No vehicles in the park" debate. I thank David Klein and David Law for their comments on the argument about quantitative studies of judging. I thank Brian MacDonald for his meticulous editing of the manuscript. In addition, I benefited from comments I received when presenting parts of the book to the law faculties at Washington University, the University of Toronto, the University of Texas, Vanderbilt University, Boston University, Rutgers University at Camden, Suffolk University, and the NYU Legal History Colloquium. The book improved substantially through testing before such knowledgeable audiences. I thank everyone who commented on these occasions. Modified versions of Chapters Five and Six have been published in *Texas Law Review*, and modified versions of Chapters Seven and Eight have been published in *Boston College Law Review*. I thank the law reviews for allowing me to reuse this material.

I thank Chuck Myers, my editor at Princeton University Press, for his enthusiastic support for this project. It is terrific to have an editor with so much knowledge and interest in the subject.

Finally, I thank my family. Honorata makes everything I do possible. Jolijt, Kats, Vinny, and Sava are understanding, supportive, and fun.

BEYOND THE FORMALIST-REALIST DIVIDE

1

○ ○ ● ● ●

INTRODUCTION

PERSPECTIVES ON JUDGING in the United States are dominated by a story about the formalists and the realists. From the 1870s through the 1920s—the heyday of legal formalism—lawyers and judges saw law as autonomous, comprehensive, logically ordered, and determinate and believed that judges engaged in pure mechanical deduction from this body of law to produce single correct outcomes. In the 1920s and 1930s, building upon the insights of Oliver Wendell Holmes, Roscoe Pound, and Benjamin Cardozo, the legal realists discredited legal formalism, demonstrating that the law is filled with gaps and contradictions, that the law is indeterminate, that there are exceptions for almost every legal rule or principle, and that legal principles and precedents can support different results. The realists argued that judges decide according to their personal preferences and then construct the legal analysis to justify the desired outcome.

This is the standard chronicle within legal circles as well as in political science, repeated numerous times by legal historians, political scientists who study courts, legal theorists, and others. A recent article on judging coauthored by two law professors and a federal judge begins:

> How *do* judges judge? According to the formalists, judges apply the governing law to the facts of a case in a logical, mechanical, and deliberative way. For the formalists, the judicial system is a "giant syllogism machine," and the judge acts like a "highly skilled mechanic." Legal realism, on the other hand, represents a sharp contrast. . . . For the realists, the judge "decides by feeling and not by judgment; by 'hunching' and not by ratiocination" and later uses deliberative faculties "not only to justify that intuition to himself, but to make it pass muster."[1] printed .

A book on judging by three political scientists lays out the same account: "Until the twentieth century, most lawyers and scholars believed that judging was a mechanistic enterprise in which judges ap-

2 · CHAPTER 1

plied the law and rendered decisions without recourse to their own
ideological or policy preferences. . . . In the 1920s, however, a group
of jurists and legal philosophers, known collectively as 'legal realists,'
recognized that judicial discretion was quite broad and that often the
law did not mandate a particular result."[2] A legal historian writes,
"Formalist judges of the 1895–1937 period assumed that law was objective, unchanging, extrinsic to the social climate, and, above all, different from and superior to politics. . . . The Legal Realists of the 1920s
and 1930s, tutored by Holmes, Pound, and Cardozo, devastated these
assumptions. . . . They sought to weaken, if not dissolve, the law-
politics dichotomy, by showing that the act of judging was not impersonal or mechanistic, but rather was necessarily infected by the judges'
personal values."[3] A legal theorist writes that "we may characterize
formalism as the descriptive theory of adjudication according to which
(1) the law is rationally determinate, and (2) judging is mechanical. It
follows, moreover, from (1), that (3) legal reasoning is autonomous,
since the class of legal reasons suffices to justify a unique outcome; no
recourse to non-legal reasons is demanded or required."[4] "Realists
were certainly antiformalists," he adds.[5] Identifying the inspiration
for legal realism, a legal sociologist writes, "Holmes's central ideas on
law are based on a rejection of the doctrine of legal formalism that
dominated American legal thought. The doctrine of legal formalism
holds that the law is an internally consistent and logical body of
rules that is independent from the variable forms of its surrounding
social institutions."[6]

The formalist-realist antithesis has migrated to shape general historical understandings. A specialist in the turn of the twentieth century
reports, "At the beginning of the Progressive Era, the judges of the Supreme Court had long followed the abstract concept of *legal formalism*.
They ruled through a deductive process that followed the logic that
had shaped preceding rulings. . . . Progressives argued that rather than
law being a set of abstract principles and accumulated precedents from
which jurists could not deviate, law had to take account of social conditions from which law arose. . . . They urged that attachment to legal
formalism be abandoned and replaced with legal realism."[7]

This ubiquitous formalist-realist narrative is not a quaint story of
exclusively historical interest: it structures contemporary debates
and research on judging. The formalists are "the great villains of contemporary jurisprudence."[8] A "formalist" judge is guilty of foolish-
ness or dishonesty—of slavish adherence to rules contrary to good
sense or manipulation under the guise of adherence. Judge Richard
Posner's *How Judges Think* is pitched as an effort to debunk the delusions of legal formalism that still beguile the legal fraternity.[9] Well over
a hundred quantitative studies of judging have been conducted by po-

litical scientists,[10] with reams more currently underway, many aiming to prove that formalism is wrong and realism is correct. Legal academics are busily developing "new legal formalism" or "new legal realism."[11] The entire legal culture has been indoctrinated in the formalist-realist divide.

A database of U.S. law journals going back two centuries provides concrete evidence of the rapid ascendance and current attention to formalism and realism.[12] Before1968, no article (*zero*) was published in a law journal with "formalism" or "formalist" in the title.[13] The first article title to include one of these terms was written by Grant Gilmore in 1968.[14] From 1968 through 1979, *nine* articles had one of these terms in the title. From 1980 through 1989, the total was *twenty-seven*; from 1990 through 1999, it was *sixty-eight*; and from 2000 through 2007, *forty-eight*.[15] A search for titles with "realism" or "realist" (subtracting other usages of these common terms) shows a similar trajectory, moving from a relatively low frequency from the 1930s through the 1950s (a low of *seven* and high of *sixteen*), going up a bit in the 1960s and 1970s (numbering in the low *twenties* each decade), then jumping to a much higher level in the 1980s (*sixty-five*), 1990s (*eighty-two*), and 2000 through 2007 (*sixty-four*).[16] Remember that this counts only titles with a reference to the formalists or the realists. Many more articles (in the thousands) and books mention or discuss them.

The pervasive influence this story exercises on contemporary thought about judging is all the more extraordinary when one realizes that the formalist-realist divide is wrong in essential respects. The story about the legal formalists is largely an invention, and legal realism is substantially misapprehended. Quantitative studies of judging are marked by a distorting slant owing to incorrect beliefs about the formalists and realists. Legal theory discussions of legal formalism are irrelevant, misleading, or empty. Debates about judging are routinely framed in terms of antithetical formalist-realist poles that jurists do not actually hold.

The objective of this book is to free us from the formalist-realist stranglehold. It consists of a web of interlocking misinterpretations and confusions bundled in a mutually reinforcing package that is now virtually taken for granted. The consequences of this collection of errors are ongoing and pernicious. Rooting out the formalist-realist story will help us recover a sound understanding of judging.

The Myth about the Legal Formalists: Part I

The key to dislodging this framework is to refute assumed beliefs about legal formalism. This effort will take some doing. Many historians and theorists have made confident assertions about what the legal formalists believed. I and others have taught a generation of students about the former dominance of legal formalism. It is stupefying to think that we could have been collectively wrong for so long about something so central and well known.

To demonstrate that the age of "legal formalism" never really existed as such is like proving that ghosts do not exist: one must dispute the credibility of ghost sightings and offer more plausible alternative explanations for the phenomena witnessed. That is the approach taken in part I. Much like chasing ghosts, investigating the formalists proves elusive because they are hard to catch a glimpse of. The formalists never speak for themselves. Every account of the legal formalists and the purportedly widespread belief in "mechanical jurisprudence" has been written by *critics* like Roscoe Pound and Jerome Frank, and by modern historians and theorists relying upon the accounts of critics. "Formalism," legal theorist Tony Sebok observed, ". . . does not really have an identity of its own: As a theory of law, it exists only as a reflection of scholars like Holmes, Pound, Llewellyn, and Frank."[17]

To break down the story, the leading accounts of mechanical jurisprudence and legal formalism—written by Roscoe Pound, Jerome Frank, Grant Gilmore, and others— will be exposed as replete with errors and falsehoods. Although Pound repeatedly *claimed* that turn-of-the century judges and lawyers believed in mechanical deduction, he offered no quotations or citations to that effect by anyone who espoused this purportedly dominant view of judging. When describing this set of beliefs, Pound relied heavily on discussions of German legal science. Frank also relied upon German legal science in his portrayal of judging, and he cited Pound. Most claims about the legal formalists trace back through a string of citations to Pound and Frank.

Abundant ironies will tumble forth as this false story is splayed open. Jurists in the late nineteenth century, it turns out, took substantial pride in the progress they had made in *overcoming* formalism in law. They thought formalism was a primitive legal stage beyond which they had evolved. Chapters 2, 3, 4, and 5 reveal that *many* people in law—including many of the most prominent lawyers, judges, and academics of the day—described judging in consummately realistic terms.

As a preview of the evidence to come, consider this 1881 passage about judging:

> It is useless for judges to quote a score of cases from the digest to sustain almost every sentence, when *every one knows* that another score might be collected to support the opposite ruling. The perverse habit of qualifying and distinguishing has been car-

ried so far that all fixed lines are obliterated, and a little ingenuity in stating the facts of a case is enough to bring it under a rule
that will warrant the desired conclusion. . . . *[T]he most honest
judge knows that the authorities with which his opinions are garnished
often have had very little to do with the decision of the court—perhaps
have only been looked up after that decision was reached upon the general equities of the case.* . . . He writes, it may be, a beautiful essay
upon the law of the case, but the real grounds of decision lie
concealed under the statement of facts with which it is prefaced. It is the power of stating the facts as he himself views them
which preserves the superficial consistency and certainty of the
law, and hides from careless eyes its utter lack of definiteness
and precision.[18]

William G. Hammond made these striking statements, as skeptical as
anything the legal realists would say five decades later, upon his instal-
lation as the first full-time dean and professor at St. Louis Law School.
He was not a legal radical. Hammond, indeed, has been identified by
legal historians as an important contributor to legal formalism.[19]

A Reconstruction of Legal Realism: Part II

The standard portrait of the legal realists as a band of pioneering jurists
shining a realistic light on judging to illuminate a previously darkened
age advances a gross misunderstanding of our legal history. Contemporary historiography paints Holmes as an iconoclast, Pound as a
bridge from Holmes to the realists, Cardozo as bravely breaking taboos
in his candor about judging, and the realists as rebellious radicals who
finally crushed the formalist resistance. Chapters 5 and 6 show that
much of this narrative is misleading. Holmes's views were presaged
by others, were not unusual among his contemporaries, and were tame
in comparison to some; what Cardozo said about judging in the 1920s
had been openly stated by leading judges decades earlier; the realists'
views of judging closely match what the historical jurists wrote in the
1880s and1890s.

Pound coined "mechanical jurisprudence" in 1908 to criticize judges
as trapped in a straightjacket of logical reasoning. Multiple accounts
by his contemporaries, however, suggest that judges were not reasoning in any peculiarly mechanical or precedent-bound manner. The
dominant theme at the time, contrary to the standard image of the formalist age, was the worrisome uncertainty of the law created by the
proliferation of inconsistent precedents and an explosion of legislation.

In 1930, in the course of attacking contemporary courts, Jerome Frank reprised and embellished Pound's characterization of judges beguiled by mechanical jurisprudence. Then in the 1970s the story was once again dusted off by critics of courts and worked into the full-blown theory of the formalist age. Loud bouts of skepticism about judging erupt periodically owing to unhappiness with law and judging, and the legal realists were one such episode.

A "Balanced Realism" about Judging

The objective of this book is to recover an understanding of judging now obscured by the formalist-realist divide that has prevailed for well over a century—what I call "balanced realism." Balanced realism has two integrally conjoined aspects—a skeptical aspect and a rule-bound aspect. It refers to an awareness of the flaws, limitations, and openness of law, an awareness that judges sometimes make choices, that they can manipulate legal rules and precedents, and that they sometimes are influenced by their political and moral views and their personal biases (the skeptical aspect). Yet it conditions this skeptical awareness with the understanding that legal rules nonetheless work; that judges abide by and apply the law; that there are practice-related, social, and institutional factors that constrain judges; and that judges render generally predictable decisions consistent with the law (the rule-bound aspect). The rule-bound aspect of judging can function reliably notwithstanding the challenges presented by the skepticism-inducing aspect, although this is an achievement that must be earned, is never perfectly achieved, and is never guaranteed.

A concise statement of balanced realism was set forth by Cardozo:

> Those, I think, are the conclusions to which a sense of realism must lead us. No doubt there is a field within which judicial judgment moves untrammeled by fixed principles. Obscurity of statute or of precedent or of customs or morals, or collision between some or all of them, may leave the law unsettled, and cast a duty upon the courts to declare it retrospectively in the exercise of a power frankly legislative in function. In such cases, all that the parties to the controversy can do is to forecast the declaration of the rule as best they can, and govern themselves accordingly. We must not let these occasional and relatively rare instances blind our eyes to the innumerable instances where there is neither obscurity nor collision nor opportunity for diverse judgment.[20]

Contrary to their image as skeptics, the legal realists viewed judging in similarly balanced terms. They did not assert that judges routinely manipulate the law to produce desired outcomes. The misleading skeptical image of the realists is perpetuated by the formalist-realist antithesis, which casts the realists as the opposite of formalism. Karl Llewellyn, realist extraordinaire, devoted a 500-page book to refuting the "Law School Skeptic,"[21] arguing at length that judicial decisions are highly predictable and determined mainly by legal factors.[22] He wrote the book to counteract the corrosive effect of facile skepticism about judging.[23]

Not only did the legal realists see judging in terms of balanced realism, so did their contemporaries, and so did many leading jurists in the late nineteenth century as well as in the twentieth century. Beneath roiling surface debates, jurists have generally viewed judging in terms of balanced realism. A theme that runs through this book is that judges, in particular, have consistently and candidly expressed a balanced realism about judging. Many judges will be heard from in these pages.

The Slant within Quantitative Studies of Judging: Part III

Quantitative studies of judging conducted by political scientists are booming, but the orientation of the field has been badly warped by the story about the formalists and the realists. Taking up the banner of legal realism, the expressed aim of the field has been to expose legal formalism as a fraud. Driven by this mission, scholars have labored for decades to prove that judging is political. Part III shows how this orientation has distorted their models of judging, the design of their studies, and the interpretation of their results. Political scientists working in this area have tended to suppress the role law plays in judicial decisions while overstating the role politics plays.

After exposing the slant that infects the field, chapter 7 conveys the many realistic things judges said about judging from the 1920s through the 1960s (when quantitative studies took off). Chapter 8 then summarizes the findings of the most recent quantitative studies of lower federal courts. This juxtaposition serves to underline a key point: the results of the studies tend to confirm the balanced-realism judges have expressed for many decades. Results that judicial politics scholars now tout as proof of the influence of politics on judging are more correctly interpreted—when the small size of the effect is considered—as providing evidence that judicial decisions are substantially determined by the law.

The results are not uniformly reassuring, however. Several recent studies that bear signs of an increasing politicization of judging are also discussed. Because political scientists are wont to assert that judging by its nature is politically driven, they have difficulty condemning in legal terms an increase in the politicization of judging. Balanced realism recognizes the inevitability of various political influences on judging, but it also identifies the appropriate role and limits of this influence. A realistic account of what the rule of law requires of judges is offered, along with suggestions to help reorient quantitative studies in a more productive direction.

Moving Past the Divide in Legal Theory: Part IV

Efforts by theorists to make sense of formalism, as chapter 9 explains, are plagued by two factors. One problem is that "formalism" was historically used as a pejorative with no theoretical content. Theorists working with this term today are in effect trying to turn what was insult into a meaningful concept, but the negative connotations cling to the word soiling whatever is produced. Another problem is that theorists are inevitably drawn to the false story about the legal formalists— that judges engage in mechanical deduction from a comprehensive, autonomous, logically ordered body of law. Theories that incorporate elements of this story do not match the common law system and impose demands that are impossible to achieve.

The two most influential contemporary theoretical formulations of legal formalism, by Duncan Kennedy and Frederick Schauer, are critically engaged to demonstrate that the notion lacks theoretical value. Furthermore, modern jurists who are developing "new formalism" accept the basic insights of balanced realism, and nothing in their position is based on anything distinctive to "formalism." When stripped to the basics, formalism comes to nothing more than rule-bound judging. The notion of formalism can be struck from the theoretical discussion without loss, saving much confusion.

The final chapter of the book, chapter 10, begins with a discussion of Judge Richard Posner's new book on judging. He pitches the book as a full-bore assault on legal formalism—still dominant, still pervasive in legal circles. When attacking this target, Posner sounds a great deal like an extreme skeptical realist. Beneath his deliberately provocative stance, however, Posner is a balanced realist, merely repeating what judges have been saying about judging for a hundred years. In his balanced realism about judging, Posner shares a great deal in common with his erstwhile targets, including the arch formalist Justice Antonin Scalia.

Drawing from the information and accounts provided in the course of previous chapters, especially relying upon the insights of judges, the basic elements of a balanced realist view of judging are briefly articulated. The recognition of balanced realism will not resolve the normative and empirical debates that surround judging, but it will make plain that there is much common ground and that the debate plays out on relatively limited (albeit important) terrain.

Balanced realism is descriptively accurate only as long as a balance exists between the skepticism-inducing aspects of judging and the rule-bound aspects. In recent decades, however, skepticism about judging has increased within the legal culture as well as in the public consciousness, fueled by the politicization of federal judicial appointments and state judicial elections. Excessive skepticism about judging harbors the potential to disrupt the balance. By dislodging the formalist-realist divide and replacing it with balanced realism, this book is an effort to resist this unhappy prospect.

PART ONE

The Legal Formalists

2

○ ○ ● ● ●

THE MYTH ABOUT BELIEFS IN THE COMMON LAW

THE STORY ABOUT LEGAL FORMALISM CONSISTS of two distinguishable yet integrally linked elements: a theory of the nature of law (the common law in particular) as developed by judges, which I take up in this chapter; and a theory of how judges mechanically apply law (precedents and statutes) to the facts in particular cases, which I consider in chapter 3. Both aspects of the story are fundamentally flawed. They cannot be kept entirely apart, for their connection is tight, but it is essential to understand each separately and to recognize their implications and interrelations.

With respect to the theory of the nature of law, the core idea is that during the formalist age jurists widely believed that the law was comprehensive and logically ordered, and in new situations judges *did not make law* (even when declaring new rules) but merely discovered and applied preexisting law. The most vociferous defender of the traditional understanding of the common law in the late nineteenth century was James C. Carter, an accomplished corporate lawyer and leader of the bar. Here is an excerpt from his 1890 address to the American Bar Association:

> That the judge can not make law is accepted from the start. That there is already a rule by which the case must be determined is not doubted. . . . It is agreed that the true rule must somehow be *found*. Judges and advocates—all together—engage in the *search*. Cases more or less nearly approaching the one in controversy are adduced. Analogies are referred to. The customs and habits of men are appealed to. Principles already settled as fundamental are invoked and run out to their consequences; and finally a rule is deduced which is declared to be the one which the existing law requires to be applied to the case.[1]

This passage appears to lend credence to the story about legal formalism, but substantial evidence casts doubt on this assertion. Carter's position clashed with key aspects of legal formalism, and, more immediately on point, many jurists at the time were dismissive of his assertions.

As a preliminary offering, consider the words of just one prominent naysayer. Oxford professor A. V. Dicey was the most renowned English constitutional scholar of the day, widely read on both sides of the Atlantic. The title of a lecture he delivered at Harvard Law School in 1898 was "Judicial Legislation." Dicey began by declaring "*As all lawyers are aware*, a large part and, as many would add, the best part of the law of England is judge made law. . . . it is, in short, the fruit of judicial legislation."[2]

Jerome Frank's Calculated Distortion

Jerome Frank's *Law and the Modern Mind*, published in 1930, is an infamous piece of legal realist literature. Frank began by laying out "The Basic Legal Myth" that dominates the legal culture.[3] Frank quoted a lengthy passage from the celebrated English jurist of the previous century Sir Henry Maine to describe the myth:

> When a group of facts comes before a court for adjudication, "the whole course of the discussion between the judge and the advocate assumes that no question is, or can be, raised which will call for the application of any principles but old ones, or of any distinctions but such has have long since been allowed. It is taken absolutely for granted that there is somewhere a rule of known law which will cover the facts of the dispute now litigated, and that, if such a rule be not discovered, it is only that the necessary patience, knowledge or acumen, is not forthcoming to detect it. The uninformed listener would conclude that court and counsel unhesitatingly accept a doctrine that somewhere . . . there existed a complete, coherent, symmetrical body of . . . law, of an amplitude sufficient to furnish principles which would apply to any conceivable combination of circumstances."[4]

Frank found this complex of ideas manifestly implausible, but asserted, "The lawyers' pretenses are not *consciously* deceptive. . . . Although it is the chiefest function of lawyers to make the legal rules visible and pliable, a large part of the profession *believes*, and therefore encourages the laity to believe, that those rules either are or can be made essentially immutable."[5] According to this vision, Frank claimed, "Law is a complete body of rules existing from time immemorial and unchangeable except to the limited extent that legislatures have changed the rules by enacted statutes. . . . But the judges are not to make or change the law but to apply it. The law, ready-made, pre-exists the judicial decisions."[6] Lawyers and judges widely believed in this farfetched vision of the law, Frank asserted, owing to a yearning or (infantile) need for certainty and comfort in a disordered world.

Frank does not identify the source for his Maine quote. The paragraph he recites tracks almost word for word Maine's discussion over two pages in his classic work *Ancient Law* (1861). Crucially, Frank neglects to indicate that he omitted several passages from Maine's original text. The pertinent middle passages taken out by Frank, which originally followed the second sentence quoted above, read: "*We now admit that the new decision has modified the law.* The rules applicable have, to use the very inaccurate expression sometimes employed, become *more elastic.* In fact they have been changed."[7] These sentences by Maine, excised by Frank, are directly contrary to what Frank writes just after the quote: "The lawyers, themselves, like the laymen, fail to recognize fully the essentially plastic and mutable character of law."[8]

Maine's very point in the passage was that lawyers *did* recognize that the law was elastic and changed through court decisions. By deleting the statements to this effect, Frank deceptively made it look like Maine was asserting the opposite—that lawyers *did not* think this. Frank committed yet another meaning-reversing omission. Immediately following the final sentence quoted by Frank—that the law is "complete, coherent, symmetrical . . . sufficient . . . to any conceivable combination"—Maine made this essential counterobservation: "*The theory was at first much more thoroughly believed in than it is now.*"[9] Note that Maine said this *seventy years* before Frank claimed that most lawyers still believed it.

Maine does not undertake to identify precisely when English lawyers had begun to lose their belief in this old fiction, although he implied that it took place well in the past. He acknowledged the power of Bentham's attack on legal fictions early in the century. John Stuart Mill likewise recognized Bentham's impact at the beginning of the nineteenth century. "Who, before Bentham," Mill remarked, "dared to speak disrespectfully, in express terms, of the British Constitution or the English law? . . . Bentham broke the spell."[10] And an American jurist in 1883 wrote: "The fact that, under the fiction of declaring the law, the judges in reality make it, has been recognized by every one who has studied the subject with candor and intelligence, since the days of Bentham, at least."[11]

Although it is impossible to identify a precise date for its collapse, by Maine's time this fiction appears to have lost its general hold. "We in England," Maine remarked, "are well accustomed to the extension, modification, and improvement of law by a [judicial] machinery which, in theory, is incapable of altering one jot or one line of existing jurisprudence. The process by which this virtual legislation is effected [by judges] is *not so much insensible as unacknowledged.*"[12] Maine described this as a knowing use of "double language" within legal circles.[13]

Frank artfully edited Maine's words—his sham facilitated by the fact that Maine was more famous than actually read—to assert that the bulk of lawyers in 1931 remained deluded by the comforting spell of this long-exposed fiction. Frank was well aware, however, that many others had said precisely the opposite. He acknowledged Dicey's observations (set forth above) that "all lawyers are aware" that judges make law. Frank also quoted the eminent turn-of-the-century English jurist Frederick Pollock: "No intelligent lawyer would in this day pretend that the decisions of the courts do not add to and alter the law."[14] To account for the inconvenient hitch these various remarks posed for his claim about the widespread belief in "The Basic Myth," Frank simply declared that they were the offerings of an enlightened minority, but "most lawyers deny the reality of judge made law."[15] Evidence showing the opposite follows shortly.

Frank committed another gross distortion. He identified Joseph Beale as the leading contemporary representative of conceiving of law as composed of unchanging principles and concepts autonomous from society. Frank went so far as to call this set of views "legal Absolutism or 'Bealism.' "[16] This passage from a 1914 article that Beale wrote *advocating* the sociological study of law, however, indicates otherwise:

> The vocation of our own age, then, is to study our law with a view to its readjustment and reform. For this purpose our study must take two directions. First, we must examine the law objectively to learn its social purpose and to see how far that purpose is being accomplished. Such a study is the object of the new sociological jurisprudence. The importance of these investigations cannot be overestimated. Every part of the law ought to be tested to find out how far it is conforming to its purpose.[17]

To his fellow legal academics, Beale urged that we "devote ourselves" to "new knowledge and new thought," which involves "the analysis of law and its adaptability to new conditions."[18] He strongly endorsed "the need of conforming the law of a people to its needs."[19] Beale thought that legal concepts and principles should be worked out in a logical and consistent manner (and it would be odd to argue otherwise), but that did not amount to the purely conceptualist position Frank attributed to him.[20] Beale asserted that judges and jurists developed and rationalized the law in connection with society: "It is not necessarily a logical process"; he wrote, "usually it does not proceed in accordance with formal logic. It 'will depend on a judgment or intuition more subtle than any articulate premise.' . . . How far does the proposed rule conform to other known rules of law; how far is it consistent with well established legal doctrine; how far is it in accordance with social or economic needs or with current morality?"[21] What Beale says is hardly distinguishable from what the legal realists advocated. As further evidence of this, take note that Beale's quotation about "judgment or intuition" is taken from Oliver Wendell Holmes[22]—Frank's realistic hero.

Two finals points reinforce that Frank's account deserves skepticism. He offered a couple of dramatic quotations about the formalistic mind-set. The first: "And so you will find lawyers saying that 'The judicial process in ascertaining or applying the law is essentially similar to the process by which we acquire our knowledge of geometry. . . . In the great majority of cases the solution of them [legal problems] is as certain and exact as an answer to a problem in mathematics.' "[23] Later in the text Frank writes, "Recently (in utter sobriety and with no satirical intention) the conventional view was stated thus: 'Every jurist whether he has been some leader of savages at the time of the dawn of civilization, or a modern judging sitting in a court of last resort, has sought for the principles which should determine his judgment in something apart from and above the experience of the race.' "[24]

Frank introduces both quotations in a manner that implicitly suggests they were the words of a true believer, but that was not the case. Both were written in a polemical critique of the law penned in 1913 by a lawyer, Everett Abbott.[25] The only source Abbott cited for these assertions was Roscoe Pound.[26] Frank also relied upon Pound. Another source Frank credited for his construction of the formalistic mind-set of judges was an article (translated from German) by Austrian jurist Karl George Wurzel, "Methods of Juridical Thinking,"[27] addressing theories about judging in the civil code system.[28]

Jerome Frank's colorful book is often relied upon as an authority for prevailing views in the formalist age. These comments reveal, however, that he produced an unreliable account, reversing Maine's meaning, distorting Beale's position, and drawing from German legal science in his characterization of the beliefs of American jurists.

Gilmore's Dubious Assertions about the "Formalist Age"

The most influential modern formulation of the story about the formalists is Grant Gilmore's lively and lucid book, *The Ages of American Law* (1977), delivered as the 1974 Storrs lecture at Yale. *Ages* has been cited in a thousand law review articles and in an unknown number of books,[29] often as an authoritative reference on legal formalism.

Following Karl Llewellyn (who in turn referred to Pound),[30] Gilmore divided American legal thought into three periods. The first period, running from the Revolution to the Civil War, was as an "Age of Discovery," during which courts flexibly applied rules and principles in a "Grand Style" to adjust law to changing circumstances and to meet social needs. In the second period, which began "about the time of the Civil War," the Grand Style "lost out to a Formal Style, which was as bad a way of deciding cases as the previous way had been good."[31] The formal style began to disintegrate in the 1920s—involving "a root and branch rejection of the formalism or . . . the conceptualism of the proceeding period"[32] —giving way to a more realistic approach by judges and jurists.

According to Gilmore,

> The post–Civil War juridical product seems to start from the assumption that the law is a closed, logical system. Judges do not make law: they merely declare the law which, in some Platonic sense, already exists. The judicial function has nothing to do with the adaptation of rules of law to changing circumstances; it is restricted to the discovery of what the true rules of law are and indeed always have been. Past error can be exposed and in that way minor corrections can be made, but the truth, once arrived at, is immutable and eternal.[33]

He put this forth as the defining faith of the formalist age, widely accepted in legal circles.

That is highly doubtful, however. As early as 1833, an American jurist wrote: "[T]he ancient customs are supposed to furnish a rule of decision for every case that can by possibility occur. . . . The supposition of an ancient and forgotten custom, is, *as every one knows, a mere fiction*. . . . And proceeding on the groundwork of this fiction in the administration of justice, the courts in point of fact make the law, performing at the same time the office of legislators and judges."[34] Particular attention should be paid to the phrase "as every one knows," uttered by this jurist fifty years before the supposed onset of the formalist age. Words to that effect—which demand audience agreement—are relatively uncommon in speeches and writing, yet they turn up here with notable regularity.

A lawyer wrote in 1871, "Though the rules of the judge-made law are enacted for the cases as they occur, the *fiction* is that they have existed from of old and are not enacted but declared."[35] Another lawyer wrote in 1883 that "*we all know* this is one of the *resplendent fictions*."[36]

Columbia law professor Munroe Smith observed in 1887, "*Nobody really believes in the fiction* [that the courts do not make law]."[37] Another commentator noted in 1888: "By a singular fiction the courts, from time immemorial, have pretended that they simply declared the law, and did not make the law; yet *we all know that this pretense is a mere fiction.*"[38] Judge Emlin McClain in 1902 described the "*fictitious assumption* that the [newly laid down] rule is already law."[39] "I don't believe it,"[40] declared a lawyer in 1904. A historical study of the common law written in 1905 called this set of ideas "the *baldest legal fiction.*"[41] Professor William Hornblower wrote in the 1907 *Columbia Law Review* that this old story was a "comfortable fiction."[42] "We of this day and generation are not disposed to accede to the eulogy of the common-law as the 'perfection of reason.' We smile at this eulogy, conscious as we are of the manifest imperfections of the common law."[43]

A specific assertion Gilmore made in connection with this set of ideas is demonstrably false. Gilmore remarked: "It was also during the post Civil-War period that the idea that *courts never legislate*—that the judicial function is merely to declare the law that already exists— *became an article of faith, for lawyers and non-lawyers alike.*"[44]

To the contrary, many legal writers explicitly acknowledged that judges "necessarily legislate."[45] Note the titles and dates of the following articles, every one of which acknowledged the fact of judicial legislation, recognized its inevitability, and noted its benefits (as well as problems): "Judicial Legislation" (1870),[46] "Judicial Legislation" (1872),[47] "Judicial Legislation: Its Legitimate Function in the Development of the Common Law" (1891),[48] "Judicial Legislation" (1902),[49] "Judge-Made Law" (1904),[50] "Legitimate Functions of Judge-Made Law" (1905),[51] "A Century of 'Judge-Made' Law" (1907),[52] and "The Process of Judicial Legislation" (1914).[53] The president of the New York Bar declaimed in an 1894 speech that "the courts have indulged in judicial legislation for centuries."[54]

Even judges openly acknowledged that they made law. Judge Thomas M. Cooley, one of the nation's most renowned judges, asserted in 1886, "The decisions continue to accumulate as causes arise which present aspects differing at all from any which preceded; and a great body of laws being made under the statute which is and can be nothing but '*judge-made law.*' "[55] Unanticipated situations regularly arise, lacking any clear preexisting determinative legal rule. In such cases, Cooley continued, "it is evident that what the law was to be could not have been known in advance of decisions, and it is also evident that when declared by the court its effect must be retroactive."[56] Judge John F. Dillon, another prominent judge, wrote in the same year that "stupendous work of judicial legislation has been silently going on" for a "long period,"[57] and "it is *no longer denied*, nor can it be, that the judges . . . are actually, though indirectly, engaged in legislating."[58]

These comments are particularly noteworthy for the purposes of this exploration because Cooley and Dillon have been identified by historians and theorists as *major contributors to legal formalism*.[59] Yet both judges asserted that judicial legislation is inevitable because judges are regularly confronted with unique and unanticipated situations that the existing law (cases and statues) does not provide for.[60] Other judges said the same. In a 1903 article with the "tell all" title "Judge-Made Law," Judge A. M. Mackey matter-of-factly declared that "a large portion of the unwritten or common law is judge-made law."[61] Also in 1903, U.S. Circuit Judge Le Baron Colt wrote that judges "have carried on judicial legislation from the infancy of the law in order that it might advance with society."[62]

To be sure, judges also can be found asserting that courts "make no laws, they establish no policy, they never enter into the domain of popular action," as Justice Brewer insisted in an 1893 speech.[63] That is the standard line demarking the proper role of judges. Behind its utterance was a defense of judicial legitimacy. "Judicial power is never exercised for the purpose of giving effect to the will of the judge," wrote Chief Justice John Marshall nearly two centuries ago. "Judicial power, as contradistinguished from the power of laws, has no existence. . . . Courts are mere instruments of law, and can will nothing."[64] Statements by judges admitting that they make law, as cited above, carry additional weight precisely because their refusal to invoke this time-honored shield (understood and accepted as such) exposed them to criticism as usurpers. They were, nonetheless, candidly admitting what they thought was obvious and not usefully denied.

The many statements and articles listed here plainly refute Gilmore's statements that lawyers and nonlawyers believed as an "article of faith" that "courts never legislate" but merely "declare the law that already exists." G. Edward White, one of today's foremost historians of the U.S. judicial tradition, has labeled this set of views the "oracular" theory of judging: "[T]he dominant understanding of judicial decision-making treated it as an exercise in 'finding' rather than 'making' law, with 'law' being conceived as a body of finite and immutable principles that existed independent of its interpreters."[65] This oracular view of judging prevailed, according to White, until the coming of sociological jurisprudence (à la Pound) in the early twentieth century. U.S. Supreme Court Justice Antonin Scalia similarly observed, "It is only in this century, with the rise of legal realism, that we came to acknowledge that judges in fact 'make' the common law."[66]

That is the conventional wisdom purveyed by the story of the formalist age. But many prominent legal professionals in the final quarter of the nineteenth century asserted that *everyone knew* this theory of judging was a fiction. It was widely recognized that judges made law. While many voices opposed judicial legislation as inconsistent with the separation of powers, many also accepted that judges inevitably create law in the course of developing the common law as well as when interpreting statutes and the Constitution.[67]

Gilmore's Erroneous Claim about Cardozo

Gilmore made yet another telling error. He identified the 1921 publication of Benjamin Cardozo's *The Nature of the Judicial Process* as *the* event that heralded the onset of the third (realistic) age in American law.[68] Cardozo wrote that, although in most cases the applicable legal rules and principles clearly dictate the decision,[69] in a number of cases there is no clear legal answer. When deciding such open cases, Cardozo asserted, judges should promote social ends. He stated forthrightly that these situations involve "judicial legislation." The judge must strive to decide in an objective fashion to further the community's view of the proper end, not the judge's own view.[70] Cardozo acknowledged the difficulty of keeping the two separate, conceding that judges cannot be entirely free of "subconscious loyalties."[71] For its nuanced, inside look at judging, *Judicial Process* is a classic.

Gilmore described the reception it received:

> The thing that is hardest to understand about *The Nature of the Judicial Process* is the furor which its publication caused. Nothing can better illustrate the extraordinary hold which the Langdellian concept of law had acquired, not only on the legal but on the popular mind. Cardozo's hesitant confession that judges were, on rare occasions, more than simple automata, that they made law instead of merely declaring it, was *widely regarded as a legal version of hard core pornography.* . . . [A] less saintly man than Cardozo might, in 1920, have found himself running close to the reefs of impeachment.[72]

Gilmore's claim that Cardozo's book generated a "furor" is untrue. As an exhaustive biography of Cardozo noted, "The applause that followed each of Cardozo's lectures at Yale was echoed in the reviews of the published work."[73] Much of what Cardozo wrote in the book, including that judges legislate, had been said well before 1920. The reviews of his book ranged from positive to effusive, with the exception of one that could be considered critical (while agreeing with much of what Cardozo said).[74]

Judges were enthusiastic about Cardozo's book. Judge Rousseau Burch wrote in the *Yale Law Journal*:

> In a sense, there is *nothing new* in the book but its method. Elements of the judicial process have been discussed before; but this account, although brief, is vivid and complete; although daring, is not sensational or exaggerated; although informed by genius and erudition, is lucid enough to be comprehended by law-school students; and the account is rendered with a combination of spirit and restraint, with that "animated moderation," which makes it as brilliant as it is convincing.[75]

After summarizing Cardozo's claims about judging, Judge Burch proclaimed: "It is true."[76] Federal appellate judge Frances E. Baker applauded Cardozo's declaration that judges make law: "Naturally judges could not confess when they were unconscious of being lawmakers. With the first glimmerings of consciousness they were so startled that they hid behind various fictions and pretenses. But now that the fictions are recognized for what they are, why not discard the camouflage?"[77]

Another federal appellate judge, Judge Charles M. Hough, enthusiastically commended the book to readers. He confirmed the presence of a "not inconsiderable number of causes wherein precedents are not ruling, where the statute or constitution does not directly and plainly cover, and where the Court has to deal with something previous lawmakers had not thought of, and therefore did not speak of."[78] Hough also affirmed Cardozo's account of the difficulty of maintaining the appropriate separation between "the subjective or individual conscience, and the objective or general conscience; and to indicate how far each can rightly sway judicial decision."[79]

Contrary to Gilmore's assertion, there is little evidence that Cardozo's book was viewed as scandalous—and remember that he was elevated to the U.S. Supreme Court to wide acclaim within a decade. His book offered an inside account of judging, a subject on which judges had traditionally remained mum, but what he said about judging was not received as radical. Harlan F. Stone, then dean of Columbia Law School, soon to be appointed to the Supreme Court, wrote that Cardozo's account manifested "balance, restraint, and clarity."[80] The enthusiastic reception of Cardozo's book, along with praise for its moderation, provides additional evidence that the age was not gripped by the formalist mind-set.

What They Meant by "Judges Do Not Create Law"

There were jurists who, like Carter, asserted that judges *do not* make law. Frequently the statement was qualified, as here by Judge Simeon E. Baldwin: "The common law on any point existed, *in theory at least*, before any case in which it may be applied. It was the practice of the people, or the rule which seemed to them naturally right."[81] Baldwin signals that the claim is a *theoretical* one (as Maine did in 1861), to be taken accordingly. In *The American Judiciary* (1905), when describing the judicial declaration of unwritten law, Baldwin was more frank: "Such opinions profess to state what the law was by which rights accrued out of a past transaction. In fact they often do much more. By declaring that to be the law, and declaring it with authority, they are the first to make it certain that it is the law. The difference between this and making law is not great."[82]

The claim was also understood by some to serve as a useful regulative ideal. Driving the development of the common law are "considerations of public policy," asserted Munroe Smith in 1888; cases were not in complete harmony because jurists have different views on these matters.[83] "Our judges are well aware that conflicting decisions cause practical inconvenience, embarrassing business and confusing family relations."[84] "*Theoretically*, the special rules of the common law are derived from a pre-existing body of general principles, and when a new question arises the answer is to be found by deducing from some recognized principle the required new rule."[85] "This conception has great and beneficent results,"[86] Smith thought, because it prompts judges to strive to reconcile contradictory results, rendering the law more systematic. Smith emphasized, in a realistic vein, that although "deduction" has a role in the derivation of legal rules, "the rules are ultimately determined by social interests; for if the rule obtained by deduction does not work well (i.e. does not correspond to the social necessities which it is designed to meet), it is discarded."[87]

Late nineteenth-century jurists who professed unreservedly that judges merely declared preexisting law, like Carter, usually were adherents of a theory of law called "historical jurisprudence." Historical jurists thought that law ultimately consists of—is determined by, is the product of—the customs, norms, and opinions of the community. The denial of judicial law making presupposed this understanding. Carter put it thus: "When courts apply the law founded upon custom, they do not *make* rules. They find rules already existing, *unconsciously made* by society, the *product*, as it were, of its life."[88] Carter asserted that "the judge can only *make* the law by making a wrong declaration,"[89] which then becomes a part of the law through stare decisis.

Another proponent of historical jurisprudence, Christopher Tiede-man, explained that this assertion—that "the court does not make law; it simply declares what is the pre-existing law"—is meant to refer to the notion that "all law is but the expression of the popular sense of right."[90] The center of legal gravity and the ultimate legal authority, according to this view, is in the community rather than in courts and legislatures: "The court, therefore, simply lays down the law so far as it gives judicial expression to this popular opinion; and whenever there is any departure by the court from the popular opinion, it will meet with successful opposition."[91] With that understanding, Tiedeman ac-knowledged, "The court does in some sense make law."[92] This set of views, it must be noted, also shows the error of repeated assertions that jurists in the formalist age viewed law as autonomous from society in some Platonic sense. Historical jurists, whom modern historians tag as formalists, insisted that law is tightly bound to and produced by soci-ety, ever changing in sync with society.

Carter's assertions that law is not made by judges appear less strange in light of this background. He knew what others meant when they insisted that judges made law, but he begged to differ because he had a more expansive definition of "law," as ultimately social in origin. Other prominent jurists at the time did not agree, and a few of his peers openly called his views out of touch with the modern age, in which legislation would rapidly become the primary source of law. Judge Thomas Ewing, in 1890, acidly labeled Carter's account of the law "purely fanciful."[93] Judge Charles M. Hough in 1922 called him "the misguided James Coolidge Carter."[94]

Civil Code versus Common Law Views of Law

Roscoe Pound bears primary responsibility for creating and perpetuat-ing the image that judges were held in the grip of the classical vision of the common law.[95] Pound insisted in 1913 that "the lawyer *believes* that the principles of law are absolute, eternal, and of universal valid-ity, and that law is found, not made."[96] He reiterated this portrayal nu-merous times over the next four decades. He became the dean of Har-vard Law School and a leading jurisprudential light. This powerful combination of repetition and reputation effectively cemented the image of formalistic judging. It helped lend credibility to Pound's ac-count, at least for later generations, that he vaguely echoed themes pre-viously raised by Oliver Wendell Holmes. In "The Path of the Law" (1897), one of the most famous legal articles ever written, Holmes took as his target the "fallacy" "that the only force at work in the development of the law is logic."[97] "The danger of which I speak is . . . the notion that a given system, ours, for instance, can be worked out like mathematics from some general axioms."[98]

Compelling reasons to doubt Pound's account will be elaborated in the following chapter. Because Pound and Frank cited German sources in their discussions of judging in the United States, it is useful to take a brief look at how German legal science presented law. A hugely influential theoretical construction of formalism was produced by Max Weber at the turn of the twentieth century.[99] Weber described the highest forms of "present-day legal science" in terms of five postulates:

> first, that every concrete legal decision be the "application" of an abstract legal proposition to a concrete "fact situation"; second, that it must be possible in every concrete case to derive the decision from abstract legal propositions by means of legal logic; third, that the law must actually or virtually constitute a "gapless" system of legal propositions, or must, at least, be treated as it if were such a gapless system; fourth, that whatever cannot be "construed" rationally in legal terms is also legally irrelevant; and fifth, that every social action of human beings must always be visualized as either an "application" or "execution" of legal propositions, or as an "infringement" thereof, since the "gaplessness" of the legal system must result in a gapless "legal ordering" of all social conduct.[100]

Here is the often-mentioned classical legal formalism of turn-of-the-century legal thought.

There is an abiding irony, however. Weber set this forth as an *idealized* account of contemporary civil code systems (and even in the civil law context it was not universally accepted). Anglo-American common law systems, Weber pointed out, stood in *contrast* with formally rational legal systems: "[N]ot every body of law (e.g. English law) claims that it possesses the features of a system as defined above."[101] As chapter 4 explains, the common law was originally built on the writ system—a collection of unplanned, unarranged causes of action—and judges relied heavily on fictions to effect change in the law. The case-by-case mode of legal development precluded systematic organization. Occasional legislation brought various changes in the law, often without consideration of potential conflicts with existing common law doctrines. Weber elaborated: "From such practices and attitudes no rational system of law could emerge, nor even a rationalization of the law as such, because the concepts thus formed are constructed in relation to concrete events of everyday life, are distinguished from each other by external criteria, and extended in their scope, as new needs arise, by means of the techniques just mentioned [extension by analogy or fictions]."[102]

The elementary error made by Pound, Frank, and others who drew liberally from German discussions when constructing the image of the formalist age is that these two systems were dissimilar in design, construction, and orientation. In civil code countries, Weber explained, legal formalism was the product of systematic rationalization in the universities—academic jurists controlled legal education and legal development. In common law countries, in contrast, lawyers were trained mainly by practitioners (as apprentices), and judges developed the law in a piecemeal fashion.[103] The late nineteenth-century rise of law schools in America generated talk about "legal science" in academic circles, but the unsystematic development of the common law system was already deeply entrenched, and its method of operation remained distinctive, as Weber recognized.

The famed English jurist Frederick Pollock, a contemporary of Pound and Weber, thought it obvious that the common law was not systematically rational: "[T]he system was not even logical, for a strictly logical adherence to consequences would have brought the business of the Courts to a dead-lock; and the partial remedies applied by legislation, or by forensic and in some cases judicial ingenuity, did not even pretend to be consistent with any systematic doctrine at all."[104] The following 1907 characterization of the common law, by James Bryce, author *American Commonwealth*, aligns with Pollock's comments:

> The Common Law is admittedly unsymmetrical. Some people might call it confused, however exact may be the propositions that compose it. There are general principles running through it, but these are often hard to follow, so numerous are the exceptions. There are inconsistencies in the Common Law, where decisions have been given at different times and have not been settled by the highest Court of Appeal or by the Legislature. There are gaps in it. Thus there has been formed a tendency among lawyers to rate principles, or, at any rate, let us say, philosophical and logical views of the law, very low compared with any positive declaration made by a court.[105]

Bryce's description, oozing with realism, comports much more closely with what people in U.S. legal circles were actually saying about the law and judging than what Pound, Frank, and Gilmore claimed.

3

○ ○ ● ● ●

THE MYTH ABOUT "MECHANICAL JURISPRUDENCE"

ROSCOE POUND'S 1908 "Mechanical Jurisprudence" was seminal in creating the image of judging as an exercise in mechanical, deductive reasoning. Pound began by posing the question: "What is scientific law?"[1] His answer is that "the marks of a scientific law are, conformity to reason, uniformity, and certainty. Scientific law is a reasoned body of principles for the administration of justice, and its antithesis is a system of enforcing magisterial caprice, however honest, and however much disguised under the name of justice or equity or natural law."[2] The danger of scientific law, Pound warned, is a "petrification" that "tends to cut off individual initiative in the future, to stifle independent consideration of new problems and of new phases of old problems, and so to impose the ideas of one generation upon the other."[3] Contemporary U.S. law, Pound claimed, was mired in this state: "[T]he jurisprudence of conceptions tends to decay. Conceptions are fixed. The premises are no longer to be examined. Everything is reduced to simple deduction from them. Principles cease to have importance. The law becomes a body of rules. This is the condition against which sociologists now protest, and protest rightly."[4] He argued that historical jurisprudence and analytical jurisprudence, the main legal theories of the day, exacerbated this stultification because they emphasized abstract concepts and logical analysis.[5]

As an example, Pound offered the notorious *Lochner* (and *Adair*) case, in which the Supreme Court invalidated for violating the liberty of contract a New York law limiting the working hours of bakers to no more than ten hours a day and six days a week.[6] "The conception of freedom of contract is made the basis of a logical deduction," wrote Pound. "The court does not inquire what the effect of such a deduction will be, when applied to the actual situation."[7] With courts paralyzed in this state, Pound argued, the only solution was for legislation to provide new starting points for the common law.[8]

This chapter produces evidence that, contrary to what Pound and others have asserted, lawyers, academics, and judges at the time did not widely believe that judging was an exercise in mechanical deduction. Before moving to examine the evidence, it is worth noting once again that, when setting out his portrayal of mechanical judging, Pound quoted no actual "formalists" making these claims, and he made repeated references to German jurists discussing German legal science.[9] It is also essential to recognize that the image of mechanical, deductive judging was deprived of its main conceptual underpinning in the preceding chapter. The earlier quotations from Pound, Frank, and Gilmore tied the mechanical view of judging directly to the traditional view of the common law: judges purportedly reasoned mechanically from the law—and were able to do so—because the law pre-existed in a comprehensive, gapless, logically ordered complex of rules and principles. If most people in legal circles did not in fact believe in this classic theory of the nature of law (updated to law as science), the theory of deductive judging loses its mooring.

Doubts from Practice about Law as Science and Deductive Judging

Pound framed his inquiry with the question "What is scientific law?", suggesting that this holds the key to how lawyers and judges understood law and judging at the time—but that is dubious. Schooled in the reality of legal practice, practitioners tended to scoff at the notion.

Talk of "law as a science" extends back at least to the mid-eighteenth century, when Blackstone asserted that law is "a rational science."[10] This assertion was repeated throughout the nineteenth and into the early twentieth century. The renowned law reformer David Dudley Field effused in 1859 that there is no science "greater in magnitude or importance" than "the science of law."[11] This phrase was not, however, always apprehended in the same way. For some it meant systematic knowledge,[12] for others "science" was a loose synonym for "philosophy";[13] for some it was meant in sociological terms (law is the science of social order and social norms),[14] for many it was an "honorific" term without real content.[15]

Nineteenth-century legal academics were especially enamored with the idea that law is a science, for that accorded it prestige worthy of a place in university studies. At the time law was considered a craft. Serving an apprenticeship, "reading law" in a legal office, was the traditional path to entering the bar. Gaining the status of a science would boost its standing to a field of learning. A lengthy brief was published in 1851 which endeavored to show that "reason and experience advise—almost *prescribe*—the scientific or academical method of legal study."[16] The stakes were evident to those involved: Dean Langdell of Harvard asserted that "[i]f law be not a science, a university will best consult its own dignity in declining to teach it";[17] "it is only by regarding law as a science that one can justify its being taught in a university,"[18] wrote the dean of Columbia Law School.

Despite (or thanks to) the uncertain references of the "law is a science" phrase, it was regularly invoked in the latter part of the nineteenth century, particularly by jurisprudence scholars. Throughout the formalist period, however, legal practitioners were openly skeptical. In 1874 the lawyer-editors of the *Albany Law Journal* marked this gap between theorists and practitioners: "This view [law is a science] is now taken by all theoretical legists; but it has not come down to the professional level, and for the most part, the jurist and the practitioner do not stop to inquire whether their system is a science."[19] "[T]he words 'science' and 'scientific' are much out of place in connection with law, and serve to darken counsel,"[20] a lawyer cautioned. Henry White, a member of the bar, wrote in the *Yale Law Journal* in 1892: "If the law were an exact science and furnished a complete system of rules which could be applied without serious difficulty and with certain results in every case, perhaps it would be better not to look beyond the written law in determining controversies. But . . . most cases of any difficulty present questions of law on which no one can confidently predict the decision. Most important battles in the courts, which do not turn on questions of fact, are fought on the frontier of the law, where the ground is unsettled, and where new rules are being formulated and new precedents made."[21] As Elihu Root, one of the nation's leading lawyers (a senator, secretary of state, and winner of the Nobel Peace Prize), observed in his 1916 president's address to the American Bar Association (ABA), "The natural course for the development of our law and institutions does not follow the line of pure reason or the demands of scientific method."[22]

An academic advocate of seeing law as science acknowledged (in 1895) the gaping divide on this issue, trenchantly articulating the practitioners' opposition:

> Much debate has been expended on this question [Is law a science?]. The assertion that it is, by jurists having high ideals, has provoked no little repugnance among practical lawyers, who see that their whole work is really to produce a mental result in the

minds of men—judges and jurors—who are influenced by mixed motives, interest, sympathy, antipathy, prejudice, passion; and that scientific accuracy does not cut much figure to their view, in the process, nor in the result.[23]

Not all academics were enamored with describing law as science. Dean Harlan Fiske Stone asserted that this (academic) perspective tended to be misleading. "In an ideal system law should, and perhaps could, be purely scientific and logical; but the fact is, as the law student discovers, when he begins his practice, logic oftentimes yields to practical considerations, which with the court outweigh his most logical arguments."[24] Pollock, as quoted at the end of the preceding chapter, thought it particularly inapt to characterize the common law as a science or logical arrangement.

The same gap in views is evident in connection with the notion that judging is a matter of mechanical or deductive logic. Although it is frequently said today that during the formalist age most people believed judging involved mechanical deduction, judging was seldom described in those terms in this period;[25] examples that turn up usually bear the imprint of a theoretical exercise or an empty claim. A jurist wrote in 1872, "If a forensic argument were thrown into an orderly series of syllogism, it would be found that the major premise of each of the syllogisms is a rule of law, the minor premise a proposition of fact; and that the resulting conclusion is a comparison of such allegations of law and fact."[26] In 1927 the realist Walter Wheeler Cook quoted an unattributed assertion as indicative of the prevailing mind-set: "Every judicial act resulting in a judgment consists of a pure deduction."[27] What Cook failed to indicate is that this statement came from a jurisprudential article by John Zane, entitled "German Legal Philosophy,"[28] and Cook offered no evidence to support his claim that lawyers and judges generally saw judging in these abstract terms.

As with the notion of law as science, practitioners tended to demur at the suggestion that judging was a matter of deduction. Austin Abbott, who became an academic dean after a long career as a lawyer, openly doubted (in 1893) the assertion that judging was mainly a matter of logical deduction (a view he associated with jurisprudence scholars):

> What is the method of reasoning that even common law courts are really pursuing? Is it simply a system of logic, having inflexible lines of a syllogism as its deductions? An examination of the current reports of the decisions will show that while many cases are decided upon that principle a considerable proportion even

of common law cases are decided upon principles of utility. . . . Cases are now frequent in which our courts of last resort are guided in their decision by considering which of several rules will work the best.

This is not the jurisprudence of a system of commands; it is the jurisprudence of common welfare wrought out by free reasoning upon the actual facts of life.[29]

Jabez Fox wrote several turn-of-the-century commentaries in the *Harvard Law Review* giving, as it were, the view from practice. "If you ask a lawyer whether he really believes that judicial decisions are mathematical deductions," Fox wrote in 1900, "he will say that the notion is absurd; that when four judges vote one way and three another, it does not mean that the three or the four have made a mistake. It means simply that the different judges have given different weights to divers competing considerations which cannot be balanced on any measured scale."[30] Fox added that, although judges must follow precedent which cannot be distinguished on some rational ground, "Beyond this the judge has a free hand to decide the case before him according to his view of the general good . . . [and] no human being can tell how the social standard of justice will work on that judge's mind before the judgment is rendered."[31] Harvard law professor James Thayer, the target of Fox's critical comments, while rebuffing other aspects of Fox's argument, concurred "entirely with the critic that our courts are not engaged in reaching 'mathematical conclusions,' or in merely logical, abstract, or academic discussions."[32] Fox tossed the same skeptical wet blanket on Holmes's famous portrayal in "The Path of the Law," responding "that the learned judge finds it necessary to expose a fallacy; namely 'the notion that the only force at work in the development of the law is logic.' " "But is this a common error?"[33] Fox asked. "I cannot believe . . . that this particular fallacy has taken a deep hold on the profession. Nor can it be admitted for a moment that the judges have failed hitherto to decide cases according to their ideas of the general good."[34]

These skeptical comments, resounding of realism born of practice, suggest that outside of jurisprudence circles, ideas about legal science and judging as logical deduction were often regarded with bemusement or indifference rather than agreement. Pound, Frank, and other legal realists asserted that *most* lawyers and jurists of the day believed that law was a science and that judging was mechanical or deductive. But it is hard to find anyone other than legal academics, theorists especially, attesting to these beliefs (although academics also expressed skepticism on this), while there are plentiful indications that lawyers found these claims ill fitting or absurd.

Contemporaneous Accounts at Odds with Pound

To scrutinize the plausibility of his characterization, Pound's observations can be juxtaposed against three contemporaneous articles. Four years earlier, in the *Yale Law Journal*, Wilbur Larremore presented the current situation as almost the opposite of Pound: "The tendency towards judicial arbitration, as distinguished from the scientific administration of the law, has been noticeable in most American State courts during the past few decades."[35] He suggested that the Court's decisions were "sympathetic with and effectuating an extra-judicial sentiment."[36] Larremore observed:

> In this condition of affairs judges indulge in the delusion that they are observing *stare decisis* merely because they cite precedents. The truth is that, much in the same manner that expert witnesses are procurable to give almost any opinions that are desired, *judicial precedents may be found for any proposition that a counsel, or a court, wishes established, or to establish.* We are not living under a system of scientific exposition and development of abstract principles, but, to a large degree, under one of judicial arbitration, *in which courts do what they think is just in the case at bar and cite the nearest favorable previous decisions as pretexts.* . . . [The Court of Appeals] has now developed the disposition to act as an independent and creative law-giver to engage in what, from any point, must be termed judicial legislation.[37]

In the same year, an article in the *Michigan Law Review* by Edward Whitney seconded Larremore's observations.[38] Whitney claimed that in both federal and state courts the doctrine of stare decisis "has already to a considerable extent been weakened."[39] Whitney suggests that some judges are reasoning in a rigid fashion, but,

> as the wilderness of authorities presented upon the briefs of counsel tends every year to become more hopeless, *the courts in general tend more and more to decide each case according to their own ideas of fairness as between the parties to that case, and to pass the previous authorities in silence, or dispose of them with the general remark . . . that they are not in conflict.* Different men, however, are of different minds. . . . the chances of difference in decision of two substantially similar cases coming before different sets of judges, or even

before the same judge in different years, tends to increase. Apparent conflicts of authority thus arise.[40]

Whitney attributed these problems to the abundance of precedents on all sides and to overburdened judges trying to get through heavy case loads.

Judge Emlin McClain of the Supreme Court of Iowa, writing in the *American Law Review*, noted the present tendency for some judges to rule in precedent-bound fashion,[41] while others used the surplus of inconsistent precedents to advance ends:

> The multiplicity of precedents has led to a greater freedom in adopting rules which shall be suitable to the attainment in general of substantially satisfactory results. No one case or series of cases has the arbitrary and inherent authority which was earlier in our judicial history accorded to the rulings of the courts. There is much greater liberality exercised in modifying, by way of restriction or expansion, rules which have once been announced. Moreover, the common law has been found to possess the capacity which all living organisms have, of getting rid of that which has become dead or useless.[42]

Judges were not trapped in mechanical jurisprudence, by this account, but rather were relatively free to modify the law in desired ways.

These contemporaneous writings in leading journals by Larremore, Whitney, and McClain establish that, at the very moment Pound set out to construct what would become the core image of the formalist age, a depiction of the situation inconsistent with Pound's claim that judges were trapped within mechanical reasoning was also in circulation.

The Struggle with Legal Uncertainty

An urgent theme within legal circles in this period, mentioned by all three jurists just discussed, was legal uncertainty. A member of the bar, Henry Craft, urgently warned in 1878 about "the magnitude and vast range of powers and discretion confided to the judiciary"[43] attributable to the "details of unsettled rules of property and personal rights—of inconsistent and conflicting decisions—of instability in adjudication made, and want of adherence to what was of old established [precedent]."[44] In an 1890 address to the Kansas bar, Judge Thomas Ewing estimated that in about 40 percent of his cases "the decisions [precedents] conflict, and a large weight of reason and authority is found on both sides."[45] "In these doubtful cases," Ewing asked rhetorically, "Who shall weigh them by reason, when the questions may be of mere arbitrary law? Who shall weigh them by conscience, when they may present no conflict solvable by the moral sense?"[46] The president of the American Bar Association, Uriah Milton Rose, remarked in his 1902 address that, owing to the proliferation of cases, judges have "discretion . . . in deciding cases . . .; for our courts can generally find precedents for almost any proposition."[47] Chief Justice Albert Savage of the Maine Supreme Court, in 1914, acknowledged that cases arise in which authority can be found on both sides or precedent is lacking and "it would be contrary to all human experience to say that his temperament and his predictions may not give color to his conception [of the law]."[48] In his 1916 speech to the ABA, Elihu Root observed, "The vast and continually increasing mass of reported decisions which afford authorities on almost every side of almost every question admonish us that by the mere following of precedent we should soon have no system of law at all, but the rule of the Turkish cadi who is expected to do in each case what seems to him to be right."[49]

All of the preceding statements were made in the heart of the so-called formalist age. They were made by leading lawyers and judges in high-profile settings. What they say is manifestly at odds with the conventional story about purportedly dominant legal formalist beliefs at the time.

Legal professionals were especially alarmed when West Publishing Company began to publish thousands of reported decisions in the late nineteenth century. Judge Oscar Fellows, in 1912, remarked, "The reported decisions in all our states so enormously multiply that the lawyer's problem is not so much where to find the law as to weigh and estimate the value of what he discovers. It is in truth more than ever 'the lawless science of the law, the countless myriad of precedents.' "[50] The problem of legal uncertainty was a regular topic of bar association speeches. One speaker endorsed an observation from another that "the lawyer hunts up the authorities and finds twenty-five on one side and twenty-six on the other, some of greater and some of lesser authority."[51]

The turn-of-the-century overflow of reported cases coincided with what many in legal circles feared was an out-of-control proliferation of legislation. "At no time and in no country has legislation been so active,"[52] remarked one commentator. Bryce wrote that "the output of legislation has of late been incomparably greater than in any previous age—greater not only absolutely but in proportion to the population of the civilized nations."[53] "In no country is the output so large as in the United States, where, besides Congress, forty-six State Legislatures are busily at work turning out laws on all imaginable subjects."[54] Many jurists looked askance at this burst of legislation, some because it threatened the dominance of the common law, but others, on a more practical level, worried that it was difficult to keep track of and generated a host of unanticipated conflicts with existing legal doctrines that judges had to reconcile without guidance.

Judge Thomas Cooley and Judge Seymour Thompson, both nationally known jurists, gave successive public speeches in the late 1880s debating the extent of legal uncertainty. Calling complaints about legal uncertainty exaggerated, Cooley argued that many areas of law (criminal, property, family, trusts, and estates) are relatively settled, that the commercial system predictably handles a multitude of economic transactions, and that society enjoys peace and order.[55] The following year Judge Thompson went to the same podium and, with apologies to Cooley, argued the opposite. He conducted a detailed doctrinal exploration showing major inconsistencies in several areas of law. Thompson asserted that "the jumble through which I have just conducted you, though full of legal technicality, is utterly destitute of any element of certainty; and every title of law abounds in such labyrinths."[56] As an indication of what others thought on the issue, the lawyer-editors of the *Albany Law Journal*—who were openly skeptical of Cooley's claims of legal certainty—praised Thompson's essay as "brilliant, vigorous, and judicious."[57] In fairness to Cooley, it must be said, he did not deny that there was legal uncertainty but rather argued that, although uncertainty was unavoidable given the complexity of law and life, law nevertheless functioned fairly well.[58]

Concerns about rampant legal uncertainty provided fuel for the debate over codification that began early in the nineteenth century and continued into the twentieth century. In 1886 Judge John Dillon summed up the case for codification:

> It is manifest from the foregoing discussion, that the Judges from the very nature of their functions, can not develop the general principles of the law so as to take in the entire subject, or do anything except (if you will pardon the expression) automatically (that is depending upon the accident of cases arising for judicial action) towards giving anything like completeness to the law or any branch of it. Not only is case law incomplete, but the multiplicty and conflict of decisions is one of the most fruitful causes of the unnecessary uncertainty, which characterizes the jurisprudence of England and America. Thousands of decisions are reported every year. An almost unlimited number can be found upon almost any subject. What any given case decides, must be deduced from a careful examination of the exact facts, and of the

positive legislation, if any, applicable thereto. A general principle will be found adjudged by certain courts. Other courts deny or doubt the soundness of the principle. Exceptions are gradually but certainly introduced. Almost every subject is overrun by a more than tropical redundancy of decisions, leaving the most patient investigator entangled in doubt.[59]

This luxuriant muddle was made worse, Dillon added, because legislation was "irregular and fragmentary," and often poorly drafted.[60] A Yale law professor in 1913 likewise urged codification—in overwrought language—to alleviate law's "tangled jungle": "The uncertainty of our law, its confusion, its startling bulkiness, redundancy and prolixity, increased annually by some 20,000 new statutes and thousands of new reported cases, make our law today the most intolerable in the world and perhaps the worst ever known to human history— all because its form and lack of uniformity are so objectionable."[61]

Distress about the unmanageable uncertainty of law, and the license this gave to judges, far more so than belief in the rigid perfection of legal science held up by Pound, characterized prevailing views of law at the turn of the century. This nigh chaotic vision of the law provided no purchase for the mechanical, deductive view of judging.

The Doubtful Charge of Excessive Conceptualism

Later generations of scholars have often repeated Pound's claims that judges engage in highly abstract conceptual reasoning with little attention to real conditions. A closer look at this claim shows that skepticism is again warranted. At the time, the main criticism of *Lochner*, the example offered by Pound that resonates the most today, was not that the judges, beguiled by an abstract understanding of liberty of contract, failed to pay attention to the facts, but the opposite. In a critical study of recent freedom-of-contract decisions, *Lochner* in particular, Ernst Freund concluded (in 1910), "No other construction can be placed upon these decisions than that the courts assume the power to look into the question of fact."[62] By Freund's account, courts were not engaging in purely abstract application of legal concepts without attention to the facts; rather, they were second-guessing legislative findings with their own reading of the facts.

Pound's list of "conceptions" included long-standing rules of procedure, evidence, and rules about jury instructions,[63] as well as words like "estoppel, malice, privity, implied intention of the testator, vested and contingent."[64] In Pound's sense, just about every legal notion is a conception. While he is correct that courts applied legal notions of this sort without rethinking their premises, this aspect of judging is routine, not something unique to judges in this period. At any given time, judges apply the bulk of legal conceptions without much thought.

Many of Pound's examples, moreover, involved pleading or procedural requirements that earlier generations of reformers had also lamented as "technicalities" with unfortunate results. This will be elaborated in a coming discussion of the traditional meaning of "formalism." For immediate purposes, the key point is that Pound failed to acknowledge that a great deal of progress had been made to rectify exactly the matters he complained about. The example he used to illustrate mechanical jurisprudence in evidence, for instance, involved a rule about the admission of scientific testimony.[65] But in 1892 the evidence scholar Wigmore observed with respect to the same rule that in practice judges "partially evaded and nullified" the requirements owing to its absurd consequences.[66] Thus, in actual practice, one of Pound's own examples represents the opposite of blind conceptualism.

In effect, what Pound did was box together sundry complaints about the defects of law and procedure, wrap them in jurisprudential packaging—discussing legal science, historical jurisprudence, and legal positivism—and ramp up their implications. What lawyers and judges had long criticized in ordinary terms as absurd or outdated rules with unfortunate consequences, Pound the jurisprudent portrayed as frozen conceptual reasoning by judges caught in the grip of abstract historical jurisprudence and legal positivism: "Through the historical school the doctrines of metaphysical jurisprudence affected profoundly the actual course of decision and of legal writing. . . . For example, the arguments of the late James C. Carter were no small factor in fashioning American judicial decisions of the last quarter of the nineteenth century."[67] This extraordinary claim about Carter's influence, for which Pound offers no support, is unlikely, given that Carter's views were out of step with the time.

The English jurist Pollock found Pound's argument implausible in two respects: he saddled historical jurisprudents with excessively abstract views they did not hold, and he erroneously asserted that judges in their decision making were strongly influenced by these abstract theories of law.[68] "So, when I am confronted with Professor Pound's unqualified assertion that a historical-metaphysical doctrine 'was dominant in the science of law throughout the [nineteenth] century,' I feel tempted to ask which of us is standing on his head."[69]

Dubious Complaints about Rigid Adherence
to Stare Decisis

There is another way to apprehend and explain the charge of "mechanical jurisprudence." The real complaint of Pound and others who echoed his argument was not that judges engaged in rigid logical deduction from abstract concepts when deciding cases but rather that judges were hewing too closely to precedents that ought to be discarded. This is an age-old complaint about judging in common law systems, voiced well before Pound invented "mechanical jurisprudence." "How often have the ablest ministers of justice been compelled to smother the cries of conscience, and sacrifice the rights of a party upon the altar of the idol, *stare decisis!*" wrote a jurist in 1833.[70]

Three points about stare decisis must be considered when evaluating this complaint. First, although critics of mechanical judging attacked courts for failing to consider public policy implications when applying the law, adherence to stare decisis was justified in *public policy* terms: reliance on settled precedents (even when wrong or obsolete), it was said, advances the stability, certainty, and predictability of the law.[71] The "much quoted" American justification for stare decisis in the nineteenth century was Chancellor Kent's observation: "If a decision has been made upon solemn argument and mature deliberation, the presumption is in favor of its correctness; and the community have a right to regard it as a just declaration or exposition of the law, and to regulate their actions and contracts by it. It would, therefore, be extremely inconvenient to the public, if precedents were not duly regarded and implicitly followed."[72] A late nineteenth-century judge explained that "one of the chief reasons why we adhere to erroneous precedents" is that, although "individual injustice may be done, but, upon the whole, the public good will be promoted, by avoiding the mischiefs of uncertainty, and long-protracted lawsuits."[73]

Hence, courts adhered to precedent not out of blind obedience in disregard of the public policy implications surrounding a given rule or case but out of the conviction that consistently following precedent was advantageous to society.[74] Oliver Wendell Holmes affirmed the wisdom of this policy: "I do not expect or think it desirable that the judges should undertake to renovate the law. That is not their province. . . . Indeed it is precisely because . . . the claim of our especial code to respect is simply that it exists, that it is the one to which we have become accustomed . . . [that] I am slow to consent to overruling precedent."[75]

The second point is that, as Holmes suggests, jurists did not view stare decisis as sacrosanct. "That maxim [stare decisis], although entitled to great weight, does not furnish an absolute rule which can never be departed from. That it does not, the number of overruled decisions, which have accumulated in the administration of the common law, abundantly proves."[76] Blackstone was quoted for holding "that precedents and rules must be followed, *unless flatly absurd or unjust*."[77] Absolute adherence to stare decisis was as ill advised as ready departures from stare decisis.[78] "*Stare decisis* is a good rule as far as it is applicable," wrote the lawyer-editors of the *Albany Law Journal* in 1873, "but it will not do to expand it into a doctrine which shall prevent all progress and deter all improvement to correspond with the ever changing condition of mankind."[79] A prominent historical jurist, Christopher Tiedeman, argued in 1895 that "the rule of *stare decisis* has its limitations."[80] "*Stare decisis* . . . [appropriately] gives way to the popular demand for a contrary ruling," he wrote.[81] Tiedeman insisted that it is necessary and proper for judges to discard precedents, openly or otherwise, that come into conflict with prevalent conceptions of right.[82]

The hard part—the always contestable nub of the matter—comes in determining when countervailing considerations are so weighty that a departure is warranted (at the perceived cost of increasing legal uncertainty and diminishing confidence in the law). Courts at the time viewed this as a heavy burden rarely met.

The third point is that legal professionals regularly remarked that judges used various techniques to alter, avoid, or overrule precedents, even when they did not openly admit it. An 1872 essay protested that the courts' *sub silentio* "method of overruling cases in fact, but not in name, is doing altogether too much reverence to the inviolability of precedents. It leads to that very uncertainty and doubt which the rule of which we speak was intended to prevent; it embarrasses both the courts and the profession."[83] "There is an 'irrepressible conflict' between the pretense of 'stare decisis' and the actuality of judicial legislation," observed the editors of the *Albany Law Journal* in 1885.[84] Columbia law professor Munroe Smith frankly described, in 1887, the process by which judges alter the law while claiming to adhere to stare decisis: "[W]hen new law is needed, the courts are obliged to 'find' it, and to find it in old cases. This can commonly be done by re-examination and re-interpretation, or, at the worst, by 'distinction.' By a combination of these means, it is even possible to abrogate an old rule and to set a new one in its place. When the old rule is sufficiently wormholed with 'distinctions,' a very slight re-examination will reduce it to dust, and a re-interpretation of the 'distinguishing' cases will produce the rule that is desired."[85] Wilbur Larremore in 1908 complained, "The most serious menace to the reliability of the law has arisen not through frank and avowed changes of mind, but through casuistical evasion of precedent, through resort to distinctions that do not distinguish. The tendency to preserve an appearance of consistency while laying down an inherently discordant principle has been on the increase in most of the state courts."[86]

Complaints during the formalist age "that courts are disposed unwarrantedly to make a fetish of precedents" appear to lend support to Pound's characterization of judges trapped in mechanical jurisprudence.[87] Throughout this period, however, jurists still spoke about the judicial use of legal fictions, subtle distinctions, and *sub silentio* over rulings to circumvent undesirable precedents. Even Roscoe Pound recognized, in an article he published the year before *Mechanical Jurisprudence*, that judges continued to utilize various interpretive techniques (including legal fictions) to see that the cases are "decided in the long run so as to accord with the moral sense of the community."[88] There is little reason to believe that judges suddenly forgot or failed to use these traditional arts within the common law system for changing the law when deemed necessary.

Dean Eugene Rostow of Yale came close to recognizing this in a retrospective look at the legal realists he published in 1961. "I sometimes wonder," Rostow remarked, "whether the lawyers of the day really believed in the 'mechanical jurisprudence' they professed, and against which Roscoe Pound's early articles inveighed with such vehemence."[89] Rostow observed that the common law has carried on for centuries without visible alteration in method, although undergoing a great deal of substantive change. What Rostow did not know was that hardly any lawyers and judges of the day actually did "profess" belief in mechanical jurisprudence.

Rapid Change, Not Strange "Mechanical Jurisprudence," Explains Complaints

The period from the 1870s through the 1930s gave birth to the modern United States. America transformed from a mostly rural society based on agricultural production to a mostly urban, industrial society. It was the age of incorporation, which brought the rise of big business and the growth of labor unions, along with the rise of consumers as the primary engines of the economy. This period introduced widespread mechanization, the use of hydroelectric power and fossil fuels (coal and oil), the electrification of the cities, the mass transportation of goods and people (canals, railroads, automobiles), and reliable means of immediate communication across vast distances (telephone, telegraph, radio). Industrial conditions were mean and dangerous, with thousands of people killed or maimed by railroads and in factories each year. Devastating depressions began in 1873, 1893, and 1929, which brought several thousand strikes and violent labor strife. Millions of immigrant laborers were absorbed from outside the previously dominant Protestant feeders (Germany, Scandinavia, and England), including Catholics from Ireland and Italy, Jews from Eastern Europe, and Chinese and Japanese. The Gilded Age witnessed the "populist" revolt of farmers in an uneasy alliance with labor, and the "progressive" reaction of middle-class reformers (who sought to reform the values of the rich as well as the poor). This period saw the growth of modern bureaucratic government, including the creation of federal Departments of Justice, Agriculture, Labor, and Commerce. A marked expansion in federal and state government activities took place, including an early version of social security (the pension for Northern Civil War veterans and their families), the regulation of railroads, the regulation of monopolies, the regulation of workplace and product safety, and the creation of mandatory education. The United States emerged as a global economic, military, and political power.

A radical makeover of American society and government, involving all of these developments, was accomplished within a short five decades.[90] This massive transformation outstripped the capacity of the slow, piecemeal mechanisms traditionally utilized by common law judges to accommodate change. These various transformations fueled a massive increase in legislation, and the growth of the administrative state. Judges need not have behaved in any peculiarly "mechanical" or "formalistic" fashion to be scorned by political critics as intransigent or harmfully reactionary. They continued to decide cases in the same old common law method and manner while the world about them underwent a rapid and complete transformation.

Prominent political scientist Henry Carter Adams, in 1886, explained popular discontent with the law thusly: "[T]he source of prevalent complaint is found in the fact that the conception of rights and duties, of liberties and constraints, of privileges and responsibilities, which lies at the basis of our juridical system, is not applied to the highly developed industrial system of the present. Difficulties have arisen because the industrial life and activity of the social organism have grown to a different plane from the one which underlies the judicial systems."[91] Juridical concepts were constructed upon individual control and responsibility, Adams noted, while modern industrial conditions were marked by social coordination and control. Tiedeman, writing in 1892, witnessed "in the last thirty years or more a strong tendency to socialism" developing in public opinion, matched unevenly and belatedly by the courts.[92] Beale wrote similarly in 1904 that in the second third of the nineteenth century a gradual shift began in social attitudes whereby "the principle of association [in contrast to the former emphasis on individualist rights] became more and more readily accepted in social and political affairs, until it has finally become the dominating idea of the time."[93] Dicey wrote about the same ongoing shift from individualism to collectivism in late nineteenth-century social attitudes, which found expression mainly in legislation.[94] Judges were trained in the older individualist-oriented ideas embodied within the common law, while social attitudes, in tune with the new reality, had shifted to embrace a more social view of responsibility.

Judges were not only handcuffed by the step-by-step changes allowed by the common law judicial craft, but many initially were also unwilling vehicles for the desired changes, which they considered unwise. Evidence supporting this explanation comes from a firsthand account by a judge. In a thoughtful retrospective look at the period written in 1927, Judge Leonard Crouch described the rapid changes in the economy and society that took place at the turn of the century. The presiding generation of judges had been trained to see law in terms defined by a bygone age:

> The 19th century was a period of individualism. In politics, a minimum of government was best; in economics, free competition was essential; and in law the preservations of the rights of persons and property, including freedom of contract, was fundamental. Except as he himself had willed the existence of a relation to which the law attached a sanction, an individual was to be free from exaction; nor was he to be liable unless for a fault.[95]

Crouch underwent his legal training when these views were still being taught, so he could appreciate them. "The long succession of decisions in the Nineties and in the first ten or twelve years of the present century, holding unconstitutional many acts of the legislature which interfered with the property rights and freedom of contract of the individual, *seemed to most of us sound law and socially desirable.*"[96] Moreover, he added, "we had been taught to regard certainty in the law as essential."[97] The failure of the courts to respond to the extraordinary changes, however, incited popular "discontent with and criticism of the courts" and "an attack on the common law itself."[98] Prompted by this agitation, he observed, courts in the first decade of the new century began to gradually move the common law in a more progressive direction.[99]

Judge Crouch's account is instructive because it provides access to both points of view: of the judges resisting the change and of the jurists who supported it. This was not a clash between judges blindly engaging in rigid stare decisis or abstract logical deduction heedless of social reality versus uniquely self-aware jurists valiantly struggling to bring an enlightened understanding to law and judging. This was a disagreement between jurists across a generational divide that spanned unprecedented changes in society who saw legal doctrine and the social welfare in contrasting terms. Owing to these differences of opinion, the reluctant judges allowed small and slow changes, found some of the desired changes contrary to long-standing law and ill advised, and in particular instances did not feel that the heavy burden required to change the law (at the cost of increasing legal uncertainty) had been met. At the same time, the jurists and public in favor of change thought desired shifts in the law were long overdue.

With this explanation, there is no need to accept Pound's argument that judges in the "formalist age" reasoned in a bizarrely mechanical manner unlike judges before or after them. Crouch's description of events is also consistent with the contemporaneous accounts reported earlier—from Larremore, Whitney, and McClain—that are directly at odds with Pound's portrayal, for they too observed that judges had begun to utilize the freedom allowed by the overflow of available precedents on all sides to move the law in new directions.

4

○ ○ ● ● ●

THE HOLES IN THE STORY ABOUT LEGAL FORMALISM

MAJOR DOUBTS WERE RAISED in the preceding two chapters about the most influential accounts of the formalist age. Roscoe Pound's claim that judges reasoned in a logical, mechanical manner is inconsistent with statements of many jurists at the time worried about the messy state of the law and the capacity of judges to construct legal justifications for whatever outcome they desired. Jerome Frank deceptively reversed the import of Maine's observations, and several of Grant Gilmore's crucial assertions about the period are demonstrably false. Contrary to what Pound, Frank, and Gilmore insisted, there is overwhelming historical evidence that *all lawyers knew*—as was often repeated—that judges made law. Pound and Frank relied on German discussions of civil law systems, whereas Max Weber argued that common law systems were *not* formally rational legal systems. Jurisprudents in the United States were enamored with saying that "law is a science," but practitioners rejected this idea and dismissed the notion that judging was a matter of pure logical deduction.

Although this counterevidence pokes large holes in the story about the formalists, the story is so widely accepted as true that it will not be easily deflated. This final chapter on the topic adds several layers of historical and theoretical depth to fill out the argument. One of the most paradoxical aspects of this story is that the generation in law we now charge with embracing formalism saw itself as successfully overcoming formalism. Another misfit is that jurists at the time agonized over the rampant use of legal fictions, which made a mockery of claims that law was logical and systematically ordered. This additional historical background provides a fuller sense of what jurists at the time thought about law, judging, and formalism.

An analytical discussion clarifies several routinely confused aspects of the story about formalism, exposing precisely why it is wrong. An examination of the strongest remaining support offered for the claim of formalism—the style of written decisions—then shows why this support is unreliable. Finally, this effort at debunking demonstrates that the story about the formalists that circulates today has a relatively recent provenance, resurrected by leftist legal historians and theorists in the 1970s, motivated by contemporary political concerns.

Twists in the story about the legal formalists appear at every turn.

The Historical Meaning of "Formalism"

Within common law systems, "formalism" is an old term with negative connotations that reach back to twelfth- and thirteenth-century England, when "forms of action" became entrenched within the common law.[1] "The system of Forms of Action or the Writ System is the most important aspect of English medieval law," wrote nineteenth-century legal historian Frederick Maitland, "and it was not abolished until its piecemeal destruction in the nineteenth century."[2] A party seeking legal redress was required to secure (for a fee) a king's writ (or summons) that called the defendant to answer;[3] writs represented forms of action; each form of action had a precise formula that the plaintiff was required to plead.[4]

In the early period, new forms of action were liberally created through variations of old forms as the need arose; at its peak, there were hundreds of forms. This practice was halted in the late thirteenth century out of concern from rivals of the king's courts about the expansion of their jurisdiction at the expense of local and ecclesiastical tribunals.[5] When writs were frozen, stultification began to set in. If no form of action fit, or if the plaintiff chose the wrong form of action, or if the plaintiff made any error or omission in meeting the required formula, the case was lost regardless of merit, and the plaintiff was liable for costs.[6]

Formalism of this sort, Frederick Pollock wrote, was present in Germanic customary law as well as in Roman law, and one can find "all the world over, professional attachment to form for form's sake."[7] The unforgiving strictness of the form system, Pollock suggested, was the product of an "irrational" desire for ritual-like exactitude, along with a rational worry about the abuse of judicial power.[8] Maitland and Pollock argued that, despite its harsh consequences, viewed in the context of this nascent period of legal development, when judges lacked legal training and corruption was rife, "formalism is the twin-born sister of liberty."[9] "[D]iscretionary powers can only be safely entrusted to judges whose impartiality is above suspicion and whose every act is exposed to public and professional criticism."[10] Those who harp on "the disorderly mass of crabbed pedantry" produced by this system, they observed, "shall do well to remember that the rule of law was the rule of writs."[11] In a less charitable light, critics pointed out that the obscure technical requirements of the form system made lawyers indispensible intermediaries. "To all but the profession, the law of forms of action is in a great measure a sealed book."[12]

The fixing of forms and the requirement of strict adherence gave birth to a proliferation of legal fictions. Situations constantly arose that did not match the formula, and society changed over time. Forms of action contained cumbersome, senseless, or archaic requirements. In response to the practical demands at hand,[13] courts invented legal fictions to meet requirements of the form, sometimes de facto creating new forms without acknowledging it.[14] As Maitland put it, courts in effect said, "Why not abbreviate the process by supposing things have been done which have in fact not been done?"[15] Pleadings would refer to fake parties—famously John Doe—doing fake things. To satisfy the requirements of trover (for damages to personal property), for example, a plaintiff would fictitiously plead that the defendant had found property lost by the plaintiff. Although untrue, this allegation complied with the required formality, and the case would proceed to the merits.[16] Over time, the common law and pleadings became suffused with fictions of this sort.[17] "We have seen a gradual process of formal decay which set in soon after the death of Edward I in 1307," wrote Maitland, "and together with this formal decay a vigorous but contorted development of substantive law brought by fiction within medieval forms."[18]

The writ system remained basically intact (with a few legislatively imposed modifications) until procedural reforms were implemented in the course of the nineteenth century in England and the United States to simplify pleading requirements, abolish forms of action, and join law and equity.[19] But the marks of the writ system, which shaped doctrinal lines, would not be erased. English jurist John Salmond wrote in 1905 that the "forms of action are dead, but their ghosts still haunt the precincts of the law. In their life they were powers of evil, and even in death they have not wholly ceased from troubling. In earlier days they filled the law with formalism and fiction, confusion and complexity."[20]

The term "formalism" drew its pejorative connotations from unforgiving forms of action that visited absurd or unjust consequences. An American jurist in 1864 plaintively inquired: "Why should he [a plaintiff] be required in his summons to give his complaint a specific name, call it an action of trespass, case, debt, or detinue—on the peril that if he makes a mistake in this particular, if he assigns a wrong name to his action, however well founded in law and justice his cause may be, he shall lose it, and be turned out of court in some instances, with the entire and irremediable loss of his claim, and in all that with a judgment against him for costs?"[21]

A subtle shift occurred over time in the pejorative application of "formalism"—although the underlying notion remained constant throughout. This condemnation was directed to express disapproval at inflexible or rigid legal thinking of any kind, not just pleading or procedural requirements. This expansion in reference was natural because "form" and "rule" are close cognates, paired in this standard definition of "formula": "A prescribed or set form; an established rule; a fixed or conventional method in which anything is to be done, arranged, or said."[22] A jurist in 1847 observed, unflatteringly, that early on in their legal training lawyers acquire "habits of pedantic formalism and slavery to precedent."[23] A lawyer in 1892 wrote: "Few things can more impair his [judge, lawyer] usefulness than confirmed *formalism*, or, as it might be called, *legalism*, which misses the real meaning and character of the law and sees the relations of men to property and to each other, only as they are established by printed rules."[24]

As these quotations reflect, by the nineteenth century, when reforms were implemented, formalism was roundly slammed as the unwelcome inheritance of a bygone age that ought to be overcome.[25] An American judge in 1857 castigated "ignorant and slavish formalism."[26] The prominent historical jurist William Hammond (quoted in the introduction) remarked in 1875: "Formerly the 'law of the land' was a rigid, *abstruse technical* system, clothing its simplest rules and principles in artificial forms and language."[27] He applauded contemporary law for its comparative transparency and simplicity. An 1876 article on legal education observed that "the archaic period . . . is the period of rigid formalism" and optimistically opined that, while residual procedural formalism remained to be rooted out, the U.S. common law system had progressed beyond the formalist stage to focus on principles.[28] An 1889 article detailing ongoing procedural and substantive reforms noted with satisfaction that in nine states "[j]ustice is administered, as it should be, without reference to the artificial and technical rules of the common law."[29] In 1892 John Henry Wigmore, the great evidence scholar, charged that judges who enforce a particularly impractical rule (on the admission of scientific testimony, mentioned in the preceding chapter) would "be guilty of a formalism which is neither creditable to the law nor beneficial to litigants."[30] "The tendency of the day is towards creating more competent trial judges and vesting in them a larger discretion, and that policy should be here exemplified."[31] In 1895 a jurist tracing out the historical progress of legal doctrine identified several instances of "a triumph of the spirit of the law over its earlier formalism."[32] At the close of the century, to call a judge "a formalist and a hairsplitter" was an insult.[33]

The condemnatory references to "formalism" that mark this period provide credence to the assertion of a jurist who, in 1893, identified "the *Zeitgeist* and its dislike of formalism."[34] This statement exposes yet another surprising twist in this exploration: a generation of jurists that saw itself as finally prevailing over senseless formalism has been contemptuously dubbed "the formalist age" by later generations.

The Embarrassing Presence of Legal Fictions

As explained, the writ system made it exceedingly difficult to accomplish legal change.[35] Legal fictions were the main expedient utilized by judges for centuries to alter the law. By the early nineteenth century, however, legal fictions were under sharp attack. Jeremy Bentham scorned legal fictions: "What you [judges] have been doing by the fiction—could you, or could you not, have done it without the fiction? If not, your fiction is a wicked lie: if yes, a foolish one."[36] "Wheresoever the use of a fiction prevails, and in proportion as it prevails, every law-book is an institute of vice; every court of judicature is a school of vice."[37] An American jurist in 1841 noted: "All manner of pleadings and proceedings, both in law and equity, are stuffed with falsehoods and lies."[38] In a sardonic essay lampooning legal fictions, the author observed with thinly disguised disgust that actions for ejectment contained not "a single tittle of truth in any one of the facts that are put upon the record."[39] Popular ditties were sung ridiculing legal fictions.[40]

Maine's *Ancient Law* (1861) contained a chapter addressing legal fictions, stating that jurists were well aware of the useful function they served.[41] He was more sympathetic to legal fictions than Bentham because he felt change was necessary within the fixed common law system and fictions met this need. But Maine agreed that the use of legal fictions was not creditable to modern legal systems, and he suggested that legal change in the future should be accomplished openly through legislation.

The vocal unhappiness with the use of legal fictions that can be found through the turn of the twentieth century provides additional evidence that jurists did not believe in the image of legal formalism.[42] Lawyers knew that the law and legal proceedings were shot through with deliberate falsehoods—belying claims about logical coherence—and lawyers knew that fictions masked (transparently) alterations in the law.[43] Fictions made a mockery of the claim of adherence to stare decisis, for compliance with precedent was maintained on the surface when lawyers were well aware that its operation had been evaded. "[T]here is many a legal fiction which both young and old [lawyers] accept with reluctance,"[44] wrote a legal editor in 1870. "At the present time," a jurist wrote in 1917, "there is no longer any need to resort to subterfuges or to employ fictional phraseology," although he made this remark in a two-part article that cataloged a long list of still-active legal fictions.[45]

The writ system and its demise left the law in an unsystematic state, exacerbated by the distorting presence of legal fictions.

Why Jurists Did Not Believe Judging Was Purely Deductive

For analytical purposes, it is essential to keep separate the two aspects set forth, respectively, in chapters 2 and 3: a theory of law and its development by judges, and a theory of how judges apply the law to individual cases.[46] The label legal formalism is regularly applied to the characterization of the common law as comprehensive, gapless, conceptually consistent and logically ordered, and autonomous, as developed by judges through the application of reason.[47] In the historical literature this is sometimes designated "classical legal thought."[48] The label legal formalism is also often applied to the description of judicial decision making as mechanically or deductively applying legal concepts, principles, precedents, or rules to the facts in a given case.[49]

Confusion arises because these two aspects are frequently discussed in tandem and because the terms "reason" and "deduction" have been invoked in connection with both. In connection with the development of legal rules, it has been said that jurists and judges utilize reason to "deduce" new rules out of existing principles to cover new situations. In connection with rendering legal decisions in particular cases, it has been said that judges reason syllogistically, deductively applying rules and principles (major premise) to the facts in a given case (minor premise) to come to the decision (necessary conclusion). Pound used "deduction" in connection with both,[50] and writings on legal formalism often fail to mark this distinction.

Nineteenth-century jurists recognized the distinction between these two aspects, as laid out in this 1833 passage:

> The science of law, then, is that knowledge whereby we distinguish between the just and unjust, reduced into a system, and

arranged so as to be conveniently taught, easily remembered and readily applied.

But it is quite obvious that the *application* of this knowledge is a very different thing from the knowledge itself.... What is abstractly just or unjust may be determined with mathematical precision, because the evidence of these abstractions is intuitive. But the relative justice and injustice depends upon so many and such complex circumstances, as to require talents of the very highest order both for the comprehension of principles and facts, to draw the distinction between them with success, and satisfaction to society.[51]

The author advocated the systematic development of legal rules and principles—"law as science"—to assist judges in completing the problem-fraught task of application. "The law then would stand the fairest chance of being heard amidst the din of litigation; and of shining forth unobscured by the clouds of passion, prejudice, and ignorance."[52] It is precisely because judges *cannot* apply the law to the facts in a mechanical fashion—"it is because judges cannot be found through whose faculties the law certainly speaks"[53]—that every effort must be made to organize the law systematically, this jurist argued.

A separate crucial distinction must be drawn in connection with the first topic (body of law): speaking about the law in the abstract or ideal versus speaking about the law generated by judges (and legislatures)—the actual state of the law. Although a number of jurists claimed that the immanent principles of law, and the subsidiary rules that followed therefrom, could be discerned through reason, they did not all mean the same thing by this assertion, and there was no agreement on how it was done. Often it was stated in nigh-ceremonial terms, or uttered as an aspiration or an expression of faith in the law, rather than presented as a concrete claim about law. Others saw it as a fiction. More to the point, even among those who believed in an idealized vision, many jurists complained that judges abjectly failed the law in this respect. An essential part of the old common law understanding was that judges' decisions were merely *evidence* of the law, not the law itself.[54] Erroneous declarations of rules of law, by this reasoning, did not tarnish the integrity of the law.[55] Such errors could nonetheless become deeply enmeshed in the law through stare decisis, wreaking havoc in the law. As an early nineteenth-century jurist remarked, "The history of the common law contains many instances of this sort, of unintended perversion by judges, of some of its most important principles, through mistaken views and fallacious reasonings."[56]

Reflecting this bifurcation of law conceived in the abstract or ideal from the actual decisions of courts, a classically oriented jurist in 1889 spoke "Of the Certainty of the Law and the Uncertainty of Judicial Decisions." He simultaneously extolled the majesty of the common law as the epitome of reason and principle, while also complaining about conflicting precedents, and confusing, poorly reasoned, and erroneous judicial decisions.[57] Hence, the same jurists who paid homage to the reason of the common law (considered abstractly or ideally), could also be fiercely critical of judges for ruining the rational structure of the common law. As legal historian A.W.B. Simpson observed, "Strong legal scientists indeed went out of their way to draw attention to the prevalence of judicial error and confusion."[58]

With the foregoing in mind, it is possible to expose the confusion at the core of the story about the formalists. Four positions must be kept apart: (1) the law conceived abstractly or ideally as logically ordered principles and rules (for those who saw law in these terms); (2) the observed actual state of the law; (3) deductive reasoning when deriving or determining the content of legal rules; and (4) deductive reasoning when applying existing precedents or rules to the facts in a given case. Contrary to standard assertions about what *most* lawyers and judges purportedly *believed* during the formalist age, legal professionals held various views about each, and the four positions did not relate to one another in any uniform way. As disclosed throughout earlier chapters, just about everyone saw law in terms of its actual *problematic* state (no. 2); a number held abstract or idealized views of law as something to strive toward (no. 1); a number asserted that new rules could be deduced from existing principles (no. 3);[59] but seldom did jurists say that judicial application of the law to the facts was a matter of pure deduction (no. 4).

The twofold error contained in present views of the formalist age can now be articulated. The first error is that, though the fourth position is now frequently cited as *the* belief characteristic of the formalist view—that judges deductively apply the law to the facts in a case to produce correct outcomes—that was the view least often expressed at the time. Jurists rarely made this claim because they had a realistic awareness of the complexities involved in judging and of the foibles of human judges (as the next two chapters detail). The second error is that the second position *was* widely held—seeing the actual state of the law as messy and uncertain—but this realistic view of the law is virtually erased by the conventional story about the formalist age.

A great deal of confusion has followed from the failure to keep these basic distinctions in mind. The jurist most often identified as a preeminent formalist,[60] Christopher Columbus Langdell, is a case in point.

This passage from the preface of his casebook is cited as indicative of his formalistic thought:

> Law, considered as a science, consists of certain principles or doctrines. . . . Each of these doctrines has arrived at its present state by slow degrees; in other words, it is a growth, extending in many cases through centuries. The growth is to be traced in the main through a series of cases. . . . It seems to me, therefore, to be possible to take such a branch of the law as Contracts, for example, and, without exceeding comparatively moderate limits, to select, classify, and arrange all the cases which had contributed in any important degree to the growth, development, or establishment of any of its essential doctrines.[61]

In a review of the book, Oliver Wendell Holmes indelibly branded Langdell when he remarked that "the end of all his striving, is the *elegantia juris*, or logical necessity of the system as a system."[62] "The Langdellians," according to legal historian Thomas Grey, "treated law as an [autonomous] intellectual discipline independent of theology, moral philosophy, economics, or political science, one that involved the application of scientific methods to common law materials."[63] Grey asserted that "the Langdellians linked formality to systematicity and autonomy in a way that made theirs the most formal of formalisms."[64]

The legal science Langdell envisioned involved systematizing legal rules and principles. He saw the cases as the raw empirical material of legal science (claiming that the library is to the jurist as the garden is to the botanist).[65] By studying the run of cases, he asserted, jurists could determine which were mistakenly reasoned, and through inductive reasoning they could discern the guiding legal principles, which could then be rationally organized; through deductive reasoning from these principles, in turn, new rules could be developed to deal with new situations.[66] Langdell was undoubtedly an enthusiast for principles and reason.

But to say that law should be organized rationally—a sensible position given the haphazard development of the common law writ system papered over with fictions—and to engage in this process are not to say that legal rules are immutable or autonomous, or that only logic matters in the development and application of law.[67] Samuel Williston (identified by Grey as a "Langdellian")[68] insisted that "Langdell's followers have recognized the necessity that rules of law should produce satisfactory economic and social effects."[69] They were not blind extremists who saw legal doctrine as a cloistered realm, but rather they "attached greater value to the simplicity and certainty" and predictability that accrues from the logical development of a relatively limited number of principles.[70] Williston argued that law does, and must, change to meet the needs of a changing society.[71] Although he emphasized principle and logic, Langdell's view was that law evolves in connection with society, which infuses law with considerations of justice and policy (although he was not entirely consistent about how his various positions hung together).[72]

Historian Bruce Kimball, the author of several recent studies disputing the charge that Langdell was a "formalist," shows that Langdell did not present the law as a geometrical system, and his inductive method presumed neither a comprehensive or entirely internally consistent system nor a deductive system.[73] Additionally, as Grey pointed out, Langdell believed that "[j]udges often did not accurately state the rules on which they decided cases. Further, the basic principles had not been properly formulated and arranged. The law consisted of a mass of haphazardly arranged cases: a 'chaos with a full index.' "[74] Langdell liberally dismissed as mistaken the grounds judges provided in their written opinions to justify their decisions.[75] Evaluated in terms of the four positions identified above, he aspired to make law more coherent and rational (a version of no. 1), and he thought induction and deduction could be used to derive principles and rules (a version of no.3 applied to scholars more so than judges); but he also considered law to be in a defective state (no. 2), and he was highly critical of the actual reasoning of judges (contrary to nos. 3 and 4). Considering this combination of positions, Langdell, often put forth as *the* exemplar of formalist thought, is a poor fit for the position typically attributed to classical legal formalists.

Although Langdell is maligned today, and was memorably abused by Holmes, others at the time received his views as an advance. As the English jurist Pollock observed in 1895, "We have long given up the attempt to maintain that the common law is the perfection of reason. Existing human institutions can only do their best with the conditions they work in."[76] Pollock credited Langdell with this more progressive approach to law. "No man has been more ready than Mr. Langdell to protest against the treatment of conclusions of law as something to be settled by mere enumeration of decided points. . . . Decisions are made, principles live and grow. This conviction is at the root of all Mr. Langdell's work, and makes his criticism not only keen, but also vital."[77] Pollock uttered these words at the Harvard commencement, Langdell's final as dean (hence the encomiums)—providing some assurance that Pollock made an effort to convey Langdell's own vision of his work. Consistent with this understanding, a legal historian has argued that, contrary to the conventional stereotype, Langdell's version of legal science was "the beginning of anti-formalism."[78]

The failure to keep track of the distinctions between law abstractly or ideally conceived and views about the actual state of the law, and how these two perspectives on law relate to deduction in judging, lies at the heart of today's misunderstandings of the "formalist age." The conventional story about the formalist age draws a straight line from the abstract faith in the perfection of the common law—which relatively few jurists espoused at the time—directly to the assertion that judges engaged in mechanical, deductive reasoning when applying the law to the facts in a particular case. But this works only for the formal rationality of German legal science in which the *actual* civil code purports to represent the *ideal*, allowing deductive reasoning to operate from the written code to the facts in cases. Pound, Frank, and Gilmore, and many others following them, connect deductive reasoning in given cases to the idealized vision of the law—position no. 4 operating directly from position no. 1—without recognizing that this skips completely over the messy actual state of the common law (the problems posed by no. 2 and no. 3 in practice).

Historian Morton Horwitz conjoined the two here: "There were . . . major advantages in creating an intellectual system which gave common law rules the appearance of being self-contained, apolitical, and inexorable, and which, by making 'legal reasoning seem like mathematics,' conveyed 'an air . . . of . . . inevitability' about legal decisions."[79] Historian William LaPiana also linked the two:

> The [historical school of thought] legal theories of thinkers like Hammond, Cooley, Bliss, Tiedeman, Phelps, Dillon, and Carter provide the basis for a "formalistic" view of law and judging. As long as the ultimate repository of law is declared to be a body of principles beyond the reach of political processes, especially legislative processes, and once the guarantees of the Constitution are proclaimed to embody these unwritten principles, the decision of cases can become the mechanical application of transcendent rules.[80]

By this account, the two elements to the formalist story deliver complementary payoffs: the law (body of legal principles and rules) is objective, and judging (mechanical, deductive) in particular cases is objective.

The connection between the two seems natural—but *only* if one fails to attend, first, to what they were saying about the poor actual state of the law and, second, to the difficulties inhering at the stage of application. Once the problematic state of the law is recognized, this tight picture falls apart because the first step—figuring out what the law is—was terribly uncertain in practice. The second step collapses as well if the first fails. A deductive view of applying the law to the facts—which, to repeat, was seldom espoused—cannot get off the ground if the law is not seen as a complete and logically ordered system. As Judge Irving Lehman remarked in 1924 about his experience upon ascending to the bench, "[I]n many cases there were no premises from which any deductions could be drawn with logical certainty."[81] This frequently lamented reality is missed by standard accounts of legal formalism. Widespread concern about legal uncertainty—not claims about legal science, the perfection of law, or deductive reasoning—was the view of law and judging most often expressed within legal circles.

Recall that Hammond, listed above by LaPiana as a major contributor to legal formalism, uttered the skeptical observations quoted in the introduction:

> It is useless for judges to quote a score of cases from the digest to sustain almost every sentence, when *every one knows* that another score might be collected to support the opposite ruling.... [T]he most honest judge knows that the authorities with which his opinions are garnished often have had very little to do with the decision of the court—perhaps have only been looked up after that decision was reached upon the general equities of the case.[82]

This passage disclaims key aspects of the standard account of what the formalists purportedly believed. Hammond did express idealized views of the common law (a pale version of no. 1); but that was a far cry from the reality of the state of the law produced by judges (no. 2), which he freely criticized, and obviously he did not believe that judicial decisions were the product of deduction (contrary to no. 4).

Judge Thomas Cooley, also identified by LaPiana above as an important contributor to legal formalism, acknowledged that tough questions regularly arise about which rules should be applied and that the application of a given rule is not a matter of simple deduction. Cooley emphasized that uncertainty in the application of law cannot be eliminated "because in the infinite variety of human transactions it becomes uncertain which of the opposing rules the respective parties contend for should be applied in a case having no exact parallel, and because it cannot possibly be known in advance what view a court or jury will take of questions upon which there is room for difference of opinion."[83] Even with respect to the interpretation and application of clear legal rules, the cases can be "numerous and variant."[84] He recognized that "just and well-instructed minds" can differ on how to interpret statutes.[85] These difficulties in the judicial application of law "must always exist so long as there is variety in human minds, human standards, and human transactions."[86] Judge Cooley sounds much like a realist when speaking about the actual task of judging.

Two Ambiguities about "Formalistic" Judicial Opinions

Pound pointed to the style of judicial opinions as his only positive proof of mechanical, deductive judging. A major question exists, however, as to whether published opinions at the time were in fact logical or deductive. An 1897 article by Henry Merwin complained about the flawed "Style in Judicial Opinions." He offered the following unreadable example, taken from a U.S. Supreme Court opinion:

> The decision of the motion was postponed to the argument upon the merits, and upon that argument counsel for plaintiffs in error, clearly recognizing the necessity they were under of showing that the State court did give effect to the subsequent legislation, in order to show the existence of a Federal question, claimed that it appeared in the record that no judgment could have been given for the defendant in error in the court below without necessarily giving effect to some of the subsequent legislation, and they claimed that an examination of the whole record would show such fact, notwithstanding the statement contained in one of the opinions of the State court already alluded to.[87]

Merwin attributed this kind of writing to haste and carelessness owing to heavy case loads, asserting that he could find "many examples of inelegance and incorrectness."[88] He characterized the style as "a narrow and technical view of the law"[89]—"so technical as to hardly rise above the level of legal slang."[90] Wigmore similarly criticized (in 1915) legal decisions for their "indifference to legal science" (by which he meant reasoned analysis).[91] A study of the written decisions of the turn-of-the-century Supreme Court concluded that different justices used different styles of analysis in their written opinions, making it dubious to lump them all together under a single "formalist" label.[92]

This brings us to a pivotal ambiguity: it is not clear what qualifies a particular decision or group of decisions as "formalistic," or how to distinguish these from decisions that are not subject to this label. There are no agreed upon criteria by which to make this distinction. Because judicial decisions in the American legal tradition are typically written in a style that reasons from precedents and statutes to results, all decisions are potentially subject to the charge of formalism—but then it would not apply to a particular period or age. This ambiguity plays out in disagreements among modern theorists and historians about precisely when judges began to commit the sin of formalistic reasoning. As will be elaborated on shortly, Robert Cover argued that antebellum judges resorted to formalism to stave off pangs of conscience for their slavery decisions, whereas Morton Horwitz and William Nelson argued that formalism emerged (for different reasons) only after the Civil War. What makes an opinion "formalist" is in the eye of the beholder.

A second pivotal ambiguity surrounding formalistic decisions was first opened up in a 1924 article, "Logical Method and the Law," by philosopher John Dewey. He elucidated an important distinction between the actual mode of judicial reasoning and the written opinion as a public justification for the decision:

> Courts not only reach decisions; they expound them, and the exposition must state justifying reasons. . . . The logic of exposition is different from that of search and inquiry. In the latter, the situation as it exists is more or less doubtful, indeterminate, and problematic with respect to what it signifies. It unfolds itself gradually and is susceptible of dramatic surprise; at all events it has, for the time being, two sides. Exposition implies that a definitive solution is reached, that the situation is now determinate with respect to its legal implication. Its purpose is to set forth grounds for the decision reached so that it will not appear as an arbitrary dictum, and so that it will indicate a rule for dealing with similar cases in the future.[93]

Dewey thus clarified that the process of coming to the decision, which is often open and uncertain, is distinct from preparing a written decision shorn of previous doubts that supports the decision and provides legal guidance for the future. Dewey added that judges at times actually do reason in a mechanical fashion, which he characterized as "routine habits of action"—for example, "making rules of pleading hard and fast"—rather than a matter of logic.[94]

Dewey straddled two alternatives. In some instances judges really do reason in a rigidly rule-bound, habitual fashion. In other cases judges reason more freely when coming to a decision, but then cast the opinion—to serve as a legal justification and as guidance on the law—in a fashion that gives the external appearance of logical deduction from legal rules and principles. Dewey said nothing about the relative proportion of one or the other, or about how to tell the difference.

This fundamental ambiguity runs throughout the literature on legal formalism, with theorists and historians taking up various positions on both sides. Pound asserted that judges of the day *genuinely* reasoned in a mechanistic fashion—it was not a guise. So insistent on this point was he that Pound made an effort to demonstrate that certain misguided decisions were logically compelled.[95] Judges were faithfully living up to their felt obligation to apply the law, in his view, which under the circumstances brought regrettable consequences. Pound thus struck a stance that was critical of prevailing legal doctrine, consistent with his Progressive political views, but not in a manner that undermined belief in law or that challenged the integrity of judges.

Gilmore identified the style of writing with the style of thinking: "The judges who thought this way and wrote this way set their faces against change."[96] He suggested that judges genuinely reasoned in a formalist fashion, abdicating or forgetting the flexibility that common law judges traditionally exercised to modify the law. Legal theorist Duncan Kennedy likewise asserted that judicial thinking reflected a genuine "experience that appears to have been common at the turn of the century: that of the compulsion by which an abstraction dictates, objectively apolitically, in a non-discretionary fashion, a particular result."[97] Legal historian Lawrence Friedman, in contrast, asserted that formalism "was less a habit of mind than a habit of style, less a way of thinking than a way of disguising thought."[98]

A number of scholars have taken *both* positions—asserting that formalistic decisions reflected rigid reasoning *and* that this reasoning concealed manipulative analysis. Frank, for example, suggested that judges sometimes in fact reasoned mechanically but also sometimes deceptively gave that appearance: "[T]hose judges who are most lawless, or most swayed by the 'perverting influence of their emotional natures or most dishonest, are often the very judges who use most meticulously the language of compelling mechanical logic."[99] Llewellyn contended that judges were truly stuck in this mode of reasoning: "[W]hatever their political or economic outlook, these . . . appellate judges . . . had grown up in and into the formal-style picture of how to go about their work."[100] But he also asserted that "we must recognize that the opinion [of the court] is often a mere justification after the event, a mere making plausible to the legal audience of a decision reached before the opinion was begun, a decision the real reasons of which we may never know. And on the other hand, we must remember that the opinion may, in any given case, reveal the true course of the decision; and that in any event it will be a factor of power in further decisions of the same or other courts."[101]

Also taking both sides of the issue, but sequentially, historian Morton Horwitz suggested that initially judges clothed themselves in the formalistic style as a guise to lock in and conceal that the substantive law operated in favor of business interests,[102] although they thereafter came to actually reason in a formalistic fashion. Robert Cover also played both sides of this ambiguity in his analysis of slavery cases, charging antebellum judges with undertaking a "retreat to formalism" in order to reduce the moral conflict they experienced when enforcing slavery statutes. "The more mechanical the judge's view of the process, the more he externalized responsibility for the result."[103] Their sought refuge in formalism offered only partial relief, Cover argued, because judges all along knew that there is sufficient leeway within the law to reach a different result if they worked at it hard enough. Thus, Cover observed, "The mechanistic view of judicial obligation and of doctrine has often been put to disingenuous use by judges."[104]

The pejorative connotations attached to the "formalist" label come in three stripes that revolve around this ambiguity. According to critics, the "formalists" were overly rigid (as Pound and Llewellyn suggested) or "stupid" (as Gilmore called Langdell)[105] for reasoning in a strictly logical fashion without heed to purposes, circumstances, consequences, or justice; or the "formalists" were frauds for hiding beneath mechanistic reasoning to manipulate the law to justify ends or results they desired. A third interpretation partakes of both alternatives: the "formalists" were self-deluded in truly believing that they were reasoning in a mechanical, deductive fashion, when (unbeknownst to them) their reasoning was subconsciously guided by personal or class biases. The essential point to recognize here is that a "formalist" decision is susceptible to any of these readings, which cannot be verified or refuted by reference to the decision itself. As Robert Cover acknowledged, "One can never be certain whether the rhetoric of formalism is dissimulation or honest self-reflection."[106] Once again, what is going on depends entirely upon the eye of the beholder.

Owing to these two central ambiguities—about what qualifies a decision as "formalistic" and about whether the written decision reflects real reasoning or is a guise to cover manipulation—there is an irreducibly slippery quality to the charge of formalism. Historians and theorists have substantial license to project their own views on the opinions. Written judicial decisions, it must be concluded from this, provide a tenuous, inadequate basis for arguments about mechanical or deductive reasoning.

The Modern Invention of the "Legal Formalism"

Although it seems much older, the "formalist age" first burst on the legal scene in the 1970s. No one at the turn of the nineteenth century called themselves formalists, which was a pejorative term. Neither

Holmes, nor Pound, nor Haines, nor Frank attached the label "formalists" or "formalism" to a prevailing theory or style of judging. Rather, they spoke in terms of legal science, logical deduction, mechanistic reasoning, and conceptual or abstract analysis. Max Weber discussed the "formal" qualities of modern law at the turn of the century, but these ideas would not penetrate U.S. legal circles for decades.[107] Llewellyn discussed the "formal style" in a 1942 essay,[108] although no one picked up the reference.

Perhaps the single-most influential work (alongside Weber's) that would contribute to the later focus on legal formalism was philosopher Morton White's intellectual history, *Social Thought in America: The Revolt against Formalism*, first published in 1949. The book described a pragmatism-inspired movement "against formalism" in turn-of-the-century American thought that swept across philosophy, economics, sociology, psychology, and law. Admitting that it was hard to pin down, he defined formalism to encompass "logic, abstraction, deduction, mathematics, and mechanics."[109] White laid out his broad thesis through a narrow focus on five thinkers who influenced Progressive thought: John Dewey (especially), Charles Beard, James Harvey Robinson, Thorstein Veblen, and Oliver Wendell Holmes. White's discussion of law, which found an audience among legal historians and theorists, almost exclusively took the form of an excursus on Holmes's writings (peppered with a few references to Pound)—whom he credited with laying the basis for a legal realist view of law and judging. Through the lens of Holmes, White described the previously dominant formalism without engaging any purportedly formalist works or thinkers.

Although it scattered the seeds of the idea, White's book did not immediately result in the use of the labels "legal formalists" or "legal formalism" within legal circles. Llewellyn again referred to the "Formal Style" in *The Common Law Tradition* (1960), asserting that characteristic of this period "Opinions run in deductive form with an air or expression of single-line inevitability."[110] Still, however, the label remained fallow. Gilmore published an article about the legal realists in 1961 without mentioning "formalism" or "the formalists," instead referring to "conceptualism" and the "predecessors" of the realists.[111] As late as 1968, a book on *American Legal Realism* also failed to use the label.[112]

Almost without warning,[113] a cluster of articles from important legal historians and legal theorists discussing the "legal formalists" and "legal formalism" arrived in the mid-1970s. Gilmore's *Ages of American Law* was published in 1977, preceded by the publication of an advance synopsis in the 1975 *Yale Law Journal*.[114] Morton Horwitz published

"The Rise of Legal Formalism," also in 1975, in the *American Journal of Legal History*.[115] Duncan Kennedy published a theoretical analysis entitled "Legal Formality" in the 1973 volume of the *Journal of Legal Studies*.[116] William Nelson extensively elaborated on the rise of legal formalism in connection with antislavery cases in a 1974 article in the *Harvard Law Review*.[117] Legal formalism was a central theme in *Justice Accused*, Robert Cover's book on judicial treatment of slavery cases.[118] All of these scholars worked at elite law schools (Harvard, Yale, and Pennsylvania), and all were politically on the left. Kennedy and Horwitz were founding members of the Critical Legal Studies Movement, which conducted a radical critique of liberal legalism from the mid-1970s until it lost steam in the 1980s.

There is unquestionably a connection between this sudden convergence of critical attention on legal formalism and the searing political events of the 1960s and 1970s—when universities and law schools were wracked by civil rights and antiwar protests. Among the Left, it was a time of seething skepticism about law.[119] The student editors of the *Harvard Law Review* wrote in 1970: "It is true that what passes for logic in some judicial opinions (and in many classrooms) is a little more than finely spun sophistry. It is also important to note that pure logic does not offer a solution to all [legal] problems."[120] Little imagination is required to see the parallels between these attitudes and the shortly forthcoming preoccupation with legal formalism. Cover drew the link in his acknowledgments, mentioning that his book was inspired by a comparison of "judicial complicity in the crimes of Vietnam" with "judicial acquiescence in the injustices of Negro slavery."[121] In the closing chapter of *Ages of American Law*, Gilmore argued that the 1970s were ushering in a "New Conceptualism" resembling that of the formalist age. "In our own history, both in the late nineteenth century and in our own time," he wrote, "the components of the formalist approach have included the search for theoretical formulas assumed to be of universal validity and the insistence that all particular instances should be analyzed and dealt with in the light of the overall theoretical structure."[122]

A group of leftist scholars deeply disaffected with the law in the 1970s thus reached back to the work of the previous episode of disaffection (Pound and the legal realists) to resurrect a portrait of what was perceived to be a common enemy. Once given a name, the notion of legal formalism and beliefs about "the formalists" swept the legal culture, rapidly ensconcing the now ubiquitous formalist-realist divide. That it came packaged in an antithesis with the already familiar legal realists made a handy pairing, easy to understand, after which each pole came to define its opposite. With evident pride of achievement,

Gilmore declared in 1979 that the previous two decades of historical research "has produced one proposition, which, so far as I know, had never been heard of before World War II, but which has, with extraordinary speed, become one of the received ideas of the 1970s. That is the proposition that the fifty year period from the Civil War to World War I was one of *legal formalism.*"[123]

A few legal historians and legal theorists expressed reservations about hopping on this bandwagon. "'Formalism is hard to measure," wrote Lawrence Friedman, "and there is always a nagging doubt whether or not this is a useful way to characterize the work of judges."[124] Legal theorist H.L.A. Hart suggested that the term was a confusing misnomer (discussed in chapter 9). Nonetheless, the label and image stuck. Among legal historians, legal theorists, and political scientists, with few exceptions,[125] the story about the legal formalists quickly became gospel, and everyone else in the legal culture, taking the word of the experts, joined along.

There were warning signs that something was amiss with the story. Indicative of an underlying lack of clarity, historians have equivocated over the appropriate label. "Between the 1870s and the 1930s," legal historical Stephen Segal declared, "American law was dominated by a jurisprudential style variously described as 'mechanical jurisprudence,' 'legal formalism,' and 'classical legal thought.'"[126] Compounding the confusion created by different but overlapping labels—merged as "Classical formalist judicial method"[127]—historians have never presented a clear or consistent statement of the content of the purportedly dominant set of formalistic beliefs. Some centered formalism on the common law, others on natural rights (or a combination of the two); often the term was invoked in vague generalities. Also problematic, scholars who have written about the legal formalists have identified different prototypical thinkers, variously picking Langdell, Cooley, Carter, Dillon, Tiedeman, Beale, and even Holmes—whom Gilmore classed as a formalist—despite the major differences among them. These elusive shape-shifting qualities have helped keep the story about the formalist age intact, for it is hard to skeptically examine a formless, moving target.

A glaring problem is that the formalists have been defined entirely by *political critics* of courts and jurists. Progressive critics (Pound above all) were responsible for the early construction of the image, and leftist historians and theorists were primarily responsible for the latest reiteration and entrenchment of the image. The suspicion that politics is what drives charges of "formalism" is heightened when one recognizes that jurists most often identified as formalists were usually conservatives of some stripe (evident in this string of names offered by historian Thomas Grey: "from the formalism of Cooley and Langdell to the formalism of Friedrich A. Hayek and Antonin Scalia").[128] Any jurist with politically conservative views who believes in liberty or in fidelity to legal rules is a prime candidate for being branded a formalist. The "formalist" label, with its ancient deprecatory connotations, has proved to be a remarkably effective group ad hominem slung at judges and jurists by their political critics. For a loose analogy, it is akin to relying entirely upon the writings of Marxists to learn about Liberalism, or vice versa—although this analogy misleads because these political theories represent a discernable cluster of ideas, whereas "formalism" appears to be largely a patched-together invention.

Scholars who insist that belief in formalism was widespread have thus far failed to satisfy a minimum test of credibility: they have not identified an affirmative statement of the full-blown formalist position by any notable jurist in the period (not talking about German legal science). What we have are various reconstructions by historians and theorists. If this was indeed the dominant view, a surfeit of articulations by eager champions of formalism should be on supply, but examples are scarce. When this absence is coupled with the many expressions of realism uttered in the period (part II), the conventional account of the formalist age appears exceedingly thin, lacking in support.

Another problem with the standard story about the formalists is that the notions that the common law is autonomous, comprehensive, and logically ordered and that judging involves mechanical deduction strike modern ears as farfetched. This reaction should have set off alarms among theorists and historians. Jurists a century ago, after all, must have been intimately familiar with all the problems thrown up by human judges working with an imperfect system of law. And indeed they were.

PART TWO

The Legal Realists

5

○ ○ • • •

REALISM BEFORE THE LEGAL REALISTS

A LEGAL THEORIST RECENTLY AFFIRMED that "American Legal Realism was, quite justifiably, the major intellectual event in 20th century American legal practice and scholarship."[1] "The conviction that legal realism has transformed American legal discourse," wrote another theorist, "is widely shared."[2] Above all else, the legal realists, with assists from Holmes, Pound, and Cardozo, are credited with bringing about a revolutionary shift in the prevailing understanding of judging, away from formalism toward realism.

The preceding chapters in part I uprooted the story about the formalists. Part II uproots the conventional understanding of the realists. There are major differences in these respective efforts at debunking, which must be stated up front: unlike the "legal formalists," self-avowed "legal realists" did exist, what they wrote has been widely read and extensively written on by historians and theorists, and the realists had a *real impact* in several ways that will be mentioned. The argument here focuses solely on their views about judging, which is what they are famous for. The popular understanding of the legal realists on judging is wrong in essential respects.

Realism about judging was commonplace decades before the legal realists came on the scene. A steady stream of frankly realistic views of judging circulated from very early on in, and throughout the course of, the legal careers of the realists, Pound and Cardozo, and even Holmes. This commentary was so prevalent that these respective generations of jurists could not help but see judging in realistic terms. It is often said "We are all realists now." The evidence presented here suggests that it can be said about jurists at least three decades before the arrival of the legal realists: "They were all realists then, too." The core points about judging announced by the legal realists in the 1920s and 1930s, it turns out, were presaged to a remarkable extent by the historical jurists of the 1880s and 1890s. This overlap shows, once again, that the story about the formalists is badly flawed, for historical jurists are today identified with legal formalism.[3] The mistake of the conventional account is not just that it erases this much earlier pervasive realism about judging, but also that it misleadingly raises the realists above their contemporaries, who understood judging in similarly realistic terms.

Another common misapprehension about the realists—a popular image that most legal historians know to be incorrect—is that they were radical skeptics about judging. They were not. Laura Kalman, in her historical study of the realists, put it concisely: "The realists pointed to the role of idiosyncrasy in law, but they believed in a rule of law—hence they attempted to make it more efficient and more certain."[4] Their goals were to explain and improve the predictability of law and judging, not to argue that judging was a fraud.

Another fundamental misapprehension is that the legal realists formed a group or movement. They did not. Historians and theorists have long been vexed by a set of identity questions about the legal realists. "The questions of *who* were the Realists and *what* was Realism are not trivial and are still contested," wrote a historian in a book about the realists.[5] Debates among historians over *who* and *what*, however, rarely entertain the possibility that beneath the label there was *nothing* distinctive—nothing unique or unifying—about the legal realists. This argument, spread over this chapter and the next, will come as a surprise to many, but it is consistent with and will explain Llewellyn's repeated admonition that realism was *not* a group or movement.

There is a widely held (often implicitly) background narrative about the pivotal role the realists played in the affairs of the day. Wielding the sharp blade of their skeptical critique of judging, according to this narrative, the realists picked up the banner of the Progressives, joined the fight against laissez-faire (formalist) judges, finally defeating obstructionist courts in 1937,[6] paving the way for the social welfare state.[7] The infamous *Lochner* case forms a standard confirming piece of this story. This too is mostly a mirage, based upon a failure to appreciate the extent of preexisting realism about judging, a lopsided view of events, and fallacious timing. As a foretaste of the basic flaw in this story, consider the first sentence of a seminal history about the New Deal: "[B]y the end of 1937 the active phase of the New Deal had largely come to an end."[8]

It might sound from the foregoing that this reconstruction aims to discredit or diminish the legal realists. That is not the case. The goal here is to rescue the realists from the distortions perpetuated by their popular image as extremists or radicals about judging. They adhered to a balanced realism, described in the introduction. They recognized the limitations of human judges and the openness and flaws of law, yet they believed that judicial decisions could be determined by rules.

The overarching aim of part II is to pry apart balanced realism about judging from the false image legal realism. The formalist-realist antithesis obscures this balanced realism, a view that the legal realists shared with their entire generation as well as with their historical jurisprudence forebears. An especially important insight about judging that was once common but is repressed today is revived here and brought to the fore—the recognition that social influences necessarily and beneficially play into judging.

The Accidental Birth of Legal Realism

Karl Llewellyn in 1930 published a modest essay with an outsized title: "A Realistic Jurisprudence—The Next Step."[9] Also in 1930, Jerome Frank published *Law and the Modern Mind*, his impudent assault on what he portrayed as prevailing delusions about law and judging, with a chapter entitled "Legal Realism." Perhaps in a pique, perhaps in haste and distracted by other pressing commitments,[10] Roscoe Pound, the target of mild criticism from Llewellyn and some sharp barbs from Frank, critically responded the following year in "The Call for a Realist Jurisprudence."[11] Llewellyn, in collaboration with Frank—both alarmed to find themselves in a brawl with the preeminent jurisprudent in legal academia (while also reveling in it)—immediately countered in "Some Realism about Realism—Responding to Dean Pound."[12] "Legal realism" was born in this skirmish.

The main protagonists were themselves unsure about what the "realist" label meant—as made plain by the later-revealed private correspondence between Pound and Llewellyn.[13] Seeking to pin down the terms of their dispute, over a three-week period Llewellyn sent Pound two overlapping but different lists of possible "realists," one with forty-four names, and he sent yet a third list of candidates to Frank.[14] Pound bemusedly responded that his own position could not be distinguished from the views expressed by several scholars on the list.[15] When reviewing Llewellyn's proposed roll of realists, Arthur Corbin protested that they "had so many and important differences as to make it highly misleading to classify them under a name"; Hessel Yntema offered the same objection.[16] Leon Green (two years later) explicitly denied that he was a "realist" or that he knew what the label meant.[17] The final list Llewellyn put forth in his published response to Pound was pared down to twenty names, including Corbin, Yntema, and

Green.[18] Llewellyn suggested that many more individuals than those named partook of realism. He also made what must be considered an odd—and since overlooked—statement: "Their differences in point of view, in interest, in emphasis, in field of work, are huge. They differ among themselves well-nigh as much as any of them differs from, say, Langdell."[19]

This slapdash origin helps explain why historians and theorists continue to dispute what the label stood for and who qualifies as a legal realist. Although the exchange with Pound cemented Llewellyn at the center of legal realism, some have argued that he was ill placed to define it, given his relative inexperience and his thin jurisprudential work to date; Llewellyn, according to historian Morton Horwitz, produced a "distorted picture of the meaning and significance of realism."[20] But if not Llewellyn and Frank—who coined "realism" as a label in the legal context—then who? A decade earlier Cardozo had used "realism" in passing connection with judging ("a sense of realism must lead us"),[21] and Felix Frankfurter used "realism" to convey the idea that courts in constitutional cases were giving greater credence to the factual basis for legislation.[22] But neither attached any jurisprudential pretensions to the term.

Beyond their shared skeptical take on the role of law in judging, the main characterizations of legal realism put forth by theorists and historians are the promotion of an instrumental view of law as a means to serve social ends,[23] the pursuit of social scientific approaches to law,[24] the efforts of reformers to transform legal education in order to improve legal practice and judging,[25] and attempts by reformers to advance a progressive political agenda in and through the law[26]— or some amalgamation of all four. The assumption that the "legal realists" were a discrete group is severely tested by these alternative characterizations for two reasons: the individuals identified as realists did not agree among themselves on these positions,[27] and others not named as realists embraced one or more of these positions.[28]

Furthermore, scholars disagree over whether realism was a school of thought, a movement, a jurisprudential theory, or just a "cynical state of mind."[29] Llewellyn denied that realism was a "school of thought."[30] He placed an exclamation point on this by closing the article with a deliberate repetition: "A *group* philosophy or program, a *group* credo of social welfare, these realists have not. They are not a group."[31] In a later work, Llewellyn obscurely clarified the term: "What realism was, and is, is a method, nothing more, and the only tenet involved is that the method is a good one. 'See it fresh,' 'See it as it works'. . . . *Realism* is *not* a philosophy but a *technology.*"[32]

With these details in mind, it is plausible to think that events would have played out quite differently had Pound not responded in a manner that magnified the significance of "realism." A number of historians and theorists take the position that Pound and Llewellyn, notwithstanding their disagreement, substantially overlap in their views of law and judging,[33] which suggests that the fight was less over substance than an unintended collision from a clash of egos. Llewellyn and Frank initially used "realism" loosely to mark an unfavorable contrast against (by demeaning as "unrealistic") what they sought to advance beyond. Neither defined the term realism when they first used it, and apparently neither initially had in mind a concrete group of realistic thinkers. By putting weight on the term realism, Pound's criticism sent them scrambling in self-defense. It became imperative for Llewellyn and Frank (unwilling to admit that they were casually spouting big claims) to come up with distinguishing content and representative jurists—a search that proved elusive.

Ideas the Legal Realists (and Forebears)
Were Exposed To

In the year of the fateful exchange, 1931, most of the people identified as core realists were between thirty-seven and forty-three years of age (Karl Llewellyn, Jerome Frank, Charles E. Clark, William O. Douglas, Thurman Arnold, Wesley Sturges, Herman Oliphant, Leon Green), just entering the prime of their professional careers;[34] a few were a decade or so younger (Felix Cohen); and a few were a decade or so older (Walter Wheeler Cook, Max Radin, Underhill Moore, Arthur Corbin). Pound was sixty years old, at the peak of his influence. With a touch of paternalism, Pound referred to the realists as "our younger teachers of law," before proceeding to set them straight.

The core group of realists completed their legal education between 1910 and 1920—a period suffused with forthright realism about judging that would have seized the attention of any intellectually curious person. In a well-publicized 1908 speech before Congress, President Theodore Roosevelt offered this appraisal of judicial decisions:

> The chief lawmakers in our country may be, and often are, the judges, because they are the final seat of authority. Every time they interpret contract, property, vested rights, due process of law, liberty, they necessarily enact into law parts of a system of social philosophy; and as such interpretation is fundamental, they give direction to all law-making. The decisions of the courts

on economic and social questions depend upon their economic and social philosophy; and for the peaceful progress of our people during the twentieth century we shall owe most to those judges who hold to a twentieth century economic and social philosophy and not to a long outgrown philosophy, which was itself the product of primitive economic conditions.[35]

This speech was a reproach of the niggardly reception some courts had accorded to legislative efforts to ameliorate the social and economic dislocations of the time.

Unfriendly court treatment of legislation also provoked a more concrete campaign to rein in the judiciary. A number of states—including California, Oregon, and Arizona—enacted recall provisions to unseat judges who rendered unpopular decisions;[36] a bill proposing the recall of federal judges was introduced (unsuccessfully), and a proposal for the recall of individual judicial decisions was also seriously debated.[37] The primary argument on behalf of these various recall provisions was that on certain issues judges make political decisions. Professor W. F. Dodd, an advocate of recall, wrote in 1909, "In this field [public policy] decisions of the courts necessarily depend not upon any fixed rules of law but upon the individual opinions of the judges on political and economic questions; and such decisions, resting as they must, upon no general principles, will be especially subject to reversal or modification when changes take place in the personnel of the courts."[38] Senator Robert L. Owen asserted (in 1911) that judicial decisions are to a degree a function "of previous predilections, of previous fixed opinion, of the point of view which has molded itself in the personal experience of the judge and become a part of him."[39] Because judges are political actors in this respect, Owen argued, they should be subject to political accountability. A pro-recall article averred that the public believes that the "great interests" influence judicial selection, and therefore citizens should have a say in the matter.[40] Bar associations vigorously fought the recall provisions, which they saw as a grave threat to judicial independence, and the issue was debated in law journals. Most everyone in legal circles would have been familiar with the charges about personal and political influences on judging.

Jerome Frank obtained his law degree in 1912. That same year, Joseph Bingham contended in the *Michigan Law Review* that "to require judicial reasoning to proceed always within the confines of promulgated rules and principles, will not prevent individual bias from affecting a decision. It could be demonstrated that judges are able to manipulate generalized expressions to suit their preferences as easily as they could plausibly justify the same decision by free reasoning. Indeed previous judicial and legislative expressions may be misused as a plausible mask to conceal the real motives or incapacity of the judge."[41] Felix Frankfurter gave a speech that year at the Harvard Law Review annual dinner asserting that "constitutional law, in its relation to social legislation, is not at all a science, but applied politics, using the word in its noble sense."[42] A 1912 book, *Our Judicial Oligarchy*, presented numerous quotations, including statements from several governors, detailing "popular distrust of the courts," distrust grounded on the widespread view that courts were biased in favor of capital interests.[43] Also in 1912, Gustavus Myers published an 800-page history of the Court making the case that "the Supreme Court as an institution has throughout its whole existence incarnated into final law the demands of the dominant and interconnected sections of the ruling class."[44] A lawyer charged in the 1912 *Yale Law Journal* that corporate lawyers who become judges bring a subconscious class bias onto the court,[45] adding: "So long as our judicial opinions are formed by the mental processes of the intellectual bankrupts these will only be crude justifications of predispositions acquired through personal or class interests and sympathy, 'moral' superstitions, or whim and caprice."[46]

Karl Llewellyn obtained his law degree in 1919. John Henry Wigmore, a respected scholar and dean of Northwestern Law School, wrote in 1917 that common law judges constantly make law and that "our own Supreme Courts have long been drawing copiously and consciously from this unbounded field of public policy."[47] In 1918 Columbia law professor (later at Harvard) Thomas Reed Powell wrote that judges decide constitutional questions based upon their "common sense" determinations.[48] "Judges argue from undisclosed premises. . . . Judges have their preferences for social policies."[49] Powell revealed that "an able judge of one of our state courts tells me that he is usually able to decide cases as his independent judgment dictates."[50] A 1918 article in the *California Law Review*, "Psychologic Study of Judicial Decisions," contended that "every judicial opinion necessarily is the justification of the personal impulses of the judge, in relation to the situation before him, and that the character of these impulses is determined by the judge's life-long series of previous experiences, with their resultant integration in emotional tones."[51] Justice Wendell Phillips Stafford of the D.C. Supreme Court gave a speech in 1919 entitled "Imagination in the Law." He said that judges knowingly utilize "solemn make-believe" (legal fictions) to change the law to meet new situations or to avoid unpalatable results "without doing violence to a venerated but harsh or outgrown rule."[52] He wondered whether people would feel reverence for the law if they knew that it was "only the resultant of contending social forces, in which very possibly their own opinions and desires have been overborne and supplanted by the opinions and wishes of others?"[53] "The eyes of the law are not truth, but policy," Stafford said.[54]

One of Llewellyn's best-known "realist" pieces was a 1950 article arguing that the canons of statutory interpretation allow judges a great deal of leeway and often come in opposing pairs.[55] In 1917, two years before Llewellyn graduated, Ernst Freund, a leading scholar, published an article disclosing the extensive leeway courts possess in statutory interpretation, providing an example in which "[e]ither of the two opposite contentions is equally plausible."[56] Freund asserted that courts have ways to override or ignore rules of construction: "And most of the current maxims stated in textbooks and judicial decisions are of little value."[57] He argued that the frequently invoked notion of legislative intent "is in reality often a fiction."[58] And he advocated that "in cases of genuine ambiguity courts should use the power of interpretation consciously and deliberately to promote sound law."[59] Bingham and Powell were on Llewellyn's list of realists, it should be noted, but none of the other above individuals who made realistic observations about judging was named (Frankfurter was on an early list but removed from the final).

The older generation of realists—including Corbin, Cook, Radin, and Moore, who earned their legal degrees between 1889 and 1902— were also saturated in realistic discourse about judging in their formative period, as were Pound and Cardozo. Pound studied law at Harvard for a year, 1889–1890, departing sans degree. Benjamin Cardozo also entered the practice of law lacking a degree, after studying at Columbia from 1889–1891. Law students and new lawyers in this period were repeatedly exposed to unadulterated realism about judging. In 1887 Columbia law professor Munroe Smith, as quoted in chapter 3, realistically described the process by which judges silently altered the law while claiming to adhere to stare decisis.[60] Smith took the view, as did Holmes and the later legal realists, that law is the product of contests over social and individual interests,[61] and that the essential purpose of law is to advance "public policy."[62] Smith advocated a "juristic science" that strives to organize legal principles and rules in "systematic form": "This is done by the science that is in constant contact with the daily life of the street and the market. It would perhaps be more accurate to call this the *art* rather than the science of law."[63]

Sylvester Pennoyer (the governor of Oregon) published a historical study in 1890 in the leading *American Law Review* that denounced judicial review, concluding with a flourish on this judicial usurpation of power: "[L]aws solemnly passed . . . are set aside at the mere whim of a body of men not amenable to the people through holding a life term of office, a body which has repeatedly and almost uniformly shown the disposition to apotheosize aggrandized wealth and corporate power above the general good."[64] Harvard law professor John Chipman Gray asserted in a jurisprudence article in the 1892 *Harvard Law Review* that one of the main sources of law is "the opinion of judges on matters of ethics and public policy; . . . [though] the judges themselves have a deprecatory habit of minimizing it, and of speaking as if their sole function was to construct syllogisms."[65]

A remarkably modern-sounding article was published in the *American Law Review* in 1893, "Politics and the Supreme Court of the United States," by Walter Coles, a St. Louis lawyer. Coles examined a series of significant Supreme Court decisions of the past century, systematically matching the political background of the justices with their decisions. He criticized several Supreme Court opinions as "vague," "weak, incoherent, and uncandid,"[66] best explained not by the stated legal reasoning but by the political views of the judges. "[T]o say that no political prejudices have swayed the court," noted Coles with consummate realism, "is to maintain that its members have been exempt from the known weaknesses of human nature, and above those influences which operate most powerfully in determining the opinions of other men."[67] Especially when no clear precedent exists, he asserted, a judge's conclusions "will be largely controlled by the influences, opinions and prejudices to which he happened to have been subjected."[68]

In 1894 renowned law professor and judge John Dillon (identified today with legal formalism), at the height of his professional eminence, published a realistic account of judging that conveyed the essence of what Cardozo would say almost thirty years later: "[I]n so far as the judges are compelled, as they not infrequently are, to exercise what is really a creative power and to make a new rule—in a word to exercise, albeit covertly or circuitously the function of legislation—it seems to be that they are rightfully, because necessarily, within the domain of ethics, and that in such cases the domains of ethics and law are not and cannot be delimited in advance, nor until the line is drawn by the judges in and by the opinion and judgment which are given in the particular cases."[69]

The following year, 1895, was memorably inauspicious for views about judging. The Supreme Court issued a surprising interpretation of the Sherman Antitrust Act in *United States v. E.C. Knight Co.*,[70] holding that the act did not apply to the Sugar Trust, which monopolized well over 90 percent of the production of sugar; the tenuous reasoning of the Court was that the trust's control of the *refining* of sugar did not involve interstate commerce. The Court then declared the income tax unconstitutional, in *Pollock v. Farmers' Loan and Trust Co.*,[71] a decision that was all the more controversial because the first vote on the case was evenly divided (one justice was ill), and a justice changed his position at the second hearing.[72] In the third case, *In re Debs*,[73] the Court upheld a lower court injunction to halt the Pullman labor strike. Howls of protest greeted each decision, which also drew critical fire in law reviews. The lesson critics drew from the trio of decisions was that the court protected the "the propertied class."[74] Judge Seymour Thompson wrote of the income tax decision, "Our judicial annals do not afford an instance of a more unpatriotic subserviency to the demands of the rich and powerful classes."[75] The Democratic platform for the 1896 presidential election asserted that "we especially object to government by injunction as a new and highly dangerous form of oppression by which Federal Judges, in contempt of the law of States and rights of citizens, become at once Legislators, Judges and executioners."[76]

Realism was also present in the generation that preceded Pound, Cardozo, and the older realists. Oliver Wendell Holmes began to practice law in 1867 and became a contributor to the *American Law Review* in 1870. The 1870s saw heightened public criticism of the courts as servants of the railroads, corporations, and the rich.[77] In a closely watched decision that created a national stir, the Supreme Court in 1870 held the Legal Tender Act (establishing the greenback) unconstitutional. Justice Miller dissented that the majority's reasoning "would authorize this court to enforce theoretical views of the genius of the government, or vague notions of the spirit of the Constitution and of abstract justice, by declaring void laws which did not square with those views. It substitutes our ideas of policy for judicial construction."[78] (Holmes would lodge a similar objection thirty-five years later in his *Lochner* dissent.) The very next year, following the appointment of two new justices, the Court reversed itself to uphold the validity of the act.[79] An editorial in the *Nation* warned that such sudden shifts in constitutional interpretation that result from the seating of new judges "will weaken popular respect for all decisions of the Court"; public suspicion is heightened when "the judges who have been added to the bench since the former decision are men who were at the bar when that decision was rendered, and were interested professionally and personally in having a different decision."[80] Public speculation was rampant that President Ulysses S. Grant appointed Justices William Strong and Joseph P. Bradley, who made the new majority, owing to their views about the act (which Grant privately confirmed).[81] His secretary of the treasury, George S. Boutwell, stated in a letter to a fellow administration official that "a court without political opinions is a myth . . . and as the Supreme Court must be political let it be right politically rather than wrong."[82]

Recognition that politics may penetrate judging was not limited to the U.S. Supreme Court. An 1870 article addressing "judge-made law" matter-of-factly observed that "the excision of politics from the judicial mind is impossible."[83] The author advocated that it is preferable to allow judges to express their views openly in political arenas (which was frowned upon), rather than "when he is compelled to retire to the bench in the political garb and colors of his party, there to fight for the cause in secret, and shelter his animosity under the pretext of law."[84] An essay about a state high court judge published in 1874 made the unadorned observation—as if was obvious—that "[e]ven on the Bench political and Constitutional questions will arise which judges must decide, and will decide according to their political convictions."[85]

Holmes's single-most famous line is "The life of the law has not been logic: it has been experience."[86] He initially wrote this in an 1880 review of Langdell's contracts casebook, when criticizing Langdell for over-emphasizing logical symmetry. Holmes was not the first to make this general point, however. In 1873 (when Holmes was still a juristic neo-phyte), the lawyer-editors of the leading *Albany Law Journal* dismissively scoffed that it is "notoriously untrue" to assert that law is the "perfection of human reason."[87] They identified this kind of talk as a "tendency of professors of all departments of knowledge" to extol their subject above all others (a statement consistent with the assertion in part I that the espousal of "law is reason" was limited to certain academic circles).[88] The editors then voiced a criticism that closely prefigures Holmes's later objection to Langdell: "If circumstances arise to make the application of the rule unfavorable to the best and broadest interests of the people or of the State, and an abrogation of it is sought on the ground of expediency, the jurist is ready with the argument that it is better that the law, once founded on reason, *should preserve its symmetry and logical continuity* than that the innovations of *experience* should be allowed to mar its beauty and endanger its 'perfected reason.' "[89] Holmes, the master of epigrams, said it more concisely, but it was said before.

An essay in the same 1873 journal expressed these bluntly skeptical views about judging:

> It is in the application of the law to individual cases, in the exercise of that license of discretion necessarily vested in the judge, that the danger lies. . . . The power to oppress has changed hands,

and the interpreter of the law has become more powerful than its maker. He has to decide upon its purposes. In the vast abyss of precedents, he will ever be liable to find those that will give him a show of authority for what he wishes to do, and can shelter himself from impeachment behind subtle distinctions.[90]

Holmes's 1905 *Lochner* dissent criticizing the majority on the grounds that the Constitution did not enact Herbert Spencer's views or laissez-faire economic theory is the most famous dissent in the history of U.S. law. A dozen years earlier, in 1893, lawyer C. B. Labatt articulated *precisely* the same argument in the *American Law Review*.[91] Labatt wrote that a Pennsylvania Supreme Court decision declaring a statute unconstitutional—striking legislation that prohibited mine owners from compensating employees in orders at company stores, an abusive practice at the time—"breathes the very spirit of Mr. Herbert Spencer himself."[92] Labatt criticized the recent trend of "freedom of contract" decisions, arguing that "there is no difficulty in escaping the preposterous conclusion which we are invited to accept, that this constitutional provision was intended to serve the purpose of stereotyping and perpetuating the *laissez faire* theories of doctrinaire economists."[93] The dismissive judicial treatment of legislation, Labatt wrote, "throws a flood of light upon the prejudiced attitude of [the courts], and strikingly illustrates the strength of the prepossessions which influence them in the consideration of these questions."[94] He suggested that the courts' tendency to disfavor labor legislation showed "the effect of the distorted medium of class prejudices through which most of the judges have viewed such questions."[95]

To recite these various realism-infused (often skeptical) observations about judging, it must be emphasized, is not to suggest that Holmes, Pound, Cardozo, and the realists actually read or knew about any particular example, but rather to show that realistic observations were swirling about early on in, and throughout, the legal careers of these respective generations of thinkers. Holmes was vocal in his realism, gifted with words, and had a superior platform (as high court judge) from which to spread his views, but he was far from the lonely iconoclast he is often painted as. By the time the legal realists arrived on the scene, realism about judging had circulated inside and outside of legal circles loudly and often for at least two generations. Historians and theorists will be tempted to explain these realistic statements away as more examples of proto-realism, a characterization which (dogmatically) preserves the realists' pride of place as the font of realistic views about judging. However, the surplusage of these observations, the range of settings in which they were made (popular press, academic books, top law reviews, political speeches, speeches to the bar, private correspondence), their straightforward tone, and the fact that they were uttered by leading political and legal figures (judges, lawyers, academics), are compelling grounds to think that realism about judging was commonplace in the late nineteenth century.

Core "Realistic" Insights about Judging Already Well Known

It is not just that realistic observations about judging were widely expressed well before the realists. Virtually every one of the core insights about judging now associated with the realists was prominently stated decades before, often by historical jurists. To demonstrate this, assertions about judging typically attributed to the realists (ignore here that the individuals identified as realists did not agree on all points) are set forth below, followed by similar assertions made around or before 1900. This arbitrary cut-off, drawn some twenty years before the claimed emergence of legal realism, is selected to dramatize the point that what are now construed as scandalous revelations by the realists were in fact old news.

The realists are known for emphasizing that legal rules can be interpreted in various ways and that how judges interpret the rules will be a function of their personal views and the surrounding social forces. Christopher Tiedeman—a well-known professor and historical jurist— forcefully made the same cluster of points in 1896:

> If the Court is to be considered a body of individuals, standing far above the people, out of reach of their passions and opinions, in an atmosphere of cold reason, deciding every question that is brought before them according to the principles of eternal and never-varying Justice, then and then only may we consider the opinion of the Court as the ultimate source of the law. This, however, is not the real evolution of municipal law. *The bias and peculiar views of the individual judge do certainly exert a considerable influence over the development of the law. . . .* The opinion of the court, in which the reasons for its judgment are set forth, is a most valuable guide to a knowledge of law on a given proposition, *but we cannot obtain a reliable conception of the effect of the decision by merely reading the opinion. This thorough knowledge is to be acquired only by studying the social and political environment of the parties and the sub-*

*ject matter of the suit, the present temper of public opinion and the scope
and character of the popular demands, as they bear upon the particular
question at issue.*[96]

Tiedeman advised that, to understand a legal ruling, one "must look
beneath the judicial opinion" and take into consideration "the pressure
of public opinion and the influences of private interests" revolving
around the case.[97]

The realists insisted that one of the main tasks of lawyers is to predict outcomes—"Our business is prophecy," said Radin[98] —and they
counseled this cannot be done well by attention to the rules only. Llewellyn asserted that not until one understands the flexibility judges
possess "do you appreciate how little, in detail, you can predict out of
the rules alone; how much you must turn, for the purposes of prediction, to the reactions of the judges to the facts and to the life around
them."[99] But this too was said much earlier. Frederick Pollock, the eminent English legal historian and jurisprudent, wrote in 1882: "The object of legal science [like natural science] . . . is likewise to predict
events. The particular kind of events it seeks to predict are the decisions of courts of justice."[100] Prediction was the job not only of the lawyer, according to Pollock; a judge as well, "following on the whole the
same process as advising counsel, makes a scientific prediction with
reference to an ideal standard [of the correct legal answer]."[101] Before
the turn of the century, the notion that lawyers were engaged in prediction was not unusual. In 1896, a year before Holmes emphasized prediction in *Path of the Law,* Tiedeman wrote "If one relies solely upon
the expression of judicial opinion his [a lawyer's] attempt to forecast
the probable decision in a pending cause of action will not amount to
much more than guess work, where there is any doubt as to the preexisting law, or where intense public feeling is enlisted in the litigated
question."[102]

The realists maintained that statutes no less than precedents are
open to different interpretations, and judges make law in the course of
applying statutes in particular situations. "For, after all, rules are
merely words and those words can get into action only through decisions," Frank pointed out; "it is for the courts in deciding any case to
say what the rules mean, whether those rules are embodied in a statute
or in the opinion of some other court."[103] The legal realists asserted that
the decision a court makes, more immediately than the applicable
rules, *is* the law. "The law of any case," Llewellyn declared, "is what
the judge decides—decisions, not rules."[104] "Law is made up not of
rules for decision laid down by the courts but of the decisions themselves," Frank asserted. "All such decisions are law."[105]

Four decades earlier Judge Thomas Cooley (a historical jurist) made a related set of points. He recognized in 1886 that "[t]he judges must decide the cases which arise, and when a case is such that just and well-instructed minds differ as to its coming within the intent of the statute, the rule laid down by the [presiding judge] or the prevailing majority of its members becomes a rule of law."[106] Along parallel lines, Tiedeman claimed in 1892, "The true rule or rules, which are produced by the enactment of a statute, are not to be found in the letter of the statute, but in the construction placed upon it by the courts."[107]

The realists argued that many rules and principles come with exceptions or counterrules and principles, which courts can invoke to support a desired outcome. Llewellyn emphasized "a common occurrence: that we turn up two cases which the two courts have put upon two inconsistent grounds: upon two different, two conflicting rules."[108] As realist Walter Wheeler Cook pithily put it, "[L]egal principles—and rules as well—are in the habit of hunting in pairs."[109] A version of this classic realist point, however, was also stated decades before. Judge Seymour Thompson observed in 1889: "Again, take the general proposition that a request is necessary to raise an implied promise. This is reiterated in many legal judgments. But it is easily shown that in many cases the law will imply a promise where there has been no request; but in what cases it will imply it and what not, who can tell? Similar doubts and infirmities seem to permeate every title of our case-made law."[110]

The legal realists argued that judges have broad leeway in connection with stare decisis. "What the courts in fact do is to manipulate the language of former decisions,"[111] declared Frank. "[T]his is achieved by taking a distinction," Llewellyn remarked, "by picking out some feature which differentiates the cases, but which neither court has stressed, and by insisting that this differentiating feature is what accounts for the results."[112] "[E]very single precedent, according to what may be the attitude of future judges, is ambiguous, is wide or narrow at need."[113] Again, however, these realist insights were hardly a revelation. William G. Hammond (a historical jurist) wrote in 1881, "The perverse habit of qualifying and distinguishing has been carried so far that all fixed lines are obliterated, and a little ingenuity in stating the facts of a case is enough to bring it under a rule that will warrant the desired conclusion."[114] The tone of the 1887 passage by Columbia law professor Munroe Smith quoted earlier evinces how utterly transparent the process was to legal observers. "When the old rule is sufficiently wormholed with 'distinctions,' a very slight re-examination will reduce it to dust, and a re-interpretation of the 'distinguishing' cases will produce the rule that is desired."[115]

The realists pointed out the substantial freedom judges have to select and characterize the facts upon which the decision is based. "[W]ith a decision already made," Llewellyn observed, "the judge has sifted through these 'facts' again, and picked a few which he puts forward as essential—and whose legal bearing he then proceeds to expound."[116] Again, the realists were not the first to divulge this. Hammond astutely observed in 1881 that "the real grounds of decision lie concealed under the statement of facts with which it is prefaced. It is the power of stating the facts as he himself views them which preserves the superficial consistency and certainty of the law, and hides from careless eyes its utter lack of definiteness and precision."[117]

The realists also made the point that judges can regularly find legal support for whatever decision they desire, working backward from the result. William O. Douglas remarked that "there are usually plenty of precedents to go around; and with the accumulation of decisions, it is not a great problem for the lawyer to find legal authority for most propositions."[118] Frank wrote: "Judicial judgments, like other judgments, doubtless, in most cases, are worked out backward from conclusions tentatively reached."[119] "A judge," he added, "eager to give a decision which will square with his sense of what is fair, but unwilling to break with the traditional rules, will often view the evidence in such a way that the facts' reported by him, combined with those traditional rules, will justify the result which he announces."[120]

Radical as they sound, these were old observations as well. Hammond said the same in 1881: "It is useless for judges to quote a score of cases from the digest to sustain almost every sentence, when *every one knows* that another score might be collected to support the opposite ruling. . . . the most honest judge knows that the authorities with which his opinions are garnished often have had very little to do with the decision of the court—perhaps have only been looked up after that decision was reached upon the general equities of the case."[121] Tiedeman asserted in 1897 that, "while the legal reason is usually considered as controlling the judgment of the court, the judgment is really dictated by the [judge's] conclusions of common sense."[122] Wilbur Larremore wrote in 1904 that "judicial precedents may be found for any proposition that a counsel, or a court, wishes established, or to establish," allowing courts to "do what they think is just in the case at bar and cite the nearest favorable previous decisions as pretexts."[123]

The realists asserted that cases arise that are not addressed by existing legislation or case law—there are gaps in the law—and in these situations judges try to work out the right outcome, making new law in the process. Judge Dillon (a historical jurist) made a similar point in

1894: "Where the legislative will is silent, and there is no customary law or precedent, the judges frequently have no guide but what is well termed in our law 'equity and good conscience.' "[124] Judges make these determinations "largely from the general sense of justice and right as interpreted and ascertained by the judges."[125] Dillon regarded this "judicial legislation" as a necessary and beneficial means through which the common law develops over time in step with society.[126]

The realists emphasized that when approaching cases judges typically respond to what they perceive as clusters of fact situations or types. Although "they are not altogether alike," situations with shared characteristics regularly recur.[127] "A generalized situation of this sort is in the judge's mind and is immediately called up," Max Radin asserted, invoking an associated set of rules or principles, and judges often render these decisions without much thought.[128] "Not only in a great many cases would the judge's mind . . . work like that, but I do not see how it could very well work otherwise,"[129] Radin added. Walter Wheeler Cook likewise asserted that established rules and principles "dispose of routine cases which do not require thought."[130] Only "a small number [of cases] will present new and unusual aspects,"[131] Cook claimed, and in these cases judges must strive to arrive at the "socially useful decision."[132] Radin elaborated that sometimes "several categories struggle in their minds for the privilege of framing the situation before them. And since there is that struggle, how can they do otherwise than select the one that seems to them to lead to a desirable result."[133] This "situation type" theory of judging—the notion that when rendering decisions judges respond to complexes of facts (which invoke rules) rather than reasoning downward from rules[134] —has been identified by a theorist as *the* distinctive innovation the legal realists brought to American jurisprudence.[135]

However, what the realists said on this subject is strikingly reminiscent of (prominent historical jurist) James C. Carter's account of judging in the 1890s:

> It is in *new cases* that nearly all the difficulty in ascertaining and applying the law arises. The great mass of transactions of life are indeed repetitions of what has before happened—not exact repetitions, for such never occur—but repetitions of all substantial features. They have once or oftener been subjected to judicial scrutiny and the rules which govern them are known. They arise and pass away without engaging the attention of lawyers or the courts. The great bulk of controversy and litigation springs out of transactions which present material features never before ex-

> hibited, or new combinations and groupings of facts. It is here
> that doubt and difficulty make their appearance. . . . Several dif-
> ferent rules—all just in their proper sphere—are competing with
> each other for supremacy.[136]

Judges commit a mistake, Carter asserted, when they force on one
transaction a rule that arose out of a different fact situation type, for
that "would be sacrificing justice for the sake of uniformity."[137] In new
situations, "the standard of justice must be *adapted* to human affairs.
Systems of law must be shaped in accordance with the actual usages
of men. It is folly to suppose that unbending rules can be made before-
hand and men be disciplined to learn them and adapt the business of
life to them."[138] Uncertainty will perpetually exist in law, Carter observed, because fact groupings "displaying new features" continually
appear and because society continually changes; cases will therefore
arise in which the law is not known until it "has been subjected to
judicial decision."[139]

Finally, the realists repeated that when rendering decisions—interpreting the law, precedent, and facts—judges are influenced by subconscious factors. Radin asserted that judges "classify events before
them into categories determined by their training, their prejudices,
their conscious or unconscious interests, their philosophy, their aesthetic leanings, or even by the chance circumstances surrounding the
particular hearing."[140] This, too, was said much earlier, exemplified in
the 1896 passage by Tiedeman set forth earlier recognizing the impact
of "the bias and peculiar views of the individual judge."[141] He emphasized, and approved of, the responsiveness of judges to prevailing
opinion: "The court is just as much influenced by public opinion as any
other honest man is."[142] "I do not say," he remarked, "that the judge
consciously obeys public opinion, or does it in any improper way. I am
speaking now of unconscious influence."[143] Walter Coles observed in
1893 that, especially when no clear precedent exists, a judge's conclusions "will be largely controlled by the influences, opinions and prejudices to which he happened to have been subjected."[144]

The Overlap with Historical Jurists (the "Formalists")

The names of prominent late-nineteenth-century historical jurists—
Tiedeman, Dillon, Hammond, Carter, Cooley—show up repeatedly in
the preceding demonstration that the core insights credited to the realists had been stated decades earlier.[145] What makes this close overlap

all the more remarkable is that contemporary historians have claimed that the "[historical] legal theories of thinkers like Hammond, Cooley, Bliss, Tiedeman, Phelps, Dillon, and Carter provide the basis for a 'formalistic' view of law and judging."[146] The legal realists are supposed to have debunked legal formalism, yet realistic views of law and judging were articulated by the very jurists now identified with formalism. This apparent contradiction shows, once again, how misguided the conventional story of the formalists and the realists is.

The strong overlap in views is mainly attributable to the primacy these respective jurists accorded to society and social factors—to social norms, social influences, social values, social interests, social attitudes—in connection with law and judging. The realists insisted that law is not autonomous from society and that law must evolve with and serve social needs. Historical jurisprudence championed the same propositions.

Leon Green, tagged as a realist notwithstanding his protest otherwise, put it succinctly: "Government and the law merely reflect the other activities of society, most of them in surprisingly clear detail."[147] Green pointed to the actions of lawyers and judges (assisted by legislation) as the primary mechanisms through which social norms and interests become embodied in the law.[148] As Llewellyn emphasized, "It is society and not the courts which gives rise to, which shapes in the first instance the emerging institution; which kicks the courts into action. It is only from observation of society that the courts can pick their notions of what needs the new institution serves, what needs it baffles. . . . In any event, if the needs press and recur, sooner or later recognition of them will work into the law. Either they will induce the courts to break through and depart from earlier molds, or the bar will find some way to put new wine into old bottles and to induce in the bottles that elasticity and change of shape which, in the long run marks all social institutions."[149] If judges don't reshape the law to conform to current social demands, Llewellyn added, it will be accomplished through legislation.[150]

James Carter, the foremost late nineteenth-century champion of historical jurisprudence, would have concurred wholeheartedly, although he put it in more old-fashioned terms. "Law *begins* as the product of the automatic actions of society."[151] "It is therefore the unconscious creation of society, or, in other words, a growth."[152] "The judges are both by appointment and tradition the experts in ascertaining and declaring the customs of life."[153] "The judge, the lawyer, the jurist of whatever name, continually occupied in the work of examining transactions and determining the customs to which they belong, and whether to those which society cherishes and favors, or to those which it condemns."[154] Carter also recognized, like Llewellyn, that courts are prone to change the law slowly owing to the constraints of the common law method,[155] so slowly that the law may fall out of sync with current needs. He allowed a legitimate (albeit circumscribed) role for legislative reform to accommodate vast changes—and he endorsed "legislation which a highly developed industrial life demands."[156]

Dillon seconded Carter's formulation. Finding "customs" too narrow, however, he expanded it to say that judges brought into law the community's sense of right.[157] Dillon summarized the defining credo of historical jurists: "that law is largely the outcome of all of the past conditions, circumstances, and customs of a people; that it ordinarily originates in or is introduced by custom (using this word in the broad sense of including judiciary law), and is supplemented by legislation, direct or oblique, when, and in general only when, the law is otherwise inadequate to meet difficult and complex or new situations and exigencies."[158] Tiedeman asserted, "[W]e cannot escape the conviction that all law, so far as it constitutes a living rule of civil conduct, whether it takes the form of statute or of judicial decision, is but an expression of the popular sense of right through the popular representative, the legislature or the court as the case may be."[159]

Deep parallels follow from the shared commitment of the realists and historical jurists to the notion that law is a reflection of social processes and that its function is to serve social needs. On his catalog of core realist propositions, Llewellyn placed first "[t]he conception of law in flux, of moving law, and of judicial creation of law."[160] Similarly, Carter wrote: "Sympathizing with every advancing movement made by society, catching the spirit which animates its progress, it is his [the judge's] aim to keep jurisprudence abreast with other social tendencies."[161] Second on Llewellyn's list of shared realist positions is "the conception of law as a means to social ends and not as an end in itself; so that any part needs constantly to be examined for its purpose, and for its effect, and to be judged in light of both and of their relation to each other."[162] Many decades earlier, Hammond wrote that "the law has no doctrines or rules that society cannot modify to its own purposes."[163] Carter wrote that the primary orientation of the judge is to ensure that the law is "fit, useful, convenient, right" for social needs.[164] Llewellyn's third proposition—"the conception of society in flux, and in flux typically faster than law"[165] —was a tenet of historical jurisprudence as well. Eighth on Llewellyn's list is "an insistence on evaluation of any part of law in terms of its effect."[166] Carter wrote: "The judges in considering whether the act was right or wrong applied to it the method universally adopted by all men; they judged it by its *consequences.*"[167]

The close parallels also extend to their respective views on the various ways in which social considerations influence judges. Historical jurists believed that judges brought society's values and sense of justice into law, subconsciously (via the internalization of social values by judges) as well as consciously (by deliberately seeking to derive or produce or match society's sense of right). "The more perfectly our judges could know and follow the popular will on all questions of legal doctrine," Hammond wrote (in 1875), "the better would our law become, the more harmoniously would every department of government work together for the common good."[168] "In short," Carter summarized, "it is the function of judges to watchfully observe the developing moral thought, and catch the improvement in customary conduct, and enlarge and refine correspondingly the legal rules."[169] Compare that with Jerome Frank's insistence: "To do justice, to make any legal system acceptable to society, the abstract preestablished rules have to be adapted and adjusted [by judges], the static formulas made alive."[170] "The will of the judge is to be directed to the just and reasonable results within the limits of the positive rule of law. Such just and reasonable results are to be aimed at consciously."[171]

For both historical jurists and legal realists, in the various ways set forth above, law was and ever must be receptive to, infused by, and permeable to morality and politics produced by society, and attentive to the purposes and needs of society.[172] Cardozo recognized this core orientation of the historical school (and the misleading term "historical"): "[M]any who profess to use the historical method in the adjudication of a cause are in truth less loyal to the significance of the historical school . . . and look more freely to the prevailing standards of welfare and utility. . . . If [historical school] assumptions be accepted, they exact, not blind reproductions of the past, but searching scrutiny of the present, for law . . . is the expression of the convictions of the present."[173] They were not the only ones who saw law in these terms. Oliver Wendell Holmes also held this view of the relationship between law and society (which he argued in *The Common Law*). The same basic set of views infused Roscoe Pound's sociological jurisprudence. Felix Frankfurter expressed (in 1912) these views with respect to judicial review of social legislation: "In so far as these questions are necessarily questions of fact, dealing with actual conditions of life and current dominant opinion, it is essential that the stream of the Zeitgeist must be allowed to flood the sympathies and the intelligence of our judges."[174] Many turn-of-the-century jurists thought of law and society connecting through judges in the similar terms.

Significant differences exist between the historical jurists and the realists that should not be overlooked. They were separated in time by several decades that involved a vast transformation in the economy, society, prevailing attitudes, and the law. When the historical jurists wrote, the common law was still the center of gravity of law (though its dominance was already threatened), at least in the minds of jurists, whereas, by the time the realists wrote, legislation had taken over primacy, and the administrative state was already a formidable presence.

Myriad implications followed from this transformation. Most relevant to this inquiry, this transformation decisively and permanently altered the relative position of judges vis-à-vis legislators. From their formerly commanding heights as the principal figures in law, in the course of the decades that ran from the heyday of historical jurisprudence to the emergence of legal realism, judges were brought down to an equal partnership with legislators or, worse, to become servants of the legislative will. Common law judges previously claimed to represent the common customs and morals of the realm, thus bearing the consent of the community,[175] but after the transition it was legislators who directly represented community consent. Although the historical jurists and the realists similarly thought of judges as the conduits through which social views were brought into law, after the transformation, with judges in a reduced position and no longer plausibly claiming to represent community consent, this notion became far more problematic.

Being of different generations, moreover, historical jurists and realists naturally had different interests and concerns. A prominent theme for a number of realists was the social scientific study of law, which historical jurists said little about (the social sciences were in their infancy in the late nineteenth century). The realists also promoted the reform of legal education, which was not a major concern of the historical jurists. The realists were less complacent than historical jurists about the possibility that judges' views reflected the interests of the elite class rather the whole society. A number of realists sought legal and social reform, which they pursued in their doctrinal analysis. The historical jurists, in contrast, were not social reformers, which their conservative doctrinal analysis reflected. On legal reform they were split—Dillon and Hammond worried about the state of the law and advocated codification to reduce uncertainty; Carter and Cooley actively opposed codification.

More than any other factor, these two groups are separated by their politics. Historical jurists are often cast by their progressive critics as laissez-faire enthusiasts,[176] but that is overdone. Cooley set and enforced railroad rates (as the first chairman of the Interstate Commerce

Commission), he supported labor arbitration, and he warned about the "merciless power of concentrated capital."[177] Tiedeman criticized miscegenation laws and opposed school bible readings; Dillon and Cooley attacked public subsidies for railroads; none of these jurists were corporate apologists.[178] Like other jurists at the time, they cherished liberty and perceived a clear distinction between the public and private spheres, and they criticized what they considered an alarming expansion of state police power and a host of intrusive legislation. These are the positions that progressive critics and later historians latched onto when branding the historical jurists, wrongly, as major contributors to the formalist age.

Judging from their mix of views, in political terms the historical jurists were moderate libertarians (in today's terminology). Two generations later, a number of realists supported New Deal reforms, and they were more enthusiastic about utilizing legislation and the administrative state to advance social objectives, situating them on the opposite pole of the political spectrum from historical jurists.[179] But the contrasting political positions of the historical jurists and the legal realists—with corresponding differences in the substantive legal doctrines they advocated—does not diminish the strong overlap of their views about judging and of the relationship between law and society.

The Insight Obscured by the Formalist-Realist Antithesis

The pivotal point to take away from the striking similarities demonstrated here is not that the realists did not say much that was new about judging, or that they had much in common with historical jurists, although both points are correct. The most profound lesson lies implicit in the positions they held in common.

Although the historical jurists said many of the same things about judging as the realists, they were *not skeptics* of judging. Cooley and Dillon were nationally known judges and law professors who had written leading legal treatises. While the historical jurists recognized that there are social influences on judicial reasoning, they did not describe this as a flaw in judging, but as an essential—necessary, beneficial—link that keeps law and society on the same plane. The grossly erroneous claim that jurists in the late nineteen century, under the spell of formalism, believed that law was *autonomous,* obscures this important insight. The constant repetition of the supposed formalist position helped entrench the picture that any factor that intrudes on the judicial reasoning machine must taint—rather than be constitutive of—the decision-making process. Only a true legal formalist would believe this, and, as earlier chapters argued, these "formalists" of legend never actually existed. A balanced realism about judging, the position held by both the historical jurists and the legal realists, understands that the social views of judges have a constructive role in their decisions.

6

○ ○ ● ● ●

A RECONSTRUCTION OF LEGAL REALISM

THE REASON THE CORE realist insights about judging were articulated decades earlier is that they are *plainly evident aspects of judging* (in common law systems). It's as simple as that. It was apparent to many that the law has inconsistencies, runs out, and routinely comes up against unanticipated situations and that judges possess a substantial degree of flexibility when working with legal materials. It was obvious to observers that the law can be interpreted differently by judges with different views. Dissenting opinions and shifts in constitutional interpretation that follow from changes in personnel are constant reminders of this.[1] The realists were astute observers of the judicial craft, to be sure, and elaborated illuminating lines of analysis. But the fundamentals of what they put out had been said much earlier by other astute and candid observers of judging, of whom there were many in the late nineteenth century.

These insights can be found even farther back. They reverberate in the words of Chief Justice Vaughan in a 1670 case:

> I would know whether any thing be more common, than for two men students, barristers, or judges, to deduce contrary and opposite conclusions out of the same case in law? And is there any difference that two men should infer distinct conclusions from the same testimony? Is any thing more known than that the same author, and place in that author, is forcibly urged to maintain contrary conclusions, and the decision hard, which is in the right?
> . . .
> A man cannot see by another's eye, nor hear by another's ear, nor can a man conclude or infer the thing to be resolved by another's understanding or reasoning.[2]

Crudely expressed by modern lights, perhaps, but the core insights about the openness and diversity of legal (and factual) judgments are there.

Another striking example can be found in a 1836 speech by a prominent lawyer urging codification, Robert Rantoul: "The judge is human, and feels the bias which the coloring of the particular case gives. If he wishes to decide the next case differently, he has only to distinguish, and thereby make new law." "Almost any case, where there is any difference of opinion," Rantoul continued, "may be decided either way, and plausible analogies found in the great storehouse of precedent to justify the decision. The law, then, is the final whim of the judge, after counsel for both parties have done their utmost to sway it to the one side or the other."[3]

In 1838, a year after Chief Justice Taney replaced the long-serving Chief Justice John Marshall on the Supreme Court, an alarmed commentator reviewing the decisions issued in Taney's first term found a wholesale "departure" underway in which the new majority endeavored to "subvert" established precedent to bring a return of "anti-federalist doctrines."[4] Another critic of the new trend disdained the "ultra-radical tirades of those friends of the administration, who exulted in the complete revolution which the judiciary has undergone, and the prospect that a new system of jurisprudence will be established on the ruins of long-settled doctrines."[5] The Supreme Court "in leaving settled principles, and depending on *private ideas of justice*, is exercising a legislative as well as a judicial function," the critic objected in 1838.[6]

In his famous 1839 book,[7] *Legal and Political Hermeneutics*, Francis Lieber declared that "the 'uncertainty of the law,' which originates in a great measure from the different interpretation to which one and the same law may be subject, has become proverbial."[8] Lieber quoted Professor Simon Greenleaf of Harvard: "The manner of the decision, too, and the reasons on which it is professedly founded, and even the decision itself, may receive some coloring and impress, from the position of the judges, their political principles, their habits of life, their physical temperament, their intellectual, moral and religious character. Not that the decision will depend on these; but only that they are considerations not to be wholly disregarded in perusing and weighing the judgment delivered."[9] Lieber added that "in decisions on all important matters, much depends upon a certain instinctive feeling, not derived from any course of reasoning, and inclination of our mind one way or the other, in nicely balanced cases, not from whim, but in consequence of long experience, and the effect of a thousand details on our mind, which details, although properly affecting a sound mind, can nevertheless not be strictly summed up."[10] Lieber was "without serious question the most eminent legal scholar in [nineteenth-century] America"[11] His book was cited twice by the U.S. Supreme Court and appeared in three editions.[12]

The historical record gets thinner (and harder to pore through) the further back one goes, but the tone and content of these various statements offer evidence that realism about judging has a lengthy heritage. Significantly, a consistent source of such insights has been judges themselves. Jerome Frank's sound and fury drown out a telling aspect of his blast against the purportedly pervasive delusions about judging. His two key skeptical chapters were filled with realistic depictions of judging by *judges*. Frank cited Holmes, Cardozo, Hutcheson, Hand, the regular standbys, along with Judges Peters, Lehman, Cuthbert Pound, and Lord Halsbury.[13] These judges all acknowledged the limitations of human judges and of law. Several dozen judges spanning more than a century are cited in this book to the same effect. Judges are intimately familiar with the often difficult, uncertain, and complex aspects of judging. They did not frequently blab about these aspects of judging, but they were by no means silent.

It is also essential to recognize that the judges who made realistic comments about judging still felt that they were genuinely engaged in the interpretation and application of law. By their accounts, it works despite the challenges, and judging is not inevitably the product of the personal biases or views of judges. Holmes, the reputed skeptic, is a prime example. "It has given me great pleasure to sustain the Constitutionality of laws that I believe to be as bad as possible," he said, "because I helped thereby to mark the difference between what I would forbid and what the constitution permits."[14] In his final dissent, opposing what he saw as a pattern of invalidating whatever happened "to strike a majority of this Court as for any reason undesirable,"[15] Holmes uttered, "I cannot believe that the [Fourteenth] Amendment was intended to give us *carte blanche* to embody our economic or moral beliefs in its prohibitions."[16]

The Legal Realists Were Committed to the Law

Now to dispel another common misunderstanding: the notion that the realists were deeply skeptical about law and judging. A leading contemporary legal philosopher characterized the realists in highly skeptical terms: "The Realists believed that decision-makers, especially judges deciding hard cases, initially make an 'all things considered' judgement about who ought to win. That preliminary judgement, taking into account moral, political, economic, and psychological factors, is not arbitrary, but is particularistic in focusing on the optimal results *for this case*. . . . To the Legal Realist, rules serve not as sources of *ex ante* guidance, but as vehicles of *ex post* legitimation of decisions reached without regard for the rules."[17]

This misconstrues their position. The realists believed in the law and fervently labored to improve it. Llewellyn unabashedly proclaimed his "faith about the Good in this institution of our law";[18] and he waxed poetically on "the esthetics of certain legal arts I deeply love."[19] In defense of the realists, Eugene Rostow, the dean of Yale Law School who knew many of the key players, remarked that "the legal realists were among our most devoted and effective reformers, both of law and of society."[20] Jerome Frank confessed, "I am—I make no secret of it—a reformer."[21]

The various goals of the realists were to increase the certainty and predictability of law, to train better lawyers, to advance legal justice, and to reform the law to better serve social needs. This constructive orientation was borne out in the legal careers of the realists, many of whom were not bookish academics but engaged jurists. Jerome Frank, Charles Clark, and Thurman Arnold became federal appellate judges.[22] Joseph Hutcheson was a federal trial judge, and later became an appellate judge. William Douglas became a Supreme Court justice. Frank, Douglas, Arnold, Felix Cohen, Wesley Sturges, and Herman Oliphant held legal positions in the federal government during the Roosevelt administration. Llewellyn took a lead role in drafting the Uniform Commercial Code, Clark in drafting the Federal Code of Civil Procedure. Arnold, Clark, Green, and Sturges served stints as law school deans. Several realists sought to reform legal education to train better-skilled lawyers,[23] with Frank an enthusiastic proponent of a "clinical-lawyer" program of education.[24] Their collective insistence that law is a powerful instrument to serve the social good, and their sustained efforts to bring this about, bespeaks their abiding faith in the law.

Rostow offered a nuanced, corrective reading of their position:

> [The realists] were alleged to believe that decisions were based on unstated interests or value preferences, and that the reasons given for decisions were in fact after-thoughts, cynical rationalizations, representing the judge not as a conscientious lawyer, working within the permissible limits of his discretion, but as a willful autocrat. By and large (though with several exceptional and occasional aberrations) the charge was not justified: the realist literature agreed with Pekelis' striking remark, amending one of Holmes' most famous quips, that "concrete cases cannot be decided by general propositions—nor without them." The realists—or most of them—were not trying to deny the inevitability of rules in a system of law that sought at any given time to decide

like cases alike. What they were trying to achieve was an awareness of the relationship between rules and policy, viewing the law as an instrument for social action in a society constantly in flux, "and in flux typically faster than the law, so that the probability is always given that any portion of law needs reexamination to determine how far it fits the society it purports to serve."[25]

Realist writings are replete with statements that support this characterization. Walter Wheeler Cook, for example, asserted, "This view does not lead to the discarding of all principles and rules, but quite the contrary. It demands them as tools with which to work; as tools without which we cannot work effectively. It does, however, make sure that they are used as tools and are not perverted to an apparently mechanical use."[26] He acknowledged, "Our legal rules and principles will give us the answer to the vast bulk of human transactions."[27]

Although Llewellyn gleefully exposed the manipulability of precedent and the openness of the rules of statutory interpretation, he consistently retracted the most radical implications of these observations, cautioning that, "while it is possible to build a number of divergent logical ladders up out of the same cases and down again to the same dispute, *there are not so many that can be built defensibly* [Llewellyn's emphasis]. And of these few there are some, or there is one, toward which the prior cases definitely press. Already you see the walls closing in around the judge."[28] A skilled lawyer asked to predict the fate of a case on appeal, Llewellyn conjectured, ought "to average correct prediction of outcome eight times out of ten, and better than that if he knows the appeal counsel on both sides or sees the briefs."[29] When identifying the sources of this high degree of reckonability, Llewellyn elaborated on several "steadying factors": judges are indoctrinated into the legal tradition such that they "see things . . . through law spectacles";[30] much legal doctrine—including rules, principles, and statutes—is reasonably clear and well developed;[31] judges follow accepted doctrinal techniques, strive to produce a just result, and strive to come up the right legal answer;[32] judges sitting together on an appellate bench interact "to smooth the unevenness of individual temper";[33] and judges' desire and commitment to live up to the obligations of the judicial role, and to earn the approval of their legal audience for appropriate judicial behavior, and their desire to avoid reversal by a higher court prompt judges to engage in a good-faith effort to conduct an unbiased search for the correct legal result.[34]

The realists harped on the various limitations of and room to maneuver allowed by legal rules, principles, statutory interpretation, stare decisis, and the finding and stating of facts in judicial decision making.

But their position is easily misunderstood if their target is not kept in mind: they were attacking the notion that judging merely entailed the logical application of legal rules and principles. Their refutation of this view—a straw man, as it was—did not mean that they embraced its polar opposite: the notion that legal rules and principles do not have a significant role in judges' decisions. Morris Cohen warned in 1916, when the core realists were just starting their legal careers, "They who scorn the idea of the judge as a logical automaton are apt to fall into the opposite error of exaggerating as irresistible the force of bias or prejudice."[35] None of the legal realists, not even Jerome Frank, made this error.

Rather, they endeavored to make plain that more is involved in the process of judging than just the application of precedents, rules, and principles, and their message was that the failure to attend to these other factors is poor lawyering. The realists did not entirely agree among themselves on what those other factors are. Llewellyn, as described above, emphasized the totality of the legal and judicial setting, including legal knowledge, legal indoctrination, approval of peers (lawyers, academics, and judges), the collaborative nature of judging, the sense of judicial obligation, and institutional constraints. For Oliphant, "The predictable element in it all is what courts have done in response to the stimuli of the facts of the concrete cases before them."[36] Other realists suggested that a complex of surrounding social factors stabilize judicial decision making. Felix Cohen recognized that "experience does reveal a significant body of predictable uniformity in the behavior of courts."[37] He speculated that dominant economic forces, the judges' class attitudes, their past experiences, and the eloquence of the lawyers in a case are some of the forces that mold judicial decisions. "We know, too, that judges are craftsmen, with aesthetic ideals, concerned with the aesthetic judgments that the bar and the law schools will pass upon their awkward or skillful, harmonious or unharmonious, anomalous or satisfying, actions and theories."[38] Like Llewellyn, Cohen also acknowledged the constraining impact of the institutional setting (including potential reversal)[39] and the judicial office: "[T]he man who dons the judicial robe with the greatest contempt for precedent finds that the pressure of his office-space compels him to follow paths that, from outside the office space, once appeared absurd."[40]

The misperception of the realists as extreme skeptics of judging is substantially attributable to Jerome Frank's spectacular cannonball splash, which soaked all the realists standing off to the side.[41] But Frank was an outlier. In his exchange with Pound, Llewellyn pointed out (with Frank's input) that Frank *alone* among the realists argued that "the rational element in law is an illusion";[42] and only Frank laid a heavy emphasis on the personality of the judge in decision making.[43] Both Llewellyn and Felix Cohen criticized Frank for this position. In a review of *Law and the Modern Mind,* Llewellyn wrote that Frank's commendable desire to smash illusions produced an unfortunate "skewing" in his account of judging, which "is much more predictable, and hence more certain, than his [Frank's] treatment would indicate."[44] "For while we may properly proclaim that general propositions do not decide concrete cases, we none the less must recognize that *ways* of deciding, *ways* of thinking, *ways* of sizing up facts 'in terms of the their legal relevance' are distinctly enough well marked in our courts. . . . It is not merely decisions, but decisions *in this setting* of their semi-regularity, which make up the core of law."[45] Felix Cohen criticized the "hunch" theory of judging and Frank's emphasis on the personal idiosyncrasies of judges for failing to recognize the "significant, predictable, social determinants that govern the course of judicial decision"[46]—within "social" Cohen included the constraints provided by the legal culture generally and the institutional context of judging.

Even Frank was not the wild skeptic given off by his fusillade. "The conscientious judge, having tentatively arrived at a conclusion," he wrote, "can check up [with the legal rules and principles] to see whether such a conclusion, without unfair distortion of the facts, can be linked with the generalized points of view theretofore acceptable."[47] Frank acknowledged that legal rules and principles "may be aids to the judge in tentatively testing or formulating conclusions; they may be positive factors in bending his mind towards wise or unwise solutions of the problem before him."[48] The purpose of his book was to explode complacency, which led Frank to press hard on every angle of skeptical realism, while saying little about the ways law constrains judicial decisions—which would have detracted from his objective. But the rule-bound side emerged in his more reflective writings. Although Frank exposed the manipulability of stare decisis, for example, he asserted that "no sensible person suggests that stare decisis be abandoned."[49] In a 1943 legal opinion (joined by Judge Learned Hand), Judge Frank acknowledged that personal values can influence a judge's decision, but he nonetheless asserted, "The conscientious judge will, as far as possible, make himself aware of his biases of this character, and, by that very self-knowledge, nullify their effect."[50] In his 1948 review of a collection of Cardozo's writings, Frank accepted as "not too wide of the mark" Cardozo's claim: "Nine-tenths, perhaps more, of the cases that come before a court are predetermined—predetermined in the sense that they are predestined—their fate established by inevitable laws that follow them from birth to death."[51] "[I]n the great majority of suits," Frank asserted, ". . . both sides agree as to the applicable rules, the disputes relating to the facts alone."[52] In the course of his career Frank shifted the focus away from legal rules and principles to identify the vagaries of fact-finding at the trial court level as the main source of uncertainty in the law.[53]

A careful reading shows that Llewellyn and Frank, and the rest of those identified as realists, all along recognized the stabilizing and constraining factors in law. Their deliberately polemical postures placed the skeptical aspects up front, but they recognized the rule-bound aspect of judging as well, and their considered views amounted to balanced realism. The author of one of the leading historical studies of the legal realists,[54] William Twining, concluded that "the image of Realism as being mainly a skeptical attack on the rationality of judicial processes does not score high marks in the minimal test of historical and textual accuracy."[55] Both Llewellyn and Frank in later editions expressed some regret about *Bramble Bush* and *Law and the Modern Mind*, respectively. It was a work of youth, Llewellyn noted (he was thirty-seven at its writing), "and a man's own ideas . . . change as he gains experience."[56] Their regret was not a retraction of the substance of their observations—which in Llewellyn's case were always balanced—but about the tone and emphasis of the presentation, which encouraged and enabled critics to misread (and easily discredit) their positions.[57]

In a touching memorial to Frank upon his death, Thurman Arnold may have offered the best way to understand this episode of realism. Arnold aptly called *Law and the Modern Mind* "shock treatment."[58] The book was published when the country was mired in the second year of the miserable depression, with government and law doing little to address the situation. "Realistic jurisprudence is a good medicine for a sick and troubled society," Arnold observed. "The America of the early 1930s was such a society."[59] Considered to be among the more radical realists, Arnold offered this broader assessment: "But realism, despite its liberating virtues, is not a sustaining food for a stable civilization."[60]

Latecomers to the Battle against Recalcitrant Judges

The final misconception that must be dispelled is the background setting against which the realists are often understood: the narrative that judges at the time were laissez-faire enthusiasts who consistently obstructed pro-labor and social welfare legislation.[61] According to this account, the realists were crucial warriors in the battle against reactionary judges, a battle finally won with the "constitutional revolution" of 1937 (following the threat of Roosevelt's court packing plan), after which courts finally halted their obstruction of economic legislation.

Credence is given to this account by well-known examples of such court actions—from *Lochner* (which Holmes explicitly tied to laissez-faire), to the Supreme Court's invalidation of four major pieces of New Deal legislation in 1935–36. Relying upon this narrative, a jurisprudent claimed that "[t]he final defeat of the Old Court majority in the exciting events of 1937 represented, no doubt, the apogee of the Legal Realists' achievements."[62]

This conventional picture, however, fails to acknowledge the massive increase of intrusive legislation that occurred from the final decade of the nineteenth century onward. "The most casual newspaper-reader and observer of legislation," an editor wrote in 1887, "must have had his attention attracted to a growing tendency in our legislation toward the regulation of private and personal concerns."[63] "At no time and in no country has legislation been so active,"[64] remarked a commentator in 1911.

A legislative onslaught it was. The broad array of subjects covered is conveyed in an annual review of "Social and Economic Legislation of the States" that began to run in 1890. The author grouped the legislation into six classes: "(1) laws concerning the family and domestic relations; (2) laws providing for the State care of the unfortunate and depraved members of society; (3) laws for the regulation of labor and the laboring classes; (4) laws for the regulation of the different forms corporate industry and concentrated capital; (5) State and local finance; (6) all legislation looking to the development of natural resources."[65]

This legislation was plentiful and reached deep into the crevasses of social and economic life. All aspects of work conditions were addressed, including hour limits, availability of bathrooms, mandatory days off, forms of payment, restrictions on child labor, and protections for labor unions (prohibiting blacklisting and disallowing the hiring of nonresidents as private security to prevent vicious treatment of striking laborers). The legislation intrusively limited contractual terms—including prohibiting waivers of employer liability to injured workers[66] —prompting the author of the survey to observe "[t]hat legislatures no longer hesitate to abridge the freedom of private contract."[67] Legislation also imposed a variety of taxes; restrictions on gambling, cigarettes, and alcohol; mandatory education, a host of health and safety regulations (including food quality and labeling requirements); banking legislation; a variety of restrictions on corporate operations; and price limits on utilities. As the author of the legislative survey noted in 1894, "While the effort to extend the functions of State government has been more noticeable, perhaps, in those parts of the country where the 'farmers' movement' has made most headway, the tendency in the direction of enlarging municipal activities is everywhere gaining strength, East and West."[68] Most of this legislation was enacted pursuant to the states' broad discretion under the "police power" to advance the health and safety of citizens.

The overwhelming bulk of this voluminous legislation survived challenges in state and federal courts. "An 1897 review of 1,639 state labor laws enacted during the preceding twenty years found that only 114 of them—7 percent—had been held unconstitutional."[69] The eminent Supreme Court historian Charles Warren, sympathetic to progressive reforms, wrote a 1913 article extolling the "progressivism" of the Supreme Court. He found that out of a total of 302 Supreme Court cases between 1873 and 1912 involving challenges to the exercise of state police power "only 36 State statutes were held unconstitutional in 40 years"[70]—an average of under *one* invalidation per year. In a separate study of cases between 1887 and 1911 in which a claim was made that state legislation violated the due process or equal protection clauses of the Constitution, Warren found that out of "560 State statutes or other form of State action adjudicated upon . . . during the last twenty-five years, the Court has upheld over 530"[71]—an average of just over *one* invalidation per year. *Lochner* was one of the latter cases (although it also bears mention that the New York high court upheld the statute before the Supreme Court struck it).[72] Consistent with Warren's analysis,[73] Munroe Smith observed in 1913 that "the attitude of the federal Supreme Court is at present satisfactory to friends of social welfare legislation."[74]

State courts were less accepting of such legislation, but even in state courts the degree of interference must not be exaggerated. Ernst Freund published a 1910 article that examined state court treatment of labor legislation. He noted that the "great mass of labor statutes have not been contested in the courts."[75] "Of those that have been questioned in the courts practically all that had any immediate bearing on safety, sanitation or decency have been sustained."[76] While state courts did show a tendency to strike certain types of labor legislation, Freund found that the states nonetheless were divided among themselves on these issues, and for each type that was struck a majority of jurisdictions nonetheless upheld similar legislation against challenge.

Courts in the period *did* invalidate legislation at a notable level. The resultant uncertainty about what would survive challenge had inhibiting effects. These actions provoked the ire of labor unions, populists, and progressives—prompting the recall initiatives mentioned earlier. But the overall picture is twisted counter to reality if one ignores the overwhelming bulk of legislation that remained on the books. The real story of the late nineteenth century—recognized by a growing number of political historians[77]—is the inexorable rise and expansion of the modern bureaucratic state (municipal, state, and federal), with its intrusive, instrumental, many-fingered forays into social and economic affairs, carried out though legislation and the administrative system. Far from standing together with arms locked in resistance against this advance out of a commitment to laissez-faire, courts largely stood by and let it happen, except for occasional obstructions that garnered a lot of attention.

The conventional laissez-faire story about the period that is told today also does not comport with what observers were saying at the time. In 1892 Tiedeman remarked that earlier in the century "laissez faire philosophy exerted the dominant influence over public opinion," "but in the last thirty years or more a strong tendency to socialism had been developed and public opinion now justifies a great many interferences with private business that would not have been tolerated fifty years ago."[78] Beale remarked in 1904, "When freedom of action is injurious to the public it not only may be, but it must be, restrained in the public interest. That is the spirit of our age, and that is the present position of the law."[79] This shift was a common topic of late nineteenth-century economic and political commentary.[80] "One of the most prominent facts of contemporary politics, both theoretical and practical," remarked a political scientist in 1888, "is the movement away from what is called 'Individualism.' "[81]

Given the unprecedented increase in the quantity, scope, and intrusiveness of legislation in the period, which chafed against traditional legal understandings, it should not be surprising that some legislation was invalidated. A considerable number of late nineteenth-century judges and jurists, though what proportion is unclear, looked askance at a good deal of this legislation. But many in law vocally supported it. There are indications that by the turn of the century judicial resistance began to diminish and thereafter to rapidly fade. The incoming generation of judges at the beginning of the century would have been trained after the broad transition in social views was underway.

As set forth in chapter 3, Judge Leonard Crouch in 1927 described the changes that began to take place after the turn of the century in judicial treatment of the law to adjust to social, political, and economic changes.[82] Others at the time reported a similar shift. A dramatic expression of the ongoing change, much of it accomplished by judges, can be found in John Wigmore's vigorous opposition, in 1914, to a proposal by the American Academy of Jurisprudence to compile a statement of legal doctrine. Wigmore sent a letter highly critical of the project to members (summarized below by historian Daniel Ernst):

> "The present decade (or even generation) is precisely the time when a formal statement of the law is inappropriate," Wigmore wrote. "The law is so obviously in a seething change that one

might as well expect to analyze a chemical reaction while the test tube is over the flame." "Take any branch of the law you like," Wigmore continued. Torts? "The old-time doctrines of liability are changing so fast that it is difficult to keep up with them." Criminal Law? "All along the line a radical re-casting is going on." Evidence? "Nobody knows how many rules are on the point of crumbling away in the next twenty years." Constitutional Law? "A prophet would be needed to tell us what its complexion will be as soon as the present unrest has subsided; certainly many existing books may be sold for old paper."[83]

A 1917 law review article entitled "The Decline of Traditionalism and Individualism" opened with the recognition that "[t]he short period of the present century has witnessed in this country many legislative and judicial changes in the law."[84] "So far as laws relative to business are concerned," the author continued, "the principle of laissez faire is giving way to that of regulation."[85] Robert Cushman in 1922 described the "new attitude of the courts" that set in after the turn the century at both the state and federal levels showing greater solicitude for collectivist views and social and economic legislation.[86] In 1924 Cardozo wrote that "the tendency today is in the direction of a growing liberalism. The new spirit has made its way gradually; and its progress, unnoticed step-by-step, is visible in retrospect as we look back upon the distance traversed. The old forms remain, but they are filled with new content. . . . We are thinking of the end that the law serves, and fitting its rules to the task of service."[87]

Judging from these accounts, it appears that by the time the realists came on the scene in the mid-1920s and 1930s the tide of attitudes within the judiciary had already decisively turned. It is true that the Supreme Court was regularly controlled by a conservative majority in this period, but that did not reflect the broader situation. Nor is there any evidence that the writings by the legal realists about judging played *any* role in the final acquiescence of judicial conservatives to social and economic legislation.

Two Realistic *Generations* in Law (at least)

Had the catchy "realism" label not been coined—initially without any precise content in mind—had the ire of Pound not been provoked, had a few rising scholars not reveled in pushing the envelope of respectability, the folks tagged as realists might not have been seen at the time (or today) as a discrete group at all. Some of the people who Llewellyn identified as realists made this objection. Several of the realists were pioneers of the social scientific study of law, others were reformers of legal education, and others pursued a progressive political agenda.

For the most part—except for the handful of realists who actually conducted social scientific studies—they were hardly distinguishable from many other law professors, judges, and legislators in the period who were busily engaged in developing substantive legal rules and doctrines in ways that adjusted to and addressed the new social, material, and economic circumstances of their vastly changed society. This transformational work was undertaken by at least two full generations of legal scholars, theirs and the one before. These jurists have been obliterated from the modern consciousness by the image of the realists as radical revolutionaries. Take, for example, William Draper Lewis—the dean of Pennsylvania Law School and head, at different times, of the Association of American Law Schools and the American Law Institute. Two decades before the realists arrived, Lewis asserted that law serves social ends, he was sharply critical of courts, and he advocated that social scientific approaches be incorporated in legal education.[88] Lewis wrote (in 1897) that "all law does depend on the proper public policy for the conditions which exist, and the changes in the conditions of life which have been going on for the past eighty years are great enough to produce the most profound changes in our law."[89]

To obtain a sense of how deep this set of views had penetrated turn-of-the-century juristic thought, consider the words of two prominent judges. Delivering the 1903 Annual Address to the American Bar Association, Second Circuit Judge LeBaron Colt insisted that it has always been the special role of courts and lawyers to "keep the law in harmony with social progress, to make it more reasonable as social necessities and public sentiment have demanded."[90]

> Ever recognizing that "the matter changeth, the custom, the contracts, the commerce, the dispositions, educations, and tempers of men and societies," they have conceived theories, invoked doctrines, and inaugurated instrumentalities to relieve the situation. They have carried on judicial legislation from the infancy of the law in order that it might advance with society. By the adoption of broad and elastic rules of interpretation, they have maintained, in large measure, the supreme law of the land in harmony with national growth.[91]

Colt frankly acknowledged that judges invoked the "doctrine of reasonableness" and "liberally" construed statutory and constitutional provisions to change the law and accommodate social changes.[92] Colt insisted, again and again: "The law should always be viewed from the standpoint of society, and not from the standpoint of the law itself. . . . The law is made for society, and not society for the law. The interests of society are primary; the interests of the law secondary. Society is the master, and the law its handmaiden."[93] Colt said this in front of a large gathering of lawyers in 1903, several years before Pound urged much the same, a generation before the realists would stake out the identical position.

Another high-profile federal circuit judge, Charles F. Amidon, in 1907, made explicit what everyone could see: "The fact that the Supreme Court in constitutional cases so frequently stands five to four, each division assigning weighty reasons for diametrically opposite views, shows plainly how much the Constitution in actual application is a matter of interpretation."[94] He added that the cases are "frequently decided not upon the language of the Constitution, but upon conflicting notions of life."[95] Given the "wide latitude for judicial construction," Amidon wrote, "the court in construing the Constitution is exercising a political power second only to that of the convention that framed the instrument."[96]

Many of the most prominent legal figures of the day—including Ernst Freund, Samuel Williston, John Henry Wigmore, Harlan Fiske Stone, William Draper Lewis—noted the openness of judging, advocated that law should change with and meet the needs of society, and promoted the reform of legal education.[97] Yet none of these jurists are thought of today as realists. Take the final example of Williston—who legal historian Thomas Grey identified as a "Langdellian."[98] Williston agreed that empirical research on law provides "necessary information" and that law is a means to social ends.[99] "I am a realist," Williston wrote, "though not so called by the group that have adopted the designation. I recognize that cases are not always decided in accordance with logical deductions from acknowledged legal principles, or for that matter in accordance with the actual facts."[100] He acknowledged that courts have "uncontrolled power to bend a general rule to the needs of the particular case."[101] "Every lawyer knows that when the equities of a case are strongly against him, the fact that logical deductions from established rules are in his favor may not save him from an adverse decision."[102]

The essential error perpetuated by current understandings is to see "the realists" as a hardy *band* of rebellious thinkers, when the views about judging they held—their balanced realism, not their skeptical pose—were shared by most jurists at the time. A big clue that points toward this conclusion can be found in Llewellyn's response to Pound. Historians have noted that, when citing examples of realistic work,

Llewellyn referred to "about sixty five people (in addition to the list of twenty)."[103] That makes roughly *eighty-five* jurists thinking along realist lines, by Llewellyn's count, including leading names of the day across a range of fields (Pound, Cardozo, Frankfurter, Landis, etc.). This *was* a *generation* of legal thinkers. Pound said as much when he objected to Llewellyn in response to his initial list of forty-four realists that "you might put almost all of us there. All of us today surely have something of what is in the juristic air we breathe."[104] On the core issues for which the realists are known—a realistic view of judging, the insistence that law must keep up with and meet the needs of society—there was broad agreement among jurists.

Llewellyn's initially odd observation about the list of twenty realists now makes more sense: "Their differences in point of view, in interest, in emphasis, in field of work, are huge. They differ among themselves well-nigh as much as any of them differs from, say, Langdell."[105] Llewellyn was not exaggerating. One example is that Francis Bohlen and Leon Green, today described as representing sharply contesting views of tort law,[106] were both on Llewellyn's initial list of realists.[107] Like every generation, this legal generation was riven by many differences. Seeing the realists as a generation also explains the final words of Llewellyn's essay: "They are not a group."[108]

The argument pressed here that the realists' views about judging were common to their generation would appear to be inconsistent with the fact that they were subjected to criticism by their peers at the time. That can be explained, however. One set of criticisms came from jurists (mainly natural law thinkers) opposed to the proposition that law is purely a means to serve social interests, a perspective that critics thought emptied law of its ethical content and reduced it to a system of power.[109] This was a troublesome implication of their position, but it was a dilemma the entire generation struggled with, for law was widely seen by that time as a means to serve social ends.[110] A few critics—including Robert Hutchins, also on Llewellyn's first list of realists[111]—were skeptical about the usefulness of shifting legal education to focus on fact situations and about the fruitfulness of social scientific studies.[112] These were legitimate doubts.

Critics who objected to the realists' views about judging fixated on their skeptical excesses, chastising the realists for failing to adequately appreciate the role played by legal rules in legal decisions. This criticism was not unfair with respect to Frank of *Law and the Modern Mind*, but, as explained above, it was a distorted reading of the realists generally—understandable given their skeptical pose—who held a balanced realism about judging. Remember that Llewellyn and Cohen criticized Frank on the same grounds.

The essential point is that the critics *also* held to a balanced realism about judging. Pound, Dickinson, and Fuller, the best-known critics, all accepted the validity of the realists' points about the openness of law and judging and the impropriety of thinking that legal rules were certain and answers easy.[113] Pound wrote, however, "It is just as unreal to refuse to see the extent to which legal technique, with all its faults, applied to authoritative legal materials, with all their defects, keeps down the alogical or unrational element or holds it to tolerable limits in practice."[114] Llewellyn and other realists, as indicated earlier, agreed with this, and protested that the critics had unfairly distorted their position.[115] No critic denied that law has open spaces, that precedent can be putty in the hands of judges, or that judges sometimes reason backward from outcomes. When properly understood in these terms, the criticism of the realists' views of judging at the time *confirms* the core argument here: that many jurists held balanced realistic views of judging (including the realists).

One clarification must be emphasized in closing. To assert that the realists expressed views about judging that were typical of their generation, although in a more rebellious tone, is not to say that the realists had no impact. Frank and Llewellyn helped prepare the way for and entrench the formalist-realist divide through their exaggerated portraits of the beliefs of their opponents; when the full-blown "formalist age" was constructed in the late 1960s and 1970s, the legal realists ended up hooked unwillingly on the opposite pole, with the realists now caricatured as well. The very *belief* that the legal realists valiantly battled against ignorant views of mechanical judging continues to have real consequences.

Furthermore, thanks in part to the work of the realists, significant changes have taken place in how casebooks are written, and the social scientific study of law is now thriving. Changes have also occurred in the style of written judicial decisions, with judges engaging in more open discussions of policy and social consequences. Nothing in this argument detracts from the historical studies that have documented the efforts of the legal realists in these respects. They were a distinguished group with many legal accomplishments. The attention they brought to the notion of realism helped crystallize shifts already underway. The thrust of this analysis is that the named realists were a few dozen individuals singled out for attention and given credit, for what was the work and success of two generational waves of jurists with similar views about judging, engaging in the same enterprise, working to bring the law into a closer match with a vastly transformed society and set of social understandings.

Repeated Bouts of Skeptical Realism

When viewed in a longer historical frame that stretches backward to the early nineteenth century and forward to the late twentieth century, the evidence presented in this and the preceding chapter suggests that skeptical-realistic insights about judging regularly emerge in the U.S. legal tradition, often linked to heightened social and political turmoil. Three examples of such skepticism were recited from the 1830s—one uttered in advocacy of codification, and two others in connection with what the authors feared was a looming constitutional crisis. Further historical excavation will likely locate additional expressions of skeptical realism in the first half of the nineteenth century.[116] Skeptical observations about judging appeared in response to the Legal Tender Decisions of 1870–71, continuing in a low key, then bursting forth in the early 1890s—a period of severe depression, strife, and dislocation. Many battles took place in legal arenas in this period.[117] Skeptical realism about judging continued apace through the turn of the century, into the first, second, and third decades, until it appears to have quieted in the 1940s. (The improvements brought by the New Deal, the final retreat of judges, and the threats of the Second World War and Communist Russia, perhaps combined to help sublimate such skepticism.). Viewed in this longer frame, it appears more accurate to situate the "legal realists" at the *tail end* of about a half-century of a continuous stream of candid realism about law and judging.

Following more than a decade of relative quiescence, a renewed episode of skeptical realism about judging in the U.S. legal culture emerged. In the late 1950s and 1960s this was manifested in southern and conservative critics who charged the Warren Supreme Court with reading their liberal values into the Constitution.[118] In the 1970s and 1980s skeptical realism was embraced by the leftist Critical Legal Studies Movement, fueled by the turmoil of race-based protests and protests against the Vietnam War.[119] In the 1990s and 2000s a steady drumbeat of skeptical realism has been directed at the courts, the Supreme Court in particular, from the left and the right.[120]

What especially stands out about expressions of skeptical realism is the similarity of the arguments across time. Rantoul in 1836, Hammond in 1881, the legal realists in the 1920s and 1930s, and Critical Legal Studies in the 1970s and 1980s (and others along the way) all argued in interchangeable terms that judges have the freedom to decide cases in accordance with their political views and to cover these decisions with legal justifications. In each case, the criticism was expressed by members of the legal fraternity.

The strikingly parallel arguments, which span nearly two centuries, lead to the surmise that realism about the openness of law and the complexities of judging is present even when not made an issue of. This is confirmed by Lieber's remark in the 1830s that the recognition that uncertainty of interpretation will arise owing to contrasting views of judges has "has become proverbial."[121] If this is correct, the expression of skeptical realism does not reflect a newfound sophisticated awareness about judging, but rather is a manifestation of unhappiness about law or judges, with critics time and again deploying already-at-hand skeptical arguments as a weapon.

The difference today is that the skeptical emphasis appears to have become a normalized aspect of discourse about judging. It dominates political science studies of courts, as the next chapter shows; the current generation of legal academics and lawyers appears prone to express a casual skepticism about judging. High-profile political attacks on courts and increasingly politicized battles over federal and state judicial appointments fan skepticism about judges among the public.[122] This is a fitting place to repeat the admonition of Judge Thurman Arnold, one of the great legal realists, that skeptical "realism, despite its liberating virtues, is not a sustaining food for a stable civilization."[123]

PART THREE

Studies of Judging

7

○ ○ ● ● ●

THE SLANT IN THE "JUDICIAL POLITICS" FIELD

POLITICAL SCIENTISTS set out in earnest, in the late 1950s and early 1960s, to conduct sophisticated quantitative (or "behaviorist") studies of judging. "Political Jurisprudence" was the name they took for their field.[1] As an early article by a leading participant, Martin Shapiro, explained, "The core of political jurisprudence is a vision of courts as political agencies and judges as political actors."[2] Today their favored label is "judicial politics."[3] These self-chosen labels openly declare a precommitment that has governed their work for the past half century: the conviction that judging is substantially political. As a critic of the field recently noted, "[R]eflecting an almost pathological skepticism that law matters, positive scholars of courts and judicial behavior simply fail to take law and legal institutions seriously."[4] This long dominant judging-is-more-politics-than-law slant shapes how quantitative studies have been designed as well as how their results have been interpreted and portrayed, belying the claim that the field produces "value-free, detached, and objective" empirical evidence about the nature of judging.[5]

This slant originated in the stories about the formalists and the realists. A 2009 description of the "history of the study of judicial politics" draws out this connection: "In the early 1900s, the legal realism school became the dominant way of thinking in the law schools, and thus as well among political scientists who studied the courts. The legal realists rebelled against the mechanical model of courts and judges, arguing instead that legal decisions were a 'mixture of law, politics, and policy' and that judges' decisions were influenced by their backgrounds, training, personality and ideology. The legal realists in political science cared about judicial behavior and judicial decision making, not just about legal structures and doctrine."[6]

The study of judging by political scientists has been warped by the false formalist-realist antithesis. Believing that the legal fraternity was under the spell of formalism, political scientists set out to refute mechanical jurisprudence; believing that the legal realists were skeptics of judging, and seeing themselves as social scientific inheritors of the realist tradition, political scientists took an extreme position that personal preferences are the driving force in judging. After exposing the distorting influence of these false beliefs on the field, this chapter demonstrates that judges have expressed a balanced realism about judging for many decades. It turns out that the results of recent quantitative studies of judging, canvassed in the next chapter, comport far more closely with what judges say about judging than with the positions taken by judicial politics scholars.

The Genesis of the Field in False
Formalist-Realist Extremes

The acknowledged forerunners of "political jurisprudence" were Oliver Wendell Holmes, Roscoe Pound, Benjamin Cardozo, and particularly the legal realists.[7] Among their political scientists forebears, most often mentioned are Edward Corwin, Robert Eugene Cushman, and Charles Grove Haines.[8] As a recent history of the field put it, these early twentieth-century forebears "scorned the mechanistic model of judging embraced by legal formalism, which viewed judges as 'value-free technicians' who do no more than discover 'the law.' "[9] A 1922 article in the *Illinois Law Review* by Haines, "General Observations on the Effects of Personal, Political, and Economic Influences in the Decisions of Judges," has earned special praise: "[T]he work of Charles Grove Haines provided the origin of what was to become behavioralism in public law."[10]

Setting out his target, Haines wrote:

> The mechanical theory which postulates absolute legal principles, existing prior to and independent of all judicial decisions, and merely discovered and applied by courts, has been characterized as a theory of a "judicial slot machine." According to this theory, it is assumed that provisions have been made in advance for legal principles, so that it is merely necessary to put the facts into the machine and draw therefrom an appropriate decision. . . . In fact, despite all influences to the contrary, American courts have clung to the belief that justice must be administered in accordance with fixed rules, which can be applied by a rather mechanical process of logical reasoning to a given state of facts and

can be made to produce an inevitable result. And it is assumed that the very nature of law requires such a mechanical application of its rules and principles. Due to the general acceptance of this view by the legal fraternity, it has become a habit of those trained in law to bestow little attention upon their individual views or prejudices and to turn attention instead to precedents which are regarded as forming the authoritative basis of the law.[11]

This is the story about the legal formalists. As earlier chapters demonstrated, every major assertion in this paragraph is false. The legal fraternity (including judges, legal academics, and lawyers) did not widely believe that legal rules were merely discovered by judges, that the rules were fixed, or that judging involved mechanical logical reasoning; and they were not oblivious to the potential influence of personal views on judging.

A familiar pattern in the legal context also played out in political science. Gaines's primary sources for these observations were articles by Roscoe Pound and a collection of works about German legal science.[12] Robert Cushman described, in 1922, the "judicial ruthlessness" of a "mechanical legalistic interpretation";[13] he asserted that in the late nineteenth century "it was the recognized theory of the judicial function that courts do not *make* law, they merely *find* or *discover* law."[14] In the footnote supporting this claim, Cushman cited a lengthy passage from Roscoe Pound which begins "A *German* writer has put the received theory thus . . ."[15]

Just as there were contemporaneous legal voices contrary to Pound, the leading political scientist Corwin did not embrace Pound's narrative. In 1909 he wrote:

> It was formerly the wont of legal writers to regard court decisions in much the same way as the mathematician regards the x of an algebraic equation: given the facts of the case and the existing law, the outcome was inevitable. *This unhistorical standpoint has now been largely abandoned.* Not only is it admitted that judges in finding the law act not as automata, as mere adding machines, but creatively, but also that the considerations which determine their decisions, far from resting exclusively upon a narrowly syllogistic basis, often repose very immediately upon concrete and vital notions of what is desirable and useful.[16]

A year after Pound claimed in "Mechanical Jurisprudence" that judges reasoned in mechanical terms, Corwin called these ideas obsolete. He discussed leading Fourteenth Amendment cases, including *Lochner*, arguing that the justices' positions were influenced by their contrasting social and political theories. According to Corwin, the decisions *were not* the product of abstract logical reasoning. The due process analysis they engaged in came down to a determination of "reasonableness," in which the justices conducted their own independent evaluation of the facts and policies at issue.[17]

Nonetheless, a dozen years later, Haines adverted to Pound's account rather than Corwin's, claiming that judges and lawyers *still* widely believed that judges discovered the law and mechanically decided cases. Pound's account became entrenched within the judicial politics field. Modern political scientists, like everyone else, swallowed whole the story about the supposed dominance of mechanical jurisprudence. C. Herman Pritchett, acclaimed as *the* progenitor of modern quantitative studies of judging, repeated this account in his influential history of the field:

> Thinking about the role of the judiciary has been stultified by the mechanical jurisprudence of the eighteenth century, which located the judge in a closed, theoretically complete, system of universal and permanent principles. Within the assumptions of the system, his only functions could be discovery and deduction. The only way the system could be extended was by analogy, and the creative role of the judge was exhausted when this task was completed.[18]

This "myth of mechanical jurisprudence," according to Pritchett, persisted "throughout the nineteenth century,"[19] its grip finally broken only through the efforts of Holmes, Cardozo, and the legal realists. Pritchett went so far as to blame the pervasive grip of this myth for stunting the early development of his own field, remarking that "[m]echanical jurisprudence and the myth of the nonpolitical character of the judicial task had rather effectively discouraged most political scientists from thinking about the courts."[20]

Preceding chapters, however, have revealed an abundance of skeptical-realistic statements in the late nineteenth century that are inconsistent with Pritchett's claim. To cite just one striking counterexample, Walter Coles's 1893 article, "Politics and the Supreme Court of the United States," set forth the core thesis of the judicial politics field: "Viewing the history of the Supreme Court at large . . . it may be said that its adjudications on constitutional questions have in their general tendencies conformed . . . to the maxims of the political party whose appointees have, for the time being, dominated the court."[21] More than a century later, judicial politics scholars have produced scores of statistical studies that hammer the same basic point:[22] Supreme Court "justices . . . vote in ways that reflect the political values of their appointing presidents."[23]

The myth at work here—a myth that *still* cripples the field—is *the myth that turn-of-the-century jurists widely believed in mechanical jurisprudence*. Political scientists who study judging also take an extreme position about the legal realists. When discussing the legal realists, Pritchett wrote that "the group was *best* represented by Jerome Frank";[24] Pritchett and Walter Murphy, another early giant, reiterated this view over a span of two decades, asserting that "[i]n 1930 Jerome Frank . . . produced the *clearest statement* of a realist position in his seminal work *Law and the Modern Mind*."[25]

The claim that this sensationalist book best represents legal realism betrays a serious misunderstanding. As chapter 6 elaborated, Frank was an outlier. Karl Llewellyn and Felix Cohen were decidedly critical of the book for exaggerating the impact of personal idiosyncrasies in judging. Llewellyn expressed concern about the potentially corrosive effect of what he called "facile" skepticism about judicial decision making.[26] And Frank himself moved away from *Law and the Modern Mind* in his more measured statements about judging.

The Slant in Alternative Models of Judging

The distorting consequences that resulted from the birth of the field in a congeries of false beliefs might have been limited if judicial politics scholars had moved beyond these initial assumptions. But they have not. A 2005 book by preeminent scholars asked impatiently, "[W]hy do so many persist in believing that judicial decisions are objective, dispassionate, and impartial? Judges are said not to have discretion; they do not decide their cases; rather it is the law or the Constitution speaking through them that determines the outcome. Judges, in short, are mere mouthpieces of the law."[27] The old (imagined) legal formalists, by this account, are alive and well. "Over the past century," the authors assert, "dominant legal models include mechanical jurisprudence, which posited that legal questions had a single correct answer that judges were to discover."[28] "Models formulated by legalists [today] rest in whole or in part on [this] mythology."[29]

Judicial politics scholars thus continue their tireless campaign, exasperated that that it is still necessary, to finally slay this deluded but resilient formalist view of judging. The three main models utilized within the field—the attitudinal model, the strategic model, and the legal model—are thoroughly informed by the formalist-realist antithesis. The formalist side is identified with the "legal model," which is denigrated within the field. The realist side is identified with the "attitudinal model," which has enjoyed decades of primacy.[30] "The attitudinal model . . . is essentially the political science version of legal realism, where judges 'decide disputes in light of the facts of the case vis-à-vis [their] ideological attitudes and values.' While the legal model assumes an almost mechanical form of jurisprudence, the attitudinal model represents the opposite extreme, suggesting that ideology alone determines judicial outcomes."[31] The newest model, the "strategic model" (explained shortly), is typically constructed in a way that lines up with the attitudinal model on the realist side of this divide.

Contemporary judicial politics scholars who recognize that there were differences among the legal realists still get their positions crucially wrong. Lawrence Baum, the author of an influential overview, distinguished the extreme from moderate realists as follows: "One version of legal realism pretty much read the law out of judges' decisions, ascribing those decisions almost solely to policy preferences. A more moderate version of realism saw judges as following their preferences within the framework and constraints of legal reasoning."[32]

The extreme version Baum describes is a doubtful reading of Jerome Frank's position. He did not "read the law out" of decisions, and he did not ascribe decisions "almost solely to policy positions." Frank made it clear that legal rules and precedents played a significant role in judicial decision making, though not necessarily dictating the outcomes in a number of cases, and he emphasized the personal idiosyncrasies of judges as much as their political views.

The more misleading characterization of the two is the purported moderate realist position, for in a crucial respect it is not moderate or realist at all. The way Baum phrases it, the *active* force behind judicial reasoning is the preferences of the judge, and the only role played by law is to place constraints on this motivated reasoning.[33] The "situation type" account of judging that several legal realists claimed operated in the large body of routine cases, however, did not accord a significant role to the preferences of judges. Standard fact types invoke an associated set of legal rules that together produce the outcomes without much thought. In open or problematic cases, according to Llewellyn, judges are oriented toward applying the law, in combination with trying to do justice (social or individual), and to formulate a legal precedent or interpretation that advances social welfare. It is true that legal realists asserted, as did other jurists, that subconscious biases had an influence on judicial reasoning. But it is tendentious to read this as the realists asserting that when deciding cases judges are "following their preferences." No legal realist, not even Frank, made this bald assertion.

Contemporary judicial politics scholars see themselves as keeping faith with the legal realists: "The attitudinal model of judicial decision making traces its roots to legal realism."[34] But their models of judging are their own invention. They present judges as "politicians in black robes,"[35] as "single-minded seekers of policy."[36] According to this perspective, ideological views or policy preferences drive the judicial reasoning process. Many judicial politics scholars appear to align the extreme position (flimsy legal chains) with judging on the Supreme Court and the moderate position (more robust but still escapable legal chains) with judging on lower courts. By the late 1970s, there was "little question that the predominant paradigm of judicial decision making places judges' attitudes at the center of the process."[37] As recently as 1998 it was affirmed that "the 'attitudinal model' . . . dominates the study of judicial politics."[38]

Even variations of this approach that allow a greater role to legal factors still accord center stage to judicial attitudes, with law operating as a constraint. Observe the sequence and phrasing of an often quoted "more inclusive" model of judging: "[J]udges' decisions are a function of what they prefer to do [policy preferences], tempered by what they think they ought to do [judicial role obligations], but constrained by what they perceive is feasible to do [institutional constraints]."[39]

It is useful to momentarily pause this account of the judicial politics field and contemplate whether, had they not been indoctrinated in the false stories about the formalists and the realists, political scientists would have modeled judges as enrobed politicians engaged in the single-minded pursuit of policy preferences. If the goal of the social scientific study of courts was to truly understand the nature of and influences on judging (rather than to prove that judging is political), would the attitudinal model have been so overwhelmingly dominant for so long? Not likely. Personal attitudes would have a place in the model, but not above all else, if only because judges don't see or describe the task this way and the institutional structure of judging is not designed this way. This perspective on judging is a contingent historical product of the misdirected effort to dispel belief in mechanical jurisprudence and a misperception of the realists.[40]

In recent years scholars have embraced the "strategic model" of judging: "There is little doubt that the field of judicial politics is undergoing a sea change that has the potential to transform the way we think about law and courts in the United States and elsewhere."[41] The introduction of the strategic model adds a rational actor dimension to the decades old social-psychological paradigm. The latter identified the determinants of judicial decisions in "social backgrounds or personal attributes, policy-oriented values and attitudes, roles, and small group influences."[42] The newer strategic approach portrays judges as rendering decisions with conscious attention to, and a calculated anticipation of, how other individuals (judges on same panel), institutional actors (legislatures, executives, higher courts), or potentially influential audiences (legal academics, the bar, interest groups, public) might react. The strategic model supposes that judges routinely calculate what course of action would best advance their policy goals. In some cases this might mean rendering a decision that stops short of their true ideological preferences if, for example, going too far risks destroying their credibility or inciting a backlash that would retard their objectives even further.

Like the attitudinal model, the strategic model as it is usually (though not by necessity) constructed does not take law seriously on its own terms. The fundamental assumption remains unchanged: strategic-reasoning judges are always striving to implement their policy goals through their decisions, within legal constraints.[43] This version in effect melds the strategic and attitudinal models, with the latter supplying the dominant judicial goal that is strategically pursued by judges. This assumed judicial goal is not inherent to the strategic model, it must be emphasized, which can be applied in conjunction with any goal or collection of goals—personal advancement or improvement of the law, for example—but the slant within the field makes it seem natural.

Political scientist David Klein elaborates on this dominant perspective in the field. Many judicial politics scholars, he asserts, "would probably argue that legal soundness is better understood as a *constraint*, whether in terms of what judges can do or in terms of what they should do. This perspective appears to be widely shared. Yet it seems to rest on an assumption that judges' only genuine desire is to shape public policy. The strictures of legal correctness may be important to judges, but only so far as obedience furthers the policy goal."[44] Seeing the law exclusively in terms of a constraint is captured in this metaphor: "[C]onsider the law to be ropes binding a judicial Houdini. The ropes may be tight or loose, possibly knotted with skill and redundancy. These ropes will strive to bind thousands of judges, each of whom possess different levels of escape skills."[45]

Klein rejects this perspective for refusing to acknowledge that "judges find the search for good answers to legal questions intrinsically rewarding."[46] It leaves no room for recognizing that judges, out of a commitment to the law or judging, genuinely reason with the primary conscious goal of faithfully applying the law. Full stop. For legally oriented judges, the law is not chains or ropes they are trying to wriggle out of but rather guideposts they are actively searching for and following to reach their destination. This is nigh inconceivable within the assumptions that govern the field, which dogmatically posit that judges are obsessed with advancing their political views.

Within the field, the "strategic conception of judicial behavior is now the closest thing to a conventional wisdom about judicial behavior."[47] An attractive quality of this theory is that it hands scholars a ready explanation for the frequent occasions when judges render decisions that *do not* align with their ideological views, even when existing legal constraints do not erect barriers against it. These decisions appear to count against the assumption that politics drives decisions. But the strategic model is enlisted to explain that, although it might appear that judges are deciding in accordance with the law, not their policy preferences, beneath it all they are still maximizing their policy agenda by electing for strategic reasons to forgo its pursuit in the immediate case because that will pay off in the long run.[48] The model thus possesses an alchemical (or casuistic) capacity to transform an apparently legally based decision into a politically calculating decision, thereby adeptly preserving the governing assumption that judging is politics.

The strategic model often paints an implausible picture of judges as magnificent Machiavellian calculators pursuing political agendas with hardly any legal integrity and an extraordinary capacity, facilitated by lots of time and information, to envision the likely consequences of their decisions among various possible audiences.[49] This position also flirts with being impervious to refutation, potentially running afoul of a basic stricture of scientific inquiry. As Baum notes, there is a "theoretical ambiguity of behavior: patterns of judicial behavior that are consistent with the assumption of policy-oriented strategy typically are consistent with other explanations as well."[50]

Not all scholars in the judicial politics field hold these positions—and not all judicial politics scholars conduct quantitative studies. A hardy band of dissenters,[51] called "institutionalists," has insisted for more than a decade that law is far more significant in judicial decisions than the attitudinal and strategic models allow for.[52] This amorphous group lacks any clear or unifying position, however, and many of these scholars engage in qualitative (especially historical) research rather than quantitative studies.

The slant within the field is reflected in the belated and begrudging reception "institutionalist" or "legal model" arguments have received. "Current judicial studies," Nancy Maveety writes in a recent overview, "are also less exclusionary in their attitudinal world view; they are *willing to admit* that judicial policy preferences *might* not explain all stages of the decision making process. Similarly, an increasing number of contemporary judicial studies are *willing to entertain* (and empirically test) the possibility that legal factors like precedent or legal rules are part of the judicial decision."[53] This statement bears repeating: not until recently, nearly a half century after the field began, were judicial politics scholars finally willing to entertain the possibility that legal rules and precedents might be an important causal factor in judging that goes beyond exclusively serving as a constraint.[54]

This is a shocking stance for a field that presents itself as a rigorous, objective social scientific inquiry into the process of judicial decision making. Leading judicial politics scholars have asserted that "challenging the theory with the best possible opposing arguments is what makes the strongest case for a theory."[55] Yet it took decades before they seriously attempted to test whether legal rules and precedents determine judicial decisions. A truly open social scientific inquiry into the judicial decision making would have placed legal elements into the mix of possibilities to be considered right from the outset.

Quantitative scholars will defend against these criticisms by saying that the attitudinal and strategic models are just simplified constructs for the purposes of testing—they are well aware that judging is more complicated. As will be shown shortly, however, judicial politics scholars routinely describe actual judging in terms of the pursuit of political preferences, so they do not treat it as a simplified model but as a descriptively accurate account of judging.

Quantitative scholars might argue in response, further, that their rigorous testing of the "attitudinal" and "strategic" models can point in the same direction: findings inconsistent with these models, or evidence that these models explain only a small percentage of judicial decisions below the Supreme Court, can be interpreted as lending support for the legal model (an inference I rely on in the next chapter). Documenting the limited explanatory power of these favored models, however, does not in itself provide direct evidence that judicial decisions are determined by legal factors. Owing to the failure of judicial politics scholars to take law seriously on its own terms, studies that test for this are still few and rudimentary.[56]

A formidable factor that inhibits researchers is the difficulty of transforming the strength of legal arguments, a qualitative judgment, into quantitative measures. But the complicated challenge this task poses is not a legitimate reason for judicial politics scholars to fail to make a concerted effort to directly test the influence of law. Otherwise they risk falling into an error of scientism: setting aside what cannot be easily measured, seeing only what can be measured, forgetting that large aspects of the psychological or social phenomena they purport to explain remain invisible because of the limitations of their methodological techniques.

The mission to prove that judging is politics, to dispel the formalist or mechanical view of judging, made the testing of the influence of law a low priority.

Slippage from Supreme Court to Other Courts

Another manifestation of the distorting slant must be exposed. Throughout its history, the judicial politics field has disproportionately conducted quantitative studies of judging on the Supreme Court. This lopsided emphasis was already flagged as a potential problem in the mid-1960s.[57] Matters did not change much until the past decade, when researchers, owing to the completion of a large database of coded opinions, have conducted a growing number of studies on federal appellate court decision making (less so on trial courts). The Supreme Court, however, still hogs most of the attention.[58]

The problem arises when scholars loosely slip from making assertions about judging on the Supreme Court to assertions about judging generally. With respect to judicial decision making, a huge chasm separates the uniquely situated Supreme Court from the lower federal courts. Political scientists do not always adequately mark the distinction.

A prime example can be found in a recent book about federal judicial appointments by Lee Epstein and Jeffrey Segal, two of the most prolific contemporary judicial politics scholars. At the beginning of the book they make the dramatic assertion that "the late great political scientist C. Herman Pritchett was far closer to the mark when he wrote that judges 'are influenced by their own biases and philosophies, which to a large degree predetermine the position they will take on a given question. Private attitudes, in other words, become public law.' "[59] But Pritchett did not quite say that. His statement was in an essay about divided opinions on the Supreme Court. The language leading up to the assertion Epstein and Segal quote reads, "*justices of the United States Supreme Court, in deciding controversial cases involving important issues of public policy,* are influenced by biases and philosophies of government . . ."[60] Epstein and Segal give a much broader scope to Pritchett's carefully circumscribed claim when, just before the crucial words "are influenced by their biases and philosophies," they insert "judge" in place of his reference to "justices" (in controversial cases!). A few sentences later they continue in this vein, asserting that "*with scattered exceptions here and there, the decisions of judges, and especially the decisions of Supreme*

Court justices, tend to reflect their own political values. More indirectly, these decisions also reflect the judges' partisan affiliation, which just so happens to coincide often with that of their appointing president."[61] Their book addresses the politics surrounding appointments at all levels of the federal judiciary, and the above assertions clearly apply to *all* federal judges.[62]

What is misleading about their statement is that, while it is correct with respect to Supreme Court justices, it creates a false impression about what quantitative studies have shown with respect to lower federal courts. After all, around 90 percent of published appellate cases are decided unanimously, which means that appellate judges concur in their legal decisions an overwhelming majority of the time regardless of differences in their ideological views or party of appointing president.[63] A recent quantitative study of federal appellate judges declares, "Frequently the law is clear, and judges should and will simply implement it, no matter who has appointed them. . . . and we shall provide considerable evidence to suggest that they do exactly that."[64] Epstein and Segal know this and note accordingly that "many of their [federal appellate decisions] are routine applications of existing law."[65] They acknowledge "that circuit judges are *not as free* as Supreme Court justices to reach decisions that correspond to their sincerely held political views."[66]

This is correct as far as it goes, but it too is potentially misleading. "Not as free" as Supreme Court justices, who have a significant degree of freedom, can still imply that circuit judges are substantially free—which is the impression the authors convey with their broad assertions throughout the book about political influences on judging. The more precisely accurate characterization of what recent studies of appellate courts have shown is that judges are "not very free" to reach decisions consistent with their policy preferences (or at least do not exercise their freedom), for these effects show up in a small proportion of cases. The evidence for this is elaborated in chapter 8. For the purposes here, the main point is that judicial politics scholars who wish to present an accurate account of what their results show should emphasize the sharp break between the Supreme Court and lower federal courts on the extent of political influences on judging. Owing to the slant in the field, what one finds instead is a blurring of the difference.

The Suspicion That Judges Are Deluded or Deceptive

Another manifestation of the slant is skepticism about the veracity or self-awareness of judges. "Judges as Liars" is the title of a 1994 essay by Martin Shapiro, a major figure in the judicial politics field. He means it. He asserts that courts "occasionally make public policy decisions or law," but judges cannot admit that they do this because they are supposed to apply preexisting law.[67] "Such is the nature of courts. They must always deny their authority to make law, even when they are making law. One may call this justificatory history, but I call it lying. Courts and judges always lie. Lying is the nature of the judicial activity."[68]

Shapiro's repeated assertion of judges' deceptive denial of law making is odd considering that in a footnote he quotes Justice Antonin Scalia, a proud legalist, for recognizing that "courts have the capacity to 'make' law"; Scalia once declared in a judicial opinion: "Judges in a real sense 'make' law."[69] Scalia has repeatedly stated that judges "*make* the law," resolving policy issues in the process.[70]

As earlier chapters documented, for more than a century prominent judges have openly admitted that they make law, from Judge Thomas Cooley and Judge John Dillon in 1886, to Judge Cardozo in 1921, to many judges since. Nonetheless, in a persistent pattern, observers of courts repeatedly assert that judges deny that they make law, and they proceed to condemn judges for denying it.

It is a commonplace among judicial politics scholars that judges are deluded or deceptive when they speak about judging. Klein, for example, observes, "Judges cannot be expected to understand their own motivations perfectly or to report them with undiluted candor."[71] Baum remarks, "Judges usually speak and write with audiences in mind, and they ordinarily present themselves in a way that they think will be received favorably. Further, they do not always understand their goals fully, and they may mislead themselves as well as their audiences"[72] Political scientists mean more than that everyone speaks and writes with audiences in mind and is self-deluded in various ways; they mean that judges, in particular and characteristically, put up false fronts and labor under self-delusions. Even scholars who more generously credit judges with honesty about judging nonetheless assert that "judicial self-reporting . . . is unreliable."[73]

Judicial politics scholars are not alone in having this view of judges. Judge Richard Posner also dismisses accounts of judging offered by his colleagues as unreliable:

> I am denying that judicial introspection, and a fortiori judges' avowals concerning the nature of judicial decision making, are good explanations for judicial action. It is a mistake to take at face value descriptions of judges as engaged always in a search for "the" correct answer, rather than exercising discretion under the

influence of personal values and preferences determined by temperament and selective life experiences rather than by a considered, somehow self-chosen judicial philosophy.[74]

In a recent book, *How Judges Think*, Posner writes that "most judges are cagey, even coy, in discussing what they do. They tend to parrot an official line about the judicial process (how rule-bound it is), and often to believe it, though it does not describe their actual practices."[75]

Judges no doubt bear some responsibility for perpetuating the belief that they are deluded or deceptive. They occasionally say things that ring false, like Justice John Roberts's claim in his Senate confirmation hearing that judging on the Supreme Court is akin to calling balls and strikes.

Two additional factors have contributed to the belief that judges are deluded or deceptive about judging. The false story about mechanical jurisprudence played a role. According to this story, judges denied that they made law and believed that they reasoned in a mechanical, deductive fashion, or at least that they claimed to reason in this fashion. These views are patently implausible, so judges evidently were either *deluded* or *lying* for (purportedly) asserting them. Once this perception of judges took hold within the legal culture, it stuck.

The second source of skepticism about the veracity of judges is the style of written decisions. They are systematically reasoned, filled with citations to precedent and legal rules, and offered as if legal conclusions necessarily follow. Seldom does an opinion reveal the uncertainties in the analysis. Justice Walter Schaefer of the Illinois Supreme Court acknowledged (in 1955) that this style of writing promotes skepticism in observers: "Some writers have therefore suggested that the ordinary judicial opinion is a fraud, in that it purports to be derived by impeccable and inevitable logic from what has already been decided, and that the judge who wrote it is either a fool for thinking the process so simple or a knave for pretending that it is."[76]

But it has long been recognized that opinions should not be interpreted to represent a judge's actual reasoning process. As Judge Schaefer noted, "[J]udicial opinions are something less than mirrors of the thinking behind the decision and . . . a judge has more freedom than the mustering of precedents makes it appear."[77] Recall that Dewey wrote, "The logic of exposition is different from that of search and inquiry."[78] The style in which the decision is presented is not meant to represent an indication of how it was reached. It is the best argument a judge can come up with to support the decision. If this distinction was not understood before, it was certainly well known after Dewey articulated it.[79] The purposes of opinions are to justify the conclusion, provide guidance for later cases, and resolve the legal issues with finality. It makes sense, therefore, that opinions are firmly stated, logically supported, and do not express doubts about the legal conclusions reached. Once the decision is made, Schaefer remarked, the judge writing an opinion "becomes an advocate" in its behalf.[80]

To know what judges think about judging, one cannot draw inferences from the style of written decisions, which are not offered as accounts of judicial decision making. Instead, one must pay attention to the very realistic things judges have been saying about judging for many decades.

Decades of Balanced Realism about Judging from Judges

The unsurpassed locus classicus of balanced realism about judging is Cardozo's *The Nature of the Judicial Process*. He stated that in the substantial bulk of cases the law is clear and the judge must rule as the law requires—"Therefore in the main there shall be adherence to precedent."[81] He also stated, however, that there are gaps in the law, uncertainties in interpretation, unanticipated fact situations, and obsolete rules that work serious injustices or harm social interests. In these situations, he advised, the judge must strive to rule in an objective fashion consistent with the community's values and interests.[82] "The standards or patterns of utility and morals will be found by the judge in the life of the community."[83] Community morality provides the "objective" view.[84] The judge is "under a duty to conform to the accepted standards of the community,"[85] even when a judge holds a different standard, Cardozo asserted. A judge should depart from this only in rare circumstances when the judge's deepest conviction calls for a standard more demanding than conventional morality.[86] He recognized, however, that it is difficult for judges to keep this entirely apart. "The perception of objective right takes the color of the subjective mind. The conclusions of the subjective mind take the color of customary practices and objectified beliefs. There is constant and subtle interaction between what is without and what is within."[87] Hence, Cardozo concluded, the distinction between the judge's subjective views of the right and the community's general view "is shadowy and evanescent."[88] Cardozo was realistic, but not fatalistic, about the ability of judges to rule in an objective fashion: "I do not mean, of course, that this ideal of objective vision is ever perfectly attained. We cannot transcend the limitations of the ego and see anything as it really is. None the less, *the ideal is one to be striven for within the limits of our capacity.*"[89]

More can be taken from Cardozo's brilliant book, but to continue this focus would merely reinforce a widespread misimpression that he was unusual among his brethren in expressing such insights. The surprising truth is that he might not have been the most candid judge about these matters even compared to his colleagues on New York's highest court. In a 1924 speech to the New York City Bar, the chief judge of the Court of Appeals, Judge Frank Harris Hiscock, reviewed a string of recent decisions and declared: "All of these cases could have been decided the other way."[90] He told his audience that constitutional questions about rights and liberties that courts are called upon to decide are less questions of law than "of policy and state craft."[91] Hence, rulings are a function of the "policy and viewpoint of a court," which can change when the membership changes.[92] Another judge on the court, Irving Lehman, delivered a reflective speech at Cornell Law School in 1924 stating that judges are sometimes confronted with conflicting precedents, or erroneous precedents, or indeed no precedents, and that they must sometimes change the law for reasons of public policy.[93] Even as a law student, he could see that "[l]aw was not an exact science founded upon immutable principles"; upon becoming a judge, he "realized that in many cases there were no premises from which any deductions could be drawn with logical certainty."[94] He added that "no thoughtful judge can fail to note that in conferences of the court, differences of opinion are based at least to some extent upon differences of viewpoint";[95] and "it is inevitable that a judge in weighing individual rights as opposed to collective benefit will to some extent be influenced by his personal views."[96] Judge Cuthbert W. Pound, also on the court, said in a 1922 speech to the bar, "The term 'constitutional right' as applied, in the first instance, to a new problem, is often of a vague and unsubstantial nature, dependent upon the proper balancing of many conflicting interests, social, public and private."[97] In a subsequent address he elaborated on the sources of uncertainty in law, observing that legal doctrines are "not infrequently reasoned away to a vanishing point. One may wade through a morass of decisions only to sink into a quicksand of uncertainty."[98] Pound observed that a degree of uncertainty is inevitable because one cannot predict how general principles will be applied in specific cases,[99] and he made the realistic observation that "lawyers and judges too often fail to recognize that the decision consists in what is done, not in what is said by the court in doing it."[100]

All of these statements were uttered by a handful of judges on a single court in the early 1920s. This was just before the emergence of the legal realists who, according to the conventional story, came on the scene to disabuse judges of their purportedly unrealistic views about judging. Subsequent to this period judges were even more explicit, as a brief sampling of such statements shows.

Associate Justice Horace Stern of the Pennsylvania Supreme Court wrote in the 1937 *Harvard Law Review* that, "however fondly we may like to delude ourselves into the belief that constitutional law is a pure science, the interpretation and evolution of which are wholly independent of political predilections, we must, if realists, recognize that courts controlled by a 'conservative' personnel and those dominated by a 'liberal' membership are more than likely to decide constitutional questions from different angles and with different results."[101] Stern recommended that judges selected for appointment (at all levels) should be measured by two standards: by professional fitness (knowledge of the law and ability to engage in legal reasoning); *and* in terms of their "attitude toward public policies and theories of political, social and economic life."[102] It bears noting that 1937 was the year of President Roosevelt's ill-fated "court packing" plan,[103] which proposed to increase the size of the Supreme Court to get a majority more compliant to his desired legislative agenda—a plan premised on the point made by Stern.

Justice Bernard L. Shientag delivered the Benjamin Cardozo Lecture to the New York Bar in 1944, with the title: *The Personality of the Judge (and the Part It Plays in the Administration of Justice)*. Shientag emphasized that the personality and beliefs of judges matter—some are thoughtful and fair, others are tyrannical, impatient, or close-minded. Although he disliked the term "hunch" because it inaccurately downplays the reasoning aspects of judgment, Shientag allowed that "intuition undoubtedly plays an important part in the deliberations and decisions of the judge."[104] Exuding the sense that what he was saying was obvious and unavoidable, he continued:

> Naturally, it is in cases where the creative faculty of the judicial process operates, where there is a choice of competing analogies, that the personality of the judge, the individual tone of his mind, the color of his experiences, the character and variety of his interests and his prepossessions, all play an important role. For the judge, in effect, to detach himself from his whole personality, is a difficult, if not an impossible, task. We make progress, therefore, when we recognize this condition as a part of the weakness of human nature.[105]

Having said that, Shientag asserted that judges are capable of screening out this influence with an effort at self-awareness, and he argued that it is a grave mistake "to exaggerate its [personal influence] existence, to over-emphasize its significance in the judicial process."[106]

By the early 1950s, judges unabashedly and regularly expressed a balanced realism about judging. Federal circuit judge Amistead Dobie in 1951 observed that, contrary to former "Utopian" dreams, a judge must deal with an imperfect legal order. "There never has been, and there never will be, a judge worthy of his salt who can be classified as a cool and clammy thinking machine. No judge, however he may try, can, in his decisions, completely and effectively divorce himself from what he has seen, has heard, has experienced and has been."[107] Clashes of interests are often involved, and the judge must choose.[108] Federal district judge Charles Wyzanski wrote in the 1952 *Harvard Law Review* about "A Trial Judge's Freedom and Responsibility." He acknowledged that judges have some freedom. "And yet from the day he takes his seat the trial judge is aware that while he has more personal discretion than the books reveal, he too is hemmed in by a developing tradition of impersonal usages, canons and legitimate expectations."[109] While judges exercise choice, Wyzanski observed, they are also disciplined by norms of judicial behavior and by the prospect of appellate reversal.

Another federal trial court judge, Leon Yankwich, wrote "The Art of Being a Judge" in 1957, in which he asserted, "This is not a mechanical craft, but the exercise of a creative art."[110] Although some "have denied altogether the importance of the personality of the judge in judicial decisions," he added that "such an attitude is unrealistic."[111] It is the necessary and proper role of courts to develop and change the law to reflect the times, Yankwich asserted, which is where the creative contribution of the judge comes into play.[112] He admitted that, although he would not change any of his decisions, some of them could justifiably have had a different outcome.[113] Federal appellate judge Calvert Magruder made a similar point in 1958: "All too often we have to realize that the case might be written up either way, in a lawyer-like opinion. The judge may not recognize that this is so, or even be conscious of the inner springs that led him to choose one result rather than the other."[114] Magruder also echoed Judge Stern's observation two decades earlier about the Supreme Court: "How far the Court should go involves an exercise in judgment. Over the long years the Supreme Court, because of changes in its membership, has oscillated between the right and the left."[115]

Federal circuit judge Albert Tate published two articles along these lines in 1959, "The Judge as a Person." and " 'Policy' in Judicial Decisions." He took it as obvious that judges' views influence their decisions.[116] "[L]ike all other human beings [judges] have limitations of vision, knowledge, intelligence, or predisposition which sometimes influence their judicial actions, however much they conscientiously try to avoid the occasion of error."[117] Tate hastened to add that in the "vast and overwhelming majority of cases the same result will be reached" regardless of who sits on the case (estimating that "90% or 95%" of appellate cases are routine),[118] but he also admitted that cases arise in which "several judges may with equal sincerity and equal reason reach different results."[119] Tate asserted with consummate realism that for all practical purposes "the correct" decision is whatever is decided by the highest appellate court to hear the case.[120] In the nonroutine cases, Tate wrote, judges must make policy decisions; on these occasions, "the judge will naturally tend to exercise what discretion is afforded him in favor of the result deemed by him to be more just or socially sound"; judges are not unconstrained when engaged in this process, which takes place within "the framework of their judicial system [including review by higher courts] and subject to the discipline of the judicial craft."[121] Through this process, general social and moral values are brought into the law, and the law stays in sync with and serves social needs, but the final product must always fit within and be expressed in "normal legal reasoning."[122]

Realistic observations by judges about judging were standard fare in the 1960s. In 1961 Judge Henry Friendly wrote that "the judge should make sure he is interpreting the long term convictions of the community rather than his own evanescent ones; but we may as well recognize this goal will not always be realized even 'by the best.' Sometimes the judge will fail of this because the community has not true convictions . . . on other occasions because it is asking too much that a judge suppress the basic beliefs by which he lives."[123] In a 1962 address at the University of Chicago Law School, Justice Roger Traynor of the California Supreme Court, one of the leading common law judges of his generation, had no qualms about acknowledging that judges must make choices in certain situations.[124] While judges should follow precedent for the sake of consistency, Traynor said, when the law is too unsatisfactory, the judge can and should abandon it;[125] he admitted that there are cases in which the decision can go either way;[126] he accepted that judges have predilections that they must struggle to overcome;[127] and he wrote that the judge must "arrive at last at a value judgment as to what the law ought to be and to spell out why."[128]

"The Limits of Judicial Objectivity" was the title of a 1963 Lecture delivered by federal circuit judge Charles Clark, an early legal realist and former dean of Yale Law School. Clark agreed with Cardozo that in a very high percentage of the cases the legal result is clear. "On the appellate level all observers place the number of cases of a predestined outcome at a very high level; Cardozo eventually went so far as to place it at 'nine-tenths, perhaps more,' of the total. At the trial level the ratio of cases turning upon certain substantive principles is obviously yet higher, though the then open contest as to the facts—the actual events—may well make the outcome less predictable."[129] In the small percentage of remaining cases, Clark wrote, the judge (after becoming as prepared and knowledgeable as he can) "is on his own for the ulti-mate result which must reflect his background, his personality, and his inner conviction."[130] In the small proportion of cases that involve genu-inely open legal questions, "judicial objectivity" does not get a judge very far, Clark remarked, so the judge has no choice but to make a decision "where there is no one and nothing to tell him how or where to go."[131]

Justice Walter Schaefer of the Illinois Supreme Court delivered a lec-ture in 1955 entitled "Precedent and Policy," published in the 1966 *Chicago Law Review*. At the outset he asserted that the "great bulk" of cases are resolved through settling questions of fact in connection with "an established legal principle."[132] Only a "minute fraction" of cases make it to appellate review; and only a "small percentage" of these appealed cases raise truly open and contestable legal questions.[133] His comments addressed this small subset of cases, wherein judges must grapple with legal uncertainty and close questions.[134] According to Schaefer, in certain contexts it is "inevitable" that judges make law:[135] when creating or adjusting the law to accommodate new situations,[136] when deciding to abandon precedent,[137] and when filling in statutes to resolve unanswered questions. They make policy decisions in these contexts. Like Cardozo, Schaefer asserted that policy decisions ought to be based upon community views and not the judge's own view,[138] but he too recognized the difficulty of keeping the two apart. "There is nothing new in the notion that the personality of the judge plays a part in the decision of cases."[139]

Additional realistic decades-old judicial accounts of judging can be recited, and similar statements by contemporary judges will be con-veyed in later chapters, but to continue here would be redundant. Judges say much the same things: a substantial bulk of the cases are routine, governed by clear law, but cases regularly arise in which they must make hard choices—because there is a gap in the law, an unantic-ipated situation has arisen, there are inconsistent precedents or the law is ambiguous, or the law is obsolete or produces a result that is deeply unjust or seriously harms the social interest. In these situations judges often must make policy choices. They should strive to adhere to the community view, but it can be difficult to keep this apart from their own views; there are sometimes contesting views within the commu-nity. Different judges can reasonably arrive at contrasting legal decisions. Judges cannot always be aware of or free from the subconscious influence of their biases. All of this has been said by judges.

Stopping this recitation in the early 1960s serves to underline a key point. Quantitative studies of judging got underway in that period to demonstrate that judges make political decisions. Compare what judges said above with Pritchett's 1969 summary of the views animating the field:

> Political jurisprudence, then, asserts that judges are inevitably participants in the process of public policy formation; that they do in fact "make law"; that in making law they are necessarily guided in part by their personal conceptions of justice and public policy; that written law requires interpretation which involves making choices; that the rule of stare decisis is vulnerable because precedents are typically available to support either side in a controversy.[140]

There are differences in tone, but multiple judges openly acknowledged everything Pritchett set out here decades before he wrote it. Apparently misled by their belief in the story about legal formalism, the political science debunkers arrived on the scene determined to strip away the false pretensions of the judicial robe, unaware that judges carried no such pretensions.

8

○ ○ ● ● ●

WHAT QUANTITATIVE STUDIES OF

JUDGING HAVE FOUND

QUANTITATIVE STUDIES of judging are burgeoning. An over-whelming proportion of these studies have been conducted on the Supreme Court. The findings can be broadly summarized in a sentence: the ideological views of Supreme Court justices have a measurable influence on their legal decisions. This does not show in all categories of cases; law still matters in various ways, and the degree of correlation between attitudes (conservative, liberal) and decisions for individual justices fall along a range.[1] A recent study of the Supreme Court found "strong evidence that legal principles are influential."[2] But it cannot be denied that the ideological views of justices have some impact on their legal decisions. As revealed in earlier chapters, this has been recognized for two centuries. Judge Richard Posner's 2005 review of the Supreme Court was plainly entitled "A Political Court."[3]

Nothing further will be said here about quantitative studies of judging on the U.S. Supreme Court. It is a unique court from which little can be gleaned about judging generally. The inordinate attention it now receives, moreover, is out of proportion to its actual impact.[4] Although there is no question that the Supreme Court makes important decisions, it must be seen in the context of judicial institutions and judging more generally. In recent years the Supreme Court has decided about 75 cases; federal appellate courts have resolved about 50,000 cases;[5] and federal trial courts have resolved more than 300,000 cases.[6] (And these numbers pale in comparison to the close to 93 million cases filed in state courts in 2001.)[7] The minuscule number of cases it hears demonstrates the error of the suggestion within the judicial politics field that the lion's share of attention the Supreme Court receives is merited because it is the chief policy maker within the judiciary. Because fewer than 15 percent of federal appellate decisions are appealed, and the Supreme Courts accepts fewer than 2 percent of those appeals, the bulk of policy making through legal decisions on the federal level is done by circuit courts, as Frank Cross observes, not the Supreme Court.[8] Because it has discretionary jurisdiction and the possibility of any given case being reviewed is remote, furthermore, it is inapt to think of the Supreme Court as checking the legal correctness of appellate decisions. The Supreme Court is more properly described as a freelance decision-making body that takes up legal questions or cases deemed compelling (whether for legal, social, political, or economic significance, or to resolve splits in circuits).

This does not purport to be a comprehensive overview of quantitative studies—which are too numerous to cover in a few pages[9]—but rather a representation of their basic findings. The emphasis will be on recent studies of federal appellate courts. Less will be said about federal trial courts and state supreme courts (which in some respects are like the U.S. Supreme Court and on other respects like lower appellate courts).[10]

Early Studies of Judicial Role Orientation

In the mid-1960s, Kenneth Vines interviewed judges on four state supreme courts, asking them how they view decision making. He divided their responses into three categories: just over half saw themselves as strictly interpreting the law (fourteen in all, whom Vines labeled "law-interpreters"); the remaining group divided almost evenly between judges who saw themselves as engaging in policy making (six, labeled "law-makers") and judges who saw themselves as doing both law interpretation and law making, with attention to achieving just outcomes (five, labeled "pragmatists").[11] Democratic appointees and Republican appointees were found in all categories, suggesting that judges with different political views can share role orientations, and that judges with the same political views can choose different role orientations.[12] When examining whether their legal decisions (in non-unanimous cases only) showed any conservative or liberal pattern, Vines found "virtually no differences among law interpreters and law makers, and while pragmatists have a somewhat more liberal position, the difference is not great."[13]

A study by John Wold of a different collection of state supreme court judges in the mid-1970s came up with a similar set of categories: twelve of the judges saw themselves as law interpreters, only three as lawmakers, and seven indentified a combination of both orientations. Conservatives fell heavily the law interpreter group. Wold found two basic conceptions in competition: "a deferential, precedent-oriented view and an innovative, policy-oriented view."[14] However, he emphasized that:

> The dissimilarities between the two views of course should not be exaggerated. Regardless of his feelings about judicial creativity, no jurist advocated an unrestrained policy-making role for his court. Even the lawmakers believed that sponsorship of change in public policy was chiefly the prerogative of the legislature, and only secondarily that of the judge ... and even some interpreters admitted the necessity of legislating in the "interstices" of the law.[15]

All the judges felt they should follow the law, and all felt the legislature had primary responsibility for law making, but the lawmakers were more willing to step in and make law if necessary.[16] Wold did not test for possible correlations between orientations, attitudes, and decisions.

At about the same time, J. Woodford Howard found a similar set of understandings distributed among judges on three federal appellate courts. Translating his labels (interpreter, innovator, realist) to match the other studies, he reported nine interpreters, five lawmakers, and twenty judges with a combination.[17] Unlike the two state supreme courts studies, the combined-orientation group in Howard's study was the largest. But the differences among judges were not marked. Avowed law interpreters, he found, recognized that there are lacunae within statutes and cases that courts must sometimes fill in.[18] Howard also found a "strong consensus" across all categories about the duty to follow the law set forth by Congress and the Supreme Court.[19] The correlations between political values and role orientation were mixed, though many moderates fell in the realist category.[20]

Howard then studied five thousand votes in several categories of cases, matching the political values of the judges with their decisions. He found *no* statistically significant correlation between their values and their legal decisions in the cases studied (with some difference showing up in civil rights cases).[21] "The data may be too weak to prove the absence of a relationship among political ideologies and voting behavior," Howard asserted, "but they are strong enough to cast doubt on a common interpretation that circuit decisions are dominated by the past political predispositions of the judges."[22] He also found that the different role orientations showed no strong correlations with decisions.[23] Howard speculated about three possible explanations for the absence of evidence showing the influence of ideological differences: there was a strong orientation among the judges to abide by stare decisis; they interpreted the applicable law along the same lines in the majority of cases; and perhaps they shared underlying policy views that spanned other political differences.[24]

Finally, a 1970s study of federal district judges found that just over half considered themselves "law interpreters," 14 percent were classified as "lawmakers," and the remainder were "pragmatists" or "realists," who felt that most cases could and should be determined based upon controlling law or precedent but recognized that on occasion they had to make law.[25]

Although early studies of judicial role orientation opened up promising lines of inquiry, this area of judicial research did not develop much further. Several studies at the appellate and trial levels suggest that role orientations can effectively dampen the influence of ideological preferences in decisions.[26] But too few such studies have been conducted to draw any firm conclusions.

These early studies suggest that judges share a common orientation of fidelity to law; beyond this common core, however, judges splinter in their views about the acceptability of rendering policy decisions. Judges who emphasize that their job is to interpret the law understand that they must sometimes make choices; judges who emphasize that they make law understand that they must follow the law when it is clear; the differences are a matter of lean and emphasis. It is a mistake to assume that judges all adopt the same template: agreement on a core legal orientation, with variation beyond that, is normal among judges.

Recent Studies of Lower Federal Courts

A 2003 study of federal appellate courts by David Klein shifted from role orientation to ask judges what their goals are when deciding cases. The two inquires overlap closely but are not the same. Role orientations—the perceived obligation of a judge—shape judicial goals, but the latter has a broader scope that draws in more general considerations related to the circumstances of judging and law. Klein interviewed two dozen judges across several federal circuits. His questions revolved around four basic goals: producing good or just decisions; producing legally correct decisions; producing coherent, uniform law (within and across circuits); and producing prompt decisions. They were asked to rate each goal along a spectrum: very important, important, moderately important, not very important, not important at all.

Above all other alternatives, the judges identified legally correct decisions as a core goal (fifteen saying very important, seven important, and no one saying anything less).[27] Perhaps surprisingly, producing prompt decisions earned the next strongest rating: ten judges rating this as very important, six as important, and six as moderately important (with none below that). Arriving at just outcomes and maintaining uniform law were also identified by a majority of the judges, but comparatively fewer rated this as a very important goal (six and five, respectively). And three judges felt that producing just outcomes was *not* very important, and another three said it was *not important at all*.

These results reinforce the point that judges exhibit core agreement with variation. They also provide a reminder that judges, like many people in many jobs, hold several goals that can sometimes conflict, and they can value highly what outsiders might assume to be less significant. Issuing a prompt decision, which drew a stronger response than doing justice, is motivated by concerns about holding up their end with colleagues, getting through work loads, and sensitivity to litigants. Getting decisions out promptly can be in tension with the other goals, which are in different ways about getting things right (however long that might take).

Klein then carefully structured the study to look at what judges do in legally uncertain cases raising issues with politically controversial implications. He looked at antitrust, search and seizure, and environmental law cases, subjects that are thought to have particular political salience. To get at legally uncertain situations, he further narrowed this down to only those cases in which new legal rules were declared.[28] Klein came up with a total of eighty-one newly declared rules, announced in sixty-two cases,[29] which he then examined against the judges' backgrounds.

As expected, Klein found a statistically significant correlation between political preferences and the rules adopted: liberal judges preferred liberal rules, whereas conservative judges preferred conservative rules.[30] His more intriguing finding was that their political preferences, while a factor in these legally open cases, did not alone explain their decisions. The perceived prestige or expertise of judges who authored opinions was statistically related with other courts following those decisions (which suggests that judges cared about getting the correct legal result); and the desire to maintain consistency among legal interpretations also had statistical support. "In short, while this study reaffirms the view that policy preferences matter, it also provides substantial evidence of the importance of legal goals."[31] The novelty of Klein's study is that, while it confirmed that political influences matter in precisely the situations one would expect—legally uncertain cases raising politically fraught issues—it also demonstrated that even in these contexts judges do not care only about politics but continue to be moved by legal considerations.[32]

A recent study of federal appellate courts focused specifically on situations of judicial disagreement. Judges have often emphasized that collegiality matters[33]—both in connection with fellow judges sitting on the same panel and with respect to lower courts. The authors, Virginia Hettinger, Stephanie Lindquist, and Wendy Martinek, attempted to discern what factors produce dissenting or concurring opinions and reversals, which they saw as disruptions of collegiality among judges. They examined a comprehensive database of published appellate opinions from 1960 to 1996; there were dissents in 9.5 percent of the cases, and concurrences in 5.5 percent of the cases.[34] As these numbers show, federal appellate judges agree on their legal decisions an overwhelming proportion of the time, regardless of differences in political views.

The attitudinal model suggests that legal disagreements are ideologically driven. Presumably, therefore, dissents and concurrences should be more likely when a panel is composed of judges with different political preferences. And that is what the authors found.[35] They also found, however, that the rate of concurrences and dissents were statistically related to other factors as well, including the perceived significance of the case, the presence of legal ambiguity, and norms within the circuit about writing separate opinions, as well as a few other factors.[36] They found that the presence of an amicus brief (reflecting salience) and circuit norms about writing separate opinions (whether this is disfavored) showed a *stronger* relationship with producing separate opinions than ideology.[37] In a separate aspect of the study, they found no evidence that circuit courts strategically shape their rules in anticipation of Supreme Court review, casting doubt on the soundness of the strategic model as an explanation of federal appellate court judging.[38]

Their most surprising finding came in connection with reversals of lower courts. About 30 percent of the cases they examined between 1960 and 1996 involved reversals (although the rates of reversal differed among circuits and over time).[39] The attitudinal model suggests that panels controlled by judges with one set of political preferences will be more likely to overturn trial judges with the opposite political preferences.[40] Contrary to their expectations, however, the authors found *no* statistically significant relation between ideological differences and the rate of reversal.[41] The presence of amicus curiae, ambiguity of legal issues, and other factors were related to the likelihood of reversal, but "panel decisions to reverse are not shaped by raw ideological disagreement with the lower court."[42]

This comprehensive 2006 study covered 994 federal judges from all the circuits in cases spanning thirty-seven years, looking at separate opinions and reversals (more than 17,000 separate positions). These are the situations with the greatest legal disagreement. Yet their results confounded several central assumptions within the judicial politics field. They found no evidence of strategic reasoning. They found that ideology was a factor in the writing of separate opinions, but also that other factors showed greater relations. Most strikingly, they found no relation between ideology and rates of reversal.[43]

A 2007 book by Frank Cross examined federal appellate court decision making in a database containing 18,000 cases decided from 1925 to 1992. He conducted quantitative analyses from just about every angle that judicial politics scholars have applied to the study of courts. This study is too detailed to relate, so its major conclusions will be summarily set forth. Although Cross found a statistically significant association between ideology and decisions, which differed with subject matter and over time, "the measured effect size for ideology is always a fairly small one."[44] To test the legal model, Cross examined procedural rules, and found that decisions varied in accordance with the required burden, demonstrating that legal rules "matter greatly in determining outcomes."[45] Cross found compelling evidence that appellate courts follow precedent set by the Supreme Court.[46] He tested a variety of personal background factors—prior employment, religion, race, gender, wealth—and concluded that "background variables matter very little."[47] Cross found no statistical support for the "strategic model" of decision making.[48] He also found little evidence that the identity of litigants (government parties, businesses, individuals) drove judicial decision making.[49] The ideological composition of the panels of judging hearing cases *did* have measurable effects on decisions, with split panels producing less ideological decisions (elaborated on more fully shortly).[50]

The dominant finding that runs through the book, Cross concluded, "is the importance of law in determining judicial outcomes."[51] "It was also noteworthy how very limited the explanatory power of the nonlegal variables was."[52] The influence of ideology shows up across the range of areas studied, but "the effect was small."[53] Ideology, gender, wealth, the identity of the litigants, the composition of appellate panels, and other factors were found to have statistically significant correlations with decisions in certain categories of cases, but the impact was not substantial in any particular instance or collectively, and all were negligible in comparison to law.

Cross's core findings about the relative insignificance of ideology and the substantial significance of legal factors in determining judicial decisions is consistent with a growing body of quantitative studies of lower federal courts. A recent study of *non-unanimous* decisions by the

Seventh Circuit from 1997 through 2003—precisely the subset of cases in which ideology is expected to show—found no statistically significant connection between ideology and dissenting behavior: "The data suggest that ideological differences do not affect judicial disagreement."[54] Studies have also found that circuit courts adhere to precedent established by the Supreme Court.[55]

An ingenious recent study designed to tease out the impact of ideology was conducted by Donald R. Songer, Martha Humphries Ginn, and Tammy A. Sarver, who examined federal appellate decisions in torts cases based upon diversity jurisdiction. In these cases, state tort law is applied by federal courts. This sizable subset of cases provides a natural experiment because the judges are virtually free from any risk of reversal from the Supreme Court or Congress.[56] Thus, the judges have unchecked rein to reach decisions based upon their policy preferences, which the attitudinal and strategic models suggests they would eagerly do. However, the authors found very small differences overall in the decisions of conservative, moderate, and liberal judges.[57] They also found that ruling patterns (for or against plaintiffs and defendants) shifted in conformity with differences in state law, which indicates that judges, whatever their policy preferences, ruled in conformity with prevailing state legal regimes. The authors then compared unanimous cases with non-unanimous cases, speculating that the latter are more open. In the former cases, ideology was not statistically significant (while legal variables were), whereas in the latter it was, a finding that suggests that political views basically come into play in hard cases with open legal questions.[58] This finding holds, it must be remembered, within a total context that shows only very small differences among judges with different political positions.

Studies of federal appellate courts are becoming more plentiful, facilitated by the creation of a large database of coded opinions. There are fewer studies of the decisions of federal trial courts, however, making it harder to draw broad conclusions. What studies of trial courts have found is generally consistent with studies of circuit courts: ideology matters, but in a relatively small proportion of cases, clustered in a few areas.

A study by C. K. Rowland and Ronald Carp of almost 28,000 federal court opinions from 1933 through 1977 in certain categories of cases (civil rights, criminal justice, labor, and economic regulation) found that the decisions of Democratic appointees were about 7 percent more liberal than Republican; they also found that this number varied over time (ranging from 1 to 11 percent), and they found that judicial rulings varied as a function of region (North-South).[59] The authors concluded that most trial court decisions are determined by controlling precedents and the evidence, with other factors coming into play when the law is open or ambiguous and the evidence is evenly divided.[60] A follow-up study by Rowland and Carp focusing on 1969–86 found an increase in partisan polarization, with the difference in decisions between Democratic and Republican appointees increasing to 12 percent (again with much fluctuation).[61] The differences on specific issues can rise to shocking levels: Carter-appointed judges upheld minority claims in race discrimination cases 78 percent of the time, whereas Reagan appointees did so 18 percent (this extreme difference was almost double the next largest disparity).[62] Other than this, the differences overall, while notable, were not large.

Based upon their findings, Rowland and Carp argued that the "attitudinal model" should be abandoned in favor of a theory of cognition.[63] What explains the differences in judgment is not that judges are striving to achieve their political preferences; rather, the authors postulate, on the whole judges render their decision in a good-faith effort to rule objectively in accordance with the law.[64] Judgments must be made with respect to ambiguous legal and factual issues, and judges approach these issues within cognitive frames that subtly influence the decisions. When rendering judgments about the facts (when assessing the probabilities about which side is correct in factual disputes), they suggested, the differences in cognitive frame account for the differences in decisions, while the shared orientation to law accounts for the substantial overlap in decisions notwithstanding ideological differences.[65]

Several studies have found that district courts duly comply with precedents established by the Supreme Court, even when the outcome is contrary to their policy preferences.[66] A study of more than two thousand cases found almost no evidence that the political backgrounds of trial judges influenced outcomes, concluding that "[i]n the mass of cases that are filed, even civil rights and prisoner cases, the law—not the judge—dominates the outcomes."[67] A recent study by Joseph L. Smith of federal district court decisions in the District of Columbia involving civil rights claims—selected for study because this subset of cases is thought likely to invoke the policy preferences of judges—found a limited ideological influence at trial and on appeal. Reagan appointees were more likely than Clinton appointees to favor defendants, showing a "noticeable, but not overwhelming, partisan tilt";[68] there were only minor differences ("no noticeable bias") in the decision patterns of Republican- and Democratic-dominated panels on appeal.[69] Smith also found that district judges shifted their decision behavior subsequent to reversals of their decisions to conform to the direction set by the appellate court,[70] which suggests that they were abiding by the legal dictates of their immediate superiors.

The evidence derived from quantitative studies of federal circuit and district court decision making is beginning to accumulate along the same lines: "The growing body of empirical research on the lower federal courts . . . reveals that ideology explains only a relatively modest part of judicial behavior and emerges on the margins in controversial and ideologically contested cases."[71]

The picture presented by these studies is not consistent across the board. A few studies have found a degree of ideological influence that is more than modest.[72] More dramatic differences tend to show up in areas in which judges have greater discretion and the issues at stake have strong ideological or personal overtones. For example, although a number of studies have found little or no gender effects on judging, a recent study of employment discrimination cases found that the likelihood of finding discrimination decreases by 10 percent for male judges compared to female judges.[73] A recent study of cases involving the voting rights act—which tends to evoke ideological divisions— found that Democratic appointees voted for liability 44 percent of the time compared to 22 percent for Republican appointees.[74] But it remains unusual to find significant differences in legal decisions owing to ideological differences.

Studies of lower courts are not numerous, and significant methodological issues have yet to be worked out, so the results reported above must be taken as tentative.[75] For example, a decade-old study has often been cited for showing significant political influences in judicial review of administrative agency decisions,[76] but a subsequent study came to a contrary finding, concluding that political backgrounds did not match decision patterns.[77] It is not clear which study is more reliable or whether they can be reconciled.

Two pivotal aspects of existing studies remain especially problematic.[78] The proposition that the judges are pursuing their policy preferences in their legal decisions cannot be tested unless one knows what those preferences are, and knows whether particular legal decisions advance them.[79] But neither of these is easy to determine because judges do not announce their policy preferences, and legal decisions revolve around legal issues without an announced or univocal political thrust. Political scientists have relied upon proxies to answer both questions. The standard way to identify the ideology of the judge is to use the political party of the appointing president—sometimes supplemented by factoring in the party that controls the Senate or the party of the home-state senators, or considering the party affiliation of the judge, previous employment, news reports surrounding the appointment, or other factors[80] —on the assumption that a conservative president will appoint a conservative judge, and vice versa.[81] There are obvious objections to this, including that judicial appointments are not driven always or purely by ideology, there are different streams within the "conservative" and "liberal" political positions, people hold various combinations of positions, they attach different significances to issues, and they have different degrees of commitment to issues.[82]

As for the second question, the standard way to code the political orientation of judicial votes is to identify the main issue at stake and to look at the alignment of the litigants in connection with that issue; for example, decisions in favor of environmental groups, criminal defendants, civil rights claimants, and labor unions are typically deemed "liberal," whereas the opposite decisions are deemed "conservative." These coding decisions are made without any consideration of the legal issues raised or the applicable law.[83] There are obvious problems with this approach, including that cases frequently involve multiple issues (so coding a case requires contestable judgments), and the way a legal issue is framed in a given case can be inconsistent with the assumed liberal or conservative alignment.[84] How one measures a judge's ideology and how one identifies the ideological orientation of a decision directly affect the results of the study. Researchers who compared different coding methods found "that efforts to estimate the impact of ideology on judicial behavior can yield significantly different results depending upon how one chooses to measure ideology."[85]

Owing to these problems, it is prudent to be cautious about making too much of the findings of current studies. But they provide useful information. And they have presented a consistent overall picture: after systematically targeting situations of legal disagreement and politically salient issues, researchers have found that politics show a limited influence on judging below the Supreme Court. A substantial proportion of the time, judges agree in their legal decisions and comply with binding legal rules. In the early 1990s quantitative studies already suggested that "ideological values play a less prominent role in the lower federal courts."[86] Recent studies have strengthened this finding.

Quantitative studies arguably were not necessary to demonstrate this, given that federal appellate courts have long rendered unanimous opinions about 90 percent of the time. Judicial politics scholars are quick, and correct, to point out that this high number does not necessarily represent agreement on the legal issues because judges may, out of collegiality or for some other reason (i.e., consider it not worth the extra work) forgo a dissent even when they disagree.[87] Judge Jon Newman acknowledged twenty years ago that "the percentage of dissenting opinions is not necessarily a true reflection of all the occasions on which one member of a panel disagrees with a panel decision," but he added that this would "not significantly increase" the number of explicit dissents.[88]

A recent critic objected that judicial politics scholars consistently focus on situations that they expect will show that judging is political.[89] But the more compelling point is that, *in spite of* this slant, judicial politics scholars have found far less political influence than expected.

Balanced Realism of Judges in Light of Quantitative Studies

As conveyed in the preceding chapter, judges have for many decades acknowledged that there are open legal questions with no clear answer, that judgments and choices must be made, and that personal biases or political preference sometimes comes into play in judicial decisions. Highly respected contemporary judges have openly and repeatedly made these same points. Judge Jon Newman, for example, wrote that "I am not so naïve as to deny that some judges in some cases permit personal predilections to determine the result. The equities sometimes matter, the rule of law is sometimes bent."[90] Judge Alex Kozinski, a self-proclaimed legalist, declared that "judges do in fact have considerable discretion in certain of their decisions";[91] that with legal principles "there is frequently some room for the exercise of personal judgment";[92] that "[p]recedent . . . frequently leaves room for judgment";[93] that "[w]e all view reality from our own peculiar perspective, we all have biases, interests, leanings, instincts";[94] and that "[i]t is very easy to take sides in a case and subtly shade the decision-making process in favor of the party you favor."[95] Judge Harry Edwards stated that a judicial panel comprised of judges with a shared ideological orientation "might use the occasion to tilt their opinion pursuant to their partisan preferences."[96] Edwards also acknowledged that in very hard cases with no clear right legal answer "it may be true that a judge's views are influenced by his or her political or ideological beliefs."[97]

In response to recent quantitative studies, Judge Patricia Wald sardonically offered "something of a *ho-hum* reaction to the notion that judges' personal philosophies enter into their decisionmaking when statute or precedent does not point their discretion in one direction or constrain it in another. . . . In such cases personal philosophies may well play a significant role in judging."[98] "But how could it be otherwise?" asked Judge Wald.[99] "[T]he judge's political orientation *will* affect decisionmaking."[100] She acknowledged that conflicting lines of precedent occasionally exist, allowing judges to "follow those precedents which they like best,"[101] and she admitted that judges can ignore or distinguish away precedents they don't like when the precedents are not precisely on point.[102] "I would be naïve to suggest that all judges reason alike," she wrote. "How could they, given their different backgrounds, experiences, perceptions, and former involvements, all of which are part of the intellectual capital they bring to the bench. The cumulative knowledge, experience, and internal bents that are in us are bound to influence our notions of how a case is to be decided."[103]

While judges candidly acknowledge these aspects of judging, they also nonetheless uniformly insist—as Judge Newman does here—that "[t]he ordinary business of judges is to apply the law as they understand it to reach results with which they do not necessarily agree. They do this every day. Distasteful statutes are declared constitutional and applied according to the legislators' evident intent; unwise decisions of administrative agencies are enforced; trial court rulings within the trial judge's discretion are upheld even though the reviewing judge would surely have ruled to the contrary; precedents of the local jurisdiction are followed that would be rejected as an initial proposition."[104] Judge Kozinski insisted that, notwithstanding the ample room for discretion and judgment, judges are "subject to very significant constraints" and can try to become aware of and attempt to counter the influence of their biases.[105]

Judges routinely admit the presence of ideological influence on decisions, but they also insist that it comes into play in a relatively small proportion of cases. In a consistent string from Benjamin Cardozo to the present, appellate judges have estimated that around 90 percent of the cases have discernible legal answers, and judges rule accordingly regardless of their political predispositions. Judge Wald estimated that difficult judgments must be made in about 15 percent of the cases.[106] Judge Edwards similarly estimated that about 5–15 percent of appellate cases are very hard, with equally strong competing legal arguments. "Disposition of this small number of cases, then, requires judges to exercise a measure of discretion, drawing to some degree on their own social and moral beliefs."[107] Even Judge Richard Posner, who revels in emphasizing the presence of legally uncertain cases (and who agrees that the percentage of unanimous cases is not a measure of legal certainty because judges sometimes forgo dissents even when they disagree),[108] nonetheless maintains that "[n]o responsible student of the judicial system supposes that 'politics' . . . or personal idiosyncrasy drives *most* decisions."[109] "The routine case is dispatched with least fuss by legalist methods."[110]

The results of quantitative studies are consistent with what judges have been saying all along. If recent trends within the field toward greater (even if begrudging) appreciation of legal factors bear out, the progress of the judicial politics field over the past half century will amount to a slow, twisted path of coming around to recover from the distorting slant built into the field by the formalist-realist antithesis.

Emphasis on the Wrong Question: *Whether* versus *How Much*

A potentially misleading concept within statistical analysis has subtly conjoined with the false story about the formalists to exacerbate the potential for mischief in the field. Quantitative studies of judging are measured by whether the results meet the standard of "statistical significance." This technical term relates to the confidence one may have in the reliability of the correlation identified, providing assurance that the finding is not likely the product of random sampling.[111] But this measure says absolutely nothing about magnitude or relevance, nothing at all about the practical or real-world significance of the finding.[112]

The test of statistical significance, as economists Stephen Ziliak and Deirdre McCloskey emphasize, "does not ask *how much*. It asks *'whether.'* "[113] A finding can meet the "statistically significant" threshold—no greater than a 1-in-20 chance that the relation found is coincidental[114] —even if the size or impact of the finding is minuscule. Scholars engaged in statistical analysis, including judicial politics scholars, are well aware that "statistical significance" says nothing about actual or substantive significance. Ziliak and McCloskey demonstrate through numerous examples across a range of fields, however, that mistaking the former for the latter is an easy, tempting, and a widely committed error in statistical analysis.

A circumstance unique to the judicial politics field encourages this error. From the outset the mission of quantitative studies was to refute the (supposed) "formalist" claim that judging is *purely* a matter of mechanical deduction. When framed in this way, the crucial point of dispute *is whether* politics matters.[115] An affirmative showing of *any* statistically significant correlation between political views and legal decisions, no matter how small, counts against the formalist view. Even if the effect is tiny, judicial politics scholars can triumphantly say to the formalist: "See, you are wrong. Contrary to your complete denial, the political views of judges influence their decisions." And that is what judicial politics scholars declare again and again. Under the sway of the false story about the formalists, "statistical significance" carries real significance because any finding that meets this threshold refutes the formalist target.

This has fundamental implications for how quantitative studies have been constructed and interpreted. If the question is *whether* political preferences influence judicial decision making, it is sensible to concentrate on legally uncertain cases (non-unanimous decisions) that implicate politically salient issues because that is where one is most likely to find affirmative evidence. As Hettinger, Lindquist, and Martinek describe, political scientists follow this chain of reasoning to justify the design of their studies:

> The empirical dynamics of judicial decision making also reveal judges do far more than simply *mechanically* apply law to resolve disputes.... In particular, dissensus among judges, whether among members of an appellate panel or between judges at different levels in a judicial hierarchy, often reflects conflict over the values inherent in different policy alternatives and indicates that judges are not always "bound" by existing precedent or other legal rules in determining case outcomes.... It is no surprise, then, that most political scientists interested in the policymaking dynamics on the bench have focused their attention on *nonunanimous* opinions, especially when constructing models of judicial voting behavior.[116]

The continuing impact of the story about the formalists—of purported belief in mechanical jurisprudence—on the design and orientation of studies of judging is manifest in this passage.

As the preceding chapter exhaustively established, however, judges have admitted for decades that personal values can have an influence on their decisions in uncertain or hard cases. Accordingly, the issue of *whether* politics matters is not disputed. Under what circumstances, in what ways, to what extent, to what effect—these are the crucial questions. These revolve around issues of *how much*. If one wants to learn about *how much* politics matters in judicial decision making, it is inappropriate to isolate solely on the subclass of cases that are most likely show political influences; decisions that show a political influence must always be described in the context of the total body of cases.

A brief return to the Hettinger, Lindquist, and Martinek study reveals how a distorted picture can be created by making statements based upon statistical significance without emphasizing *how much*. As described above, their study found that ideological differences among judges showed a statistically significant relationship in connection with an increased likelihood of a dissent or a concurrence. Now consider the actual impact they found in increasing the probability of a separate opinion:

> Comparing the baseline predicted probabilities of observing, respectively, a concurrence and a dissent when ideological difference is at its maximum observed value ... gives us a sense of the substantive effects of ideological difference. The difference in absolute terms is rather small, with slightly less than a 0.01 increase in the probability of a concurrence and a 0.02 increase in the probability of a dissent. This means that for both concurrences and dissents, the probability increases approximately 50 percent over the baseline. The fact that these changes are small in absolute terms is not at all surprising given that the likelihood of a concurrence or dissent is quite small to begin with. When we consider the effects in terms of percentage change, however, the effects are quite substantial.[117]

The main point of this passage warrants repeating. When judges with different ideological views sit on the same panel there was an increased probability of 0.02 for dissents and 0.01 for concurrences. This marginal increase in probability was the actual impact of ideological difference in the total body of cases examined. The authors gloss this by emphasizing that it represents a 50 percent increase over the baseline rate of dissent, but a 50 percent increase over a very small number is still a very small number.

If the bottom line is *how much* significance does ideology have in producing separate opinions, the resounding answer provided by this study is this: not much, hardly any, surprisingly little. This conclusion is reinforced when one also considers that other factors they tested—the presence of amicus briefs and circuit norms for separate opinions—showed an equal or higher increase in probability than ideological difference.

To their credit, the authors do not ignore the actual impact of ideological difference. But they mention it once and then play it down, relying upon on the statistical significance of their finding to issue broad assertions that ideology matters—without saying again how little it matters. Take their summary at the close of the chapter: "The findings presented in this chapter indicate that judicial behavior on appellate courts is *deeply embedded* within, and structured by, judges' ideology, interpersonal relationships, and institutional context."[118] A few sentences later they assert that "both dissents and concurrences are functions of ideological disagreement."[119] In view of the exceedingly small (albeit statistically significant) impact of their findings, these are dubious assertions.

Keep in mind, furthermore, that in the second main component of the study the authors found that ideological differences between the appellate panel and the trial court showed no statistically significant increased rate of reversal. This important finding cuts directly against the prevailing assumption within the field "that judges are motivated to embody their policy preferences in the law."[120]

When all of the results are taken together, this study, covering decisions by almost a thousand judges over nearly four decades, is a powerful demonstration of the marginal impact the political preferences of judges have in federal appellate decision making. Succumbing to the slant in the field, however, in the end the authors portray it in the opposite way by offering a potentially distorting "balanced" characterization: "Because separate opinions and reversals constitute behavioral manifestations of judges' discretionary authority, studies of dissensus shed light on critical questions related to the effective functioning and *legitimacy of our legal system and the rule of law.* . . . Our findings cut both ways. The evidence we have presented in the preceding pages of this book demonstrates that *judging is both a legal and a political activity* and that, in either case, it is an activity that takes place in an institutional context that substantially shapes the enterprise."[121]

To suggest that politics pervades judging, as political scientists often do, is just as misleading as the suggestion that politics has absolutely no impact on judging (which no jurist asserts). Only by ignoring the issue of *how much* can the phrase "judging is both legal and political" be uttered in connection with the findings of this study. Strictly speaking their statement is accurate—as it would be true even if politics show a tiny impact—but to phrase it that way nonetheless perpetuates an inaccurate impression.[122] The legitimacy of judging, the rule of law, depends entirely on questions about how much.

Measuring a Threat to the Rule of Law

The final study to be discussed here, published in 2006 by Cass R. Sunstein, David Schkade, Lisa M. Ellman, and Andres Sawicki, focused on the consequences of differences in the composition of appellate panels. In an alarmist fashion, the authors announce, "We show that variations in panel composition lead to dramatically different outcomes, in a way that creates *serious problems for the rule of law.*"[123] In an editorial in the *New York Times* describing the findings of their study,

Sunstein and Schkade wrote: "[H]ow much does ideology matter once judges are on the bench? . . . it matters a lot."[124] The authors demonstrated several different panel effects in connection with ideology, involving amplification, dampening, and conformity. Panels composed of all Democratic appointees are twice as likely to vote liberal as are panels with only Republican appointees (amplification).[125] On mixed panels, the ideological pattern of voting is substantially reduced (dampening); interestingly, Democratic appointees are more likely to vote conservative when sitting with two Republicans (conformity). Evidently, the votes of individual judges are influenced by whom they sit with.[126] These results suggest that the fates of litigants may turn upon the luck of the draw in the randomly assigned ideological mix of the panel of presiding judges. This is not consistent with the rule-of-law principle that the law be applied equally to all.

A closer look, however, presents a less worrisome picture. As the authors acknowledge, the subset of cases appealed following trial are more likely to have "a degree of indeterminacy in the law."[127] Their study, moreover, was limited to published cases, which represents only about 20 percent of opinions.[128] Appellate courts follow a policy of publishing decisions that have value as precedents,[129] which suggests that the unpublished bulk of cases are likely to be routine in legal terms, as the authors recognize.[130] Judge Patricia Wald observed that "omitting unpublished opinions will tend to exaggerate the partisan nature of judicial decisionmaking."[131] This observation is supported by the significantly lower rate of dissent when unpublished opinions are counted. In 2000 the D.C. Circuit dissent rate for all cases was 1.6 percent, but 7.8 percent when only published cases were counted; in 2001 the dissent rate for all cases was less than 1 percent, but 4.8 percent in published cases.[132]

The authors, furthermore, focused only on issues they thought were likely to show ideological influences. Of these, in five major areas no ideological effect was evident.[133] In most areas in which ideological differences did show, the differences, they admit, "are not huge"[134] (statistically significant ideological voting was mainly clustered in two categories—employment discrimination and disabilities).[135] Overall, Democrats voted liberal 52 percent of the time while Republicans voted liberal 40 percent of the time.[136] "There is a substantial overlap between the votes of Republican appointees and those of Democratic appointees."[137] The law is often clear, the authors acknowledge, and in these cases judges vote the same way no matter who appoints them.[138]

Do these findings reveal "serious problems for the rule of law"? In a separate paper summarizing the findings of recent quantitative studies of judging, Cass Sunstein and Thomas Miles again suggest that these findings have direct implications for the rule of law:

> Committed realists, emphasizing the importance of political judgments, will want to declare a clear victory. They will stress the evident disagreement, in many domains, between Republican and Democratic appointees—and thus point to the clear impact of political convictions on judicial decisions. But on the data as it stands, judicial policy preferences are only part of the picture. In most domains, the division between Republicans and Democratic appointees, while significant, is far from huge; the law, as such, seems to be having a constraining effect. We are speaking, moreover, of the most contested areas of the law, where political differences are most likely to break out—and also of appellate cases, where the legal materials are likely to have a degree of indeterminacy. For those who believe in the rule of law, and in the discipline imposed by the legal system, the results of the New Legal Realism need not be entirely discouraging. The glass is half-empty, perhaps, but it also half-full.[139]

It is ironic that self-proclaimed realists would make these assertions. Only someone who demands perfection of law and judges—only someone who believes in mechanical jurisprudence—would conclude that the rule-of-law glass is " half-empty" merely based upon a showing that political influences come into play in a subset of contested legal issues. Only "a disappointed absolutist" who "has found that the rules are not all they would be in a formalist's heaven" would declare on the basis of this finding that the rule of law is not being met.[140]

That is an unrealistic stance. No judicial system manned by humans can stamp out all possible ideological influence. Federal district judge Alvin Rubin wrote three decades ago, "The rule of law is not the doctrine of perfect decision. . . . [I]n many cases a conscientious decision is as much as can be expected, and . . . there is no ultimate 'right' answer."[141] Open questions and hard cases are inevitable in law, judges are humans subject to cognitive biases and motivated reasoning, and judges perceive their role in various ways (beyond a common orientation to apply the law). One might take the position that the rule of law is *impossible* owing to these limitations inherent to law and human reasoning, but a realistic construction of the rule of law would instead accept these factors as given, unavoidable conditions of judging.

Just as a full glass of milk is not filled to the brim, a "full glass" of the rule of law, to continue with Sunstein's metaphor, would have empty space between the surface of the milk and the lip of the glass. This space represents the irreducible play of ideological factors and the irreducible uncertainty of law. That is inevitable even in a well-functioning rule-of-law system. To say that the glass is half-full requires a showing that the level of milk is significantly below the normal level one would expect of a full glass.

Quantitative studies of judging have demonstrated that the glass is not filled to the brim, but that is to be expected. What quantitative studies have not yet shown is that the level is below what one would consider reasonably full given the inherent limitations of human reasoning and law. For that to be established, judicial politics scholars must first identify what is the reasonably full level—the rule-of-law baseline—which they have made no attempt to formulate. Only by reference to a standard of this sort can it be asserted that the level of ideological influence identified reflects a threat to the rule of law, rather than a manifestation of the irreducible normal consequence of the openness of law and the complexity of judging.

The baseline must take into account different types legal provisions, and different types of issues. Legal standards like reasonableness or fairness, for example, call for judges to make value-based judgments; some legal decisions, like criminal sentencing, are committed to the discretion or judgment of judges. By their nature, these types of decisions will be susceptible to greater variation.[142] When the rules are clear and straightforward and the facts tend to be uncomplicated, in contrast, one would expect a high degree of consistency.

Many legal issues arise that have no ideological overtones, moreover, or that turn on technical issues of law. Judge Patricia Wald objected that it is unrealistic to assume "that judges feel strongly about each of the hundreds or thousands of cases in which they participate each year and that they are constantly on the ready to jump in with their personal preferences at a moment's notice when there is no one around to object—and even when law may exist to the contrary."[143] "A large proportion of our cases," she wrote, " . . . have no apparent ideology to support or reject at all."[144]

By all accounts, the degree of legal uncertainty is a major factor in the capacity of legal rules to determine legal decisions. The proportion of legally uncertain cases undoubtedly differs across courts. As Judge Harry Edwards remarked, "[T]he [Supreme] Court considers many 'very hard' cases," but "the same is not true of courts of appeals," where "a great many are easy."[145] Higher court judges typically confront more legal uncertainty and hence must make more choices. Given this essential difference, different-level courts would have different baselines.

Finally, any attempt to measure the rule of law must not forget the full range of contexts in which law operates in legal cases that are invisible to studies of judicial decisions. Fewer than 2 percent of the cases now filed in federal court go through a full trial. A decision to resolve a case, generally speaking, is based upon an evaluation of the relevant law as it applies to the provable facts in the case (determining the probability of success), measured against the cost of continuing. The overwhelming proportion of cases resolved before trial is thus determined by the law in a concrete sense, even in the absence of a judicial ruling.[146] The same can be said of outcomes not appealed. As Judge Posner observed, "Most cases are not even appealed, because the outcome of the appeal is a foregone conclusion, usually because the case is 'controlled' by precedent or clear statutory language. For the same reason, many potential cases are never even filed. So legalism has considerable sway, and the lower the level at which a legal dispute is resolved, the greater that sway."[147]

Concrete Signs That Judging *Is* Becoming More Political

The slant within the field disables judicial politics scholars from rendering a critical assessment of judges and judging. Certain judges, relative to their similarly situated brethren, manifest a far greater influence of their ideological views in their legal decisions, whether by consciously pursuing political ends or by less effectively checking their subconscious biases. These judges *are* behaving like "politicians in black robes." Some decisions *are* made on political grounds.[148] Some courts do appear to render ideologically infused decisions an inordinately high percentage of the time.[149] Even judges have asserted, as District Court Judge Stanley Sporkin did about the D.C. Court of Appeals, "It's an ideological court up there."[150] Judge Harry Edwards, a judge on the D.C. Circuit, confirmed that in his early days on the court "judges of similar political persuasions too often sided with one another . . . merely out of partisan loyalty, not on the merits of the case."[151] Because judicial politics scholars constantly repeat the refrain that judging is political, however, it is hard to sound a genuine alarm when judges truly are deciding in a highly political fashion.

It is essential to be able to make such critical judgments because there are signs that judging might indeed be shifting in a more political direction. For most of the nation's history, until recent decades, presidents (with the exception of Franklin D. Roosevelt) did not engage in close ideological screening for their judicial appointments beneath the Supreme Court.[152] Federal judgeships were awarded mainly as patronage or to shore up local support. Ronald Reagan was the first president to systematically screen lower court appointees for their ideological views. The practice has continued ever since, especially vigorously by Republican presidents, at the urging and under the close scrutiny of conservative and liberal interest groups.[153]

Scholars who have compared judicial decision making over time have found that, when patronage dominated the appointment process, there were relatively small differences in the decision patterns of federal appellate court judges appointed by presidents from different parties.[154] This began to change with the implementation of systematic ideological screening of judicial appointees. Political cleavages in judicial voting behavior "have grown deeper in the past two decades."[155] Recent research suggests that the increasing gap is attributable to a growing penchant for conservative judges to rule in an ideologically oriented fashion. Cross, for example, found that "[t]he judges appointed by Presidents Reagan and G.H.W. Bush appear to be particularly ideological."[156]

A dramatic increase in ideologically infused judging was exposed in Judge Posner's recent book on judging. Because judicial appointments are made by the president and approved by the Senate, the most latitude to seat desired judicial candidates exists when the same party controls both. Posner constructed one table of judicial votes on the federal courts of appeals from 1925 to 2002, and a second table of judicial votes in the same courts limited to all currently serving judges.[157] Judges appointed by Republican presidents and confirmed by Republican-controlled Senates in the first table (1925–2002) voted conservative 55.8 percent of the time; judges appointed by Democratic presidents and Senates voted conservative at a rate of 49.6 percent. The 6.2 percent gap in voting behavior is notable but not large. The votes of *currently sitting* judges in these same categories, in contrast, are 66.9 percent and 49.7 percent—a gap of 17.2 percent. Note that the sizable expansion of the gap between Republican and Democratic appointees is *entirely* attributable to a spurt in conservative voting by Republican appointees. As Posner commented, the difference in votes has become more pronounced "consistent with the strong Republican push beginning with Reagan to tilt the ideological balance of the courts rightward."[158]

This study and the studies described above simultaneously help illustrate the strengths of quantitative studies of judging as well as the flaws in the currently dominant orientation. The strengths are that these studies can provide information about judicial decision-making patterns covering a vast number of judges and decisions over time that cannot be obtained in any other fashion. The fundamental flaw comes in how judicial politics scholars view judging. Although judicial politics scholars can make comparative findings of this sort, their assumption that judging *is* political limits the way these findings can be interpreted. The current cohort of conservative judges cannot be condemned for allowing their political preferences to determine their decisions, for perforce (by judicial politics' lights) that is what all judges are doing. By way of condemnation, the most that can be said is that these judges are less self-restrained in the pursuit of their political objectives, but it is not clear why such restraint is laudable if judging is fundamentally political in nature anyway. A judicial politics scholar might warn, in strategic terms, that by abusing their advantage conservative judges are risking a backlash. But this argument about possible future consequences is hardly persuasive when measured against the immediate gains in entrenching the conservative agenda in law—and this objection is devoid of normative import.

From a standpoint that views judging as politics, the only solution is to aggressively pursue the appointment of liberal judges, who will then be encouraged to offset the conservative judges by voting for liberal outcomes in a higher percentage of their cases. Extrapolating from Posner's statistics for the purposes of illustration, if this strategy were successful, conservative judges would vote conservative 67 percent and liberal 25 percent of the time (the remaining percentage of cases do not fall in one category or the other), whereas liberal judges would vote conservative 25 percent and liberal 67 percent of the time.[159] The gap in voting behavior would be 42 percent. This way lies a breakdown of the rule of law, with cases determined a high percentage of the time by the luck of the draw that seats judges on a given panel.

A different approach exists that does not lead down this path. For the purposes of illustration (again using Posner's statistics), assume that *legally* determined decisions fall in a range between 49 and 56 percent in the conservative direction, consistent with the long-term historical pattern (ignoring that the latter number is skewed upward by currently sitting judges). Assume that the difference between these two numbers represents the irreducible play of ideological factors in good-faith judging involving legally uncertain cases, which cannot be eliminated. It is then possible to condemn for being excessively ideological any individual judge or group of judges whose decisions substantially and consistently fall outside this range. This might prove to be an effective check, for this condemnation strikes at role orientation and self-esteem of judges. In contrast to the previous scenario, the effect would be to provide pressure to keep the run of decisions to within a relatively narrow range of difference.

This is just an illustration. Too many factors play into the historical numbers Posner produced to make clear assertions about what they represent. Many complicated issues must be considered before coming up with rule-of-law baselines for different kinds of legal issues and different levels of courts. The refusal of judicial politics scholars to take law seriously on its own terms, the slant that plagues the field, has kept them from exploring and developing a realistic understanding of judging that would produce the sorts of standards that are required to make such judgments about the influence of politics in judging. This potentially valuable work goes wanting.

These comments have focused on federal circuit courts, but the selection of state judges, most of whom face an election of some sort, has in recent years also become politicized to an unprecedented degree.[160] There are reasons to be concerned about the corrosive impact of the increasingly pervasive assumption that judging is political—which is not limited to the appointments context but is widespread in the legal culture. Judge Wald and Judge Edwards have engaged in heated debates with political scientists and law professors over quantitative studies of judging, insisting that the studies exaggerate the degree of political influence on decisions.[161] Judge Kozinski scorned the "cynical view" "spawned in the halls of academia" that judges reach results based upon their political preferences.[162] None of these judges denied that there are political aspects to judging, or that judges have subconscious biases, or that some judges sometimes make decisions in a consciously political fashion. Their argument is that this describes only a small proportion of the cases, and it is a serious error to suggest otherwise.

The thrust this chapter is that the judges were basically right. Nonetheless, the erroneous assumption that judging is largely political may yet have deleterious effects. Judge Edwards urged that "we should at least consider the idea that judges, told often enough that their decisionmaking is crucially informed by their politics, will begin to believe what they hear and to respond accordingly."[163] In light of the recent indications that judging on the federal level is becoming more political, Judge Edwards's worry might prove prescient. Then judicial politics scholars will finally be vindicated in their assumption that judging is political—and they might even deserve a bit of credit for helping bring this about.

PART FOUR

Legal Theory

9

THE EMPTINESS OF "FORMALISM" IN LEGAL THEORY

IN A CELEBRATED 1958 article, H.L.A. Hart, a giant of twentieth-century legal philosophy, expressed bafflement about the term "formalism":

> What precisely is it for a judge to commit this error, to be a "formalist," "automatic," a "slot machine"? Curiously enough the literature which is full of the denunciation of these vices never makes this clear in concrete terms; . . . it is said that in the formalist error courts make an excessive use of logic, take a thing to "a dryly logical extreme," [citing Roscoe Pound] or make an excessive use of analytical method. But just how in being a formalist does a judge make an excessive use of logic? It is clear that the essence of his error is to give some general term an interpretation which is blind to social values and consequences (or which is in some other way stupid or perhaps merely disliked by critics).[1]

Hart thought that the charge of formalism or excessive logic was perhaps a "misnomer for something else"—a tag for a judge "who either does not see or pretends not to see that the general terms of this rule are susceptible of different interpretations and that he has a choice left open uncontrolled by linguistic conventions."[2] "Formalism and Rule-Skepticism" was the title of a chapter in his classic book, *The Concept of Law*,[3] but again Hart expressed perplexity—"It is not always clear precisely what vice is referred to in these terms [formalism, mechanical jurisprudence]."[4]

Nearly a half century later, Cass Sunstein similarly remarked, "It is not easy to define the term formalism."[5] Despite the uncertainty that surrounds the term, talk about formalism is ubiquitous in legal theory, with jurists of various stripes working in the name of "new legal formalism," drawing fire from avowed "realists." Sunstein's remark came in a 1999 symposium issue of the *University of Chicago Law Review* dedicated to the theoretical exploration of formalism.

Every theoretical discussion of "formalism" must specify what is meant by this uncertain term. A common strategy when giving it content is to resort to the story about classical legal formalists. In his analysis of formalism, Richard Pildes asserts that the "classical formalists" believed in "a scientific system of rules and institutions that were *complete* in that the system made right answers available in all cases; *formal* in that right answers could be derived from autonomous, logical working out of the system; *conceptually ordered* in that ground-level rules could all be derived from a few fundamental principles; and socially *acceptable* in that the legal system generated normative allegiance."[6] Brian Leiter's account of formalism has similar echoes: "[W]e may characterize formalism as the descriptive theory of adjudication according to which (1) the law is rationally determinate, and (2) judging is mechanical. It follows, moreover, from (1), that (3) legal reasoning is autonomous, since the class of legal reasons suffices to justify a unique outcome; no recourse to non-legal reasons is demanded or required."[7] Sunstein asserts that formalism is "*deductive*, in the sense that judges decide cases mechanically on the basis of preexisting law and do not exercise discretion in individual cases."[8]

Any approach that defines "formalism" in these terms has doubtful validity, as earlier chapters demonstrated. These ideas were *not* widely held in the U.S. legal tradition, if they were held by any jurists at all.[9] Duncan Kennedy, who has written seminal historical and theoretical studies of formalism, concluded that this version of formalism was "invented by its adversaries rather than by any known American proponents"[10] (although Kennedy invents his own version as well).

The historical question aside, a more immediate reason not to view "formalism" in these terms for theoretical purposes is that it has absolutely no purchase today. The U.S. legal culture, with its pervasively instrumental view of law,[11] does not think of law as complete and logically ordered, does not think of law as autonomous, and does not view judging as a matter of mechanical deduction. To have relevance today, formalism must be construed differently.

A second approach to defining formalism draws from contemporary applications of the term. But this, too, gets nowhere. As Kennedy observed in a recent encyclopedia entry on formalism, " 'Legal formalism' is an important category in the history of law, the sociology of law, comparative law, and the cultural study of law, as well as in the philosophy of law and the interdisciplinary field currently called 'legal theory.' It is used in different senses in these different fields, and within each field it is a contested concept, rather than a well-established term with a clear meaning."[12] Put more plainly, legal formalism has been given all sorts of inconsistent meanings, and no one is sure what it stands for. In just the single Chicago symposium issue, Pildes found that theorists used three versions of formalism. "Because both the structure of these modern formalisms and their underlying justfications differ so sharply," Pildes observed, "it is implausible to see them as representing any unified, coherent vision of modern legal formalism."[13]

There is a compelling reason why Hart was baffled about the meaning of "formalism" a half century ago and why legal theorists do little better today. As chapter 4 explained in connection with the writ system, the term "formalism" has traditionally served to register scorn. It was a reproach directed at a judge or lawyer or a condemnation of a particular decision. "Even a cursory look at the literature," Frederick Schauer remarked, "reveals scant agreement on what it is for decisions in law, or perspectives on law, to be formalistic, except that whatever formalism is, it is not good."[14] The term is an "epithet."[15] The "*demon* of formalism," Cardozo called it.[16] The U.S. Supreme Court invoked this pejorative sense in a 2008 decision when stating, "Habeas is not 'a static, narrow, *formalistic* remedy'; its scope has grown to achieve its grand purpose."[17] It was precisely for this deprecatory thrust against courts that critics branded the turn-of-the-century as the "formalist age." A masterful rhetorical move it was—labeling one's opponents with a censure, which everyone subsequently mistook as a substantive notion.

Formalism has always served as a term of abuse with no real theoretical content. Contemporary theorists, therefore, embark upon an ill-fated mission when they try to attach genuine theoretical meaning to the term. Any term can be given content, so the objective itself is not the problem. The problem is that *this term* carries too much baggage that is false or negative. The false baggage is the old story about the legal formalists, which infects every attempt by theorists to construct a viable meaning of the term.[18] The negative baggage comes from the centuries-old use of the term as an insult. Note the contrasting visceral reactions to these two statements: "Judges should decide in a formalistic fashion"; "Judges should decide in a rule-bound fashion." Not the same. A theoretical term that cannot be read clean of unwanted connotations is compromised.

Theorists have nonetheless forged ahead in the effort to give theoretical meaning to formalism. The two most sophisticated and influential theoretical articulations of the meaning and implications of formalism, produced by Duncan Kennedy and Frederick Schauer, are examined in this chapter. Both theorists construe "formalism" in elaborate terms that revolve around the unthinking application of rules.[19]

This chapter demonstrates that formalism possesses a great potential for confusion with no compensating, redeeming theoretical value. The most demanding constructions of formalism impose conditions that are impossible for judges to meet and that poorly fit common law judging. These accounts are more misleading than informative. The less demanding constructions of formalism add nothing to the idea of "rule-bound" and thus are empty of independent meaning and can be discarded without loss. Contemporary efforts to construct a viable "new formalism," furthermore, have absorbed the major insights of balanced realism, leaving nothing distinctive to the claim of being "formalistic."

Much of the analysis is presented in negative terms, as a critical engagement with leading contemporary theories of formalism. But there is an underlying positive component to the analysis: the critique is informed by, and reflects the sensibilities of, a balanced realist position, which will be filled out in chapter 10.

Kennedy and Schauer on Formalism

Duncan Kennedy sets his argument at a high level of abstraction—liberal democratic political theory. Borrowing from Max Weber, Kennedy posits two alternative ways of structuring decisions: through rule application *or* oriented toward achieving ends. The former is formal legal rationality, and the latter is substantive rationality.[20] Liberal systems, according to Kennedy, separate these two methods of decision making: legislatures engage in substantive rationality; judges engage in formal legal rationality.

This allocation follows from the cultural and political understandings that support and legitimate liberal democratic systems. Liberal societies are comprised of individuals and groups with conflicting goals, purposes, values, ends, and desires, which must be decided upon or balanced. To respect the autonomy and reflect the consent of individuals, these decisions, which are contestable and value based, must be made by democratically accountable institutions. Elected legislative bodies concretize in law their decisions about the best mix among competing purposes and interests (choosing, balancing, allocating, distributing).[21] The role of judges is to carry out the legislative decisions faithfully by applying the law to situations that arise. "*Formality* consists in the attempt to accomplish substantively rational results—i.e., to achieve outcomes that 'maximize' a set of conflicting purposes—through the substantively rational formulation and mechanical application of rules rather than directly through substantively rational decision processes."[22] "The essence of rule application," Kennedy says, ". . . is that it is *mechanical*."[23]

Judges are prohibited from considering whether the mechanical application of rules in given instances produces results that comport with the purposes of the legislature, according to Kennedy, because that would involve judges in substantively rational decision making, which destroys legal formality.[24] He underscores this by insisting that "formality consists *not* in the activity of *following* rules, but in the process of their rigid application. The judge who reaches his decision by substantively rational processes is not acting formally."[25]

Unanticipated situations inevitably arise in which the mechanical application of the rules will have unintended, undesired, unjust, or immoral consequences—too bad. That is the cost of legal formalism. The advantages of formalism are that it is certain, predictable, and orderly.[26] Certainty and predictability enhance the autonomy of individuals— maximizing their liberty—by allowing them to plan and conduct their affairs with awareness of potential legal consequences.[27] With this knowledge, "they will be able to control precisely and completely the part that the rule appliers and the rules play in their lives."[28]

Thus, two distinct rationales justify the mechanical straightjacket of formalism placed on judges: a judge who looks at outcomes will usurp the power and function of the democratic legislature; and blind rule application maximizes individual autonomy and aggregate social welfare because it facilitates the individual pursuit of projects.[29]

Kennedy took a novel tact in his analysis of formalism. Most U.S. theorists, following Pound, have been highly critical of "mechanical" rule application as wrongheaded or a pretense by judges. Rather than criticize formalism, however, Kennedy ratcheted up its demands and lashed the demon to the post of liberalism, insisting that mechanical rule application is required of judges within liberal democracy. Thereby saddling the liberal system with an extreme version of rulebound judging, he proceeded to challenge the coherence of the entire liberal arrangement (including the impossible demands of formalism within it).[30]

Kennedy's model captures the standard legitimating discourse about law as the product of democratic consent, placing judges in a subservient role as loyal servants who carry out the dictates of legislatures, with no independent role in the creation of law. The U.S. legal culture is dominated by a "widely shared premise that judges must act as 'faithful agents' of the legislature."[31] His model also captures the discourse surrounding "the rule of law" within liberalism, which emphasizes the judicial enforcement of public rules declared in advance.[32] These qualities lend plausibility to his account.

Frederick Schauer eschews political theory in his approach to formalism, centering instead on the basic material of law—language and rules. He notes that negative references to formalism typically lament the denial of choice by judges; using this as the point of departure, he analyzes why, how, and to what extent judges are constrained in their decisions. The essence of formalism lies in the nature of rules. "Formalism is the way in which rules achieve their 'ruleness' precisely by doing what is supposed to be the failing of formalism: screening off from a decisionmaker factors that a sensitive decisionmaker would otherwise take into account."[33] Deciding according to rule, Schauer asserts, requires that the judge not think about the purposes behind the rule or the consequences of the application of the rule to the situation at hand.

Schauer arrives at this position in a few steps. Rules are set forth in general terms in advance to achieve purposes. There is an irreducible open texture or indeterminacy in the meaning and application of legal rules owing to ambiguities in language, unanticipated fact situations, and the failure to fully work out the choices among goals.[34] Despite these limitations, rules usually have a settled core meaning stabilized through language—conventional social meaning, or legal terminology conventionally understood within the legal community—which judges are charged with applying.

The rule itself constitutes an independent, authoritative basis for a decision. A judge is prohibited from evaluating whether the purposes behind a binding rule are served by applying the rule to a given situation because to engage in such an evaluation would undermine the rule's authoritative status.[35] This prohibition generates a number of outcomes that are inconsistent with the reasons behind the rules because rules inevitably reach situations they should not (they are overinclusive) and rules fail to reach situations they should (they are underinclusive). These undesirable results are the costs of adopting a rule-based system.

Age requirements for a driver's license can serve to illustrate Schauer's argument. A minimum age is selected, say sixteen, to identify drivers who are physically and emotionally mature enough to drive in a reasonably safe fashion. In coming up with this cutoff, the dangers attendant to driving are balanced against the utility of allowing people to drive. There are individuals younger than sixteen who are mature enough to drive safely—and social utility would be advanced if they were allowed to drive—but the rule prohibits them licenses. Conversely, there are immature eighteen-year-olds who are eligible to drive despite lacking the requisite maturity the rule seeks to identify. Eligibility could instead be determined on a case-by-case basis, with an official evaluating the maturity of each individual seeking a license (decision making focused on ends rather than rules). But this policy would be burdensome and inefficient, and it raises concerns about arbitrary judgments by decision makers.

If a judge were to order, notwithstanding the terms of the law, that a license be granted to a particularly mature fifteen-year-old or denied to a particularly immature eighteen-year-old, the judge's decision would advance the purposes behind the rule, while depriving the rule of its status as an independent, authoritative basis for decision. According to Schauer, "When a rule's prescribed treatment is unsuitable, if the decisionmaker were to ignore the rule, the rule would not be a real rule providing a reason for decision but would be a mere rule of thumb, defeasible when the purposes behind the rule would not be served. If every application that would not serve the reason behind the rule were jettisoned from the coverage of the rule, then the decision procedure would be identical to one applying reasons directly to individual cases, without the mediation of rules."[36] Under such a system, Schauer argues, the rules are not really "rules," because decisions are based on how best to achieve ends, which deprives rules of independent authority.

"Formalism in this sense is indistinguishable from 'rulism,'" he asserts, "for what makes a regulative rule a rule, and what distinguishes it from a reason, is precisely the unwillingness to pierce the generalization even in cases in which the generalization appears to the decisionmaker to be inapposite."[37]

Although rules suffer from over- and underinclusiveness, they foster predictability and enhance certainty in rule application[38] —anyone younger than sixteen need not bother to apply for a license, everyone over this age can count on getting it (if they pass the driving test). Rules foster formal equality by holding everyone to the same requirements in accordance with their terms. Rules also foster reliance; they make decisions more efficient because there is no need to weigh the full panoply of purposes anew in each situation; they promote stability; and they facilitate cooperation and coordination by establishing known, shared ground rules for social interaction.[39] Rules also have the capacity to restrict decision makers by limiting the factors they consider in the course of rendering decisions.[40] "Formalism therefore achieves its value when it is thought desirable to narrow the decisional opportunities and the decisional range of a certain class of decision makers."[41]

Kennedy built his conception of formalism from the top down (liberal political theory) and Schauer from the bottom up (language and rules). Yet they erected parallel analytical structures and arrive at the same position: formalism entails rule-bound judging that prohibits consideration of purposes or consequences. Neither theorist endorsed formalism as described, it must be emphasized. They were elaborating what they thought was theoretically entailed by the notion of formalism. Both raised additional complex theoretical issues that have been bypassed in this summary. What matters for the purposes here is what can be gleaned about formalism from their analyses.

At the center of their parallel analytical structures lie three closely overlapping axes: (1) both posit a sharp divide between the making of a rule and the application of a rule, with judges confined to the latter; (2) both posit a fundamental distinction between decision making controlled by preestablished general rules and end-oriented or purpose-oriented decision making that pays attention to consequences; and (3) both posit a distinctively legal realm of rules and principles versus nonlegal (lacking in legal status) norms, rules, principles, customs, values, policies, purposes, goods, or ends. These familiar distinctions evoke a cluster of classic contrasts within legal theory: legal versus substantive justice; rule-based versus khadi decisions; rule orientation versus outcome orientation; law versus equity; legal rules and principles versus moral principles or social purposes and policies.

A closer critical look at their accounts of formalism follows shortly. It is worth observing in passing here that none of these three positions comport with the accounts of judging offered by many judges and jurists for more than a century, as conveyed in this book. Against the first axis, judges and jurists have long acknowledged that judges make as well as apply law, not just in relation to the common law but also when filling gaps in statutes or dealing with unanticipated situations. Against the second axis, judges and jurists have long insisted that purposes and consequences matter. Against the final axis, judges and jurists have long asserted that, in subconscious and conscious ways, considerations external to the law—social, moral, religious—make their way into the law in the context of judging. A great deal of disagreement surrounds these topics over what is going on, how it should be characterized, and what is proper or desirable, but seldom are any one of these axes understood in the strictly separated terms demanded by the formalism constructed by Kennedy and Schauer.[42]

It is also relevant to note that, beginning in the mid-1970s, a chorus of jurists called attention to a noticeable shift away from rule-bound decision making by judges toward increasing use of standards and balancing tests, and greater consideration of social justice, individual justice, and social policies and purposes.[43] Legal sociologists Philippe Nonet and Philip Selznick argued that the U.S. legal system was evolving to a new stage of "responsive law" in which judicial decision making, while still mostly rule bound, was becoming more open to achieving desired outcomes (justice, policies, and purposes behind the law).[44] English jurist Patrick Atiyah bore witness to a greater willingness among Anglo-American judges to do individual justice in a case, setting aside the legal rules when necessary.[45] Legal theorist Roberto Unger observed that the increasing resort to open-ended clauses and general standards in statutes and administrative regulations require judges to engage in ad hoc balancing among interests (unlike rule-based decision making) and to evaluate nonlegal sources and factors.[46] Abraham Chayes, a doctrinal scholar and theorist, wrote about the explosive rise of "public law litigation," fueled by statutes that set forth broad policy goals—in diverse areas, including education, environment, employment, and business regulations—and required judges to make forward-looking public policy decisions.[47] These were so unlike traditional rule-application, Chayes remarked, that "the proceeding is recognizable as a lawsuit only because it takes place in a courtroom before an official called a judge."[48] Thus, in the very period in which Kennedy and Schauer were articulating their stringent accounts of legal formalism, observers from a range of theoretical perspectives noted that an increasingly greater proportion of judicial decision making did not fit within a narrow rule-bound framework.

The Artificial Separation of Purposes from Rule Interpretation

Kennedy did not elaborate on what he meant by "mechanical" application; his reference to this smacks of "unthinking." That is perhaps appropriate for routine or typified fact situations or for basic rules applied to basic facts—Speed Limit 65—but, beyond that, the term "mechanical" is inapt.[49] "Fact situations do not await us neatly labeled, creased, and folded," Hart observed, "nor is their legal classification written on them to be simply read off by judges."[50] Legal rules inevitably have areas of indeterminacy and ambiguity, he added, so "deductive reasoning" "cannot serve as a model for what judges . . . should do in bringing particular cases under general rules."[51]

Schauer's detailed analysis offers a more tractable point of departure. Formalism, to repeat his central claim, prohibits judges from considering the purposes behind a rule when applying it to the facts at hand. The literal meaning of the rule controls.

This claim raises an immediate threshold question as to whether judges indeed understand rules by interpreting their literal meaning without consideration of their purposes. If the answer is no, then

Schauer's strict separation between rule and purpose cannot be maintained. Schauer knows that in practice, when confronted with ambiguity or uncertainty in meaning, judges often refer to legislative purposes—that is not the philosophical question in dispute. He frames the issue more narrowly: formalism demands that rules be applied according to the literal meaning of their terms, which have a core meaning that can be understood without consideration of purposes.

The classic analysis on this point in legal theory is the debate between H.L.A. Hart and Lon Fuller over a rule that says, "No vehicles in the park." Hart insisted that this rule has a core meaning conveyed by its terms (automobiles prohibited). Only at the margins or penumbra, according to Hart, is the application of this rule open or uncertain (to bicycles and roller skates, for example); a judge must make a decision about what the rule means in these situations, assisted by consideration of purposes.[52]

In response, Fuller argued that the interpretation of rules *always* involves consideration of underlying purposes.[53] He posed a question to illustrate his point: does the rule prohibit the placement of a World War II truck in the park as a war memorial? Fuller asked whether this is within the core or the penumbra of the rule, and what places it there.[54] The standard riposte to Fuller's argument is that a functional truck, even if intended as a memorial, is clearly prohibited by the terms of the rule because it indubitably is a "vehicle"; his example merely serves to illustrate that rules, when applied literally, can have unintended or undesirable results. Many theorists appear to be of the opinion that Hart had the better argument, which is Schauer's position as well.[55]

That is too hasty a conclusion, however. What makes Fuller's challenge powerful is that it is not about adverting to purpose to resolve ambiguities in the application of a rule. (Hart agreed that judges should consider purpose when dealing with ambiguity.)[56] Fuller, rather, insisted that purpose is essential to interpretation even with respect to what is thought to be a rule's nonambiguous core (although purpose need not be consciously considered). It is purpose, not unadorned literal meaning, that tells judges what falls within the core of a rule.

To see why Fuller has a strong argument, consider two standard definitions of "vehicle": "1) any means in or by which someone travels or something is carried or conveyed. . . . ; 2) a conveyance moving on wheels, runners, tracks, or the like, as a cart, sled, automobile, or tractor."[57] Now ask: What in the literal meaning of "No vehicles in the park" says that automobiles are in the obviously prohibited core, while (as Hart contended)[58] application to bicycles and roller skates is ambiguous? A limitless number of possible conveyances come with the definition of "vehicle"—wheelchair, skateboard, child's wagon—none distinguished by the literal terms of the rule. Hart thought it obvious that an automobile is a paradigm example of a vehicle, which is correct, but no more so than a bicycle—used by many people as their primary means of transportation. Perhaps Hart thought that application of the rule to bicycles was ambiguous because he had in mind a sedate city park where people ambled along in quiet conversation, an atmosphere that bicycles would disrupt, yet he also knew of more active parks with bicycles. But that is precisely an exercise in thinking about purpose to interpret the rule. Indeed, the evident influence of Hart's own implicit assumptions about purpose when he gave meaning to this rule, unbeknownst to himself, shows how consideration of purpose can operate at a deep subconscious level; he denied that purpose mattered even as it shaped what he considered to be the self-evident, literal core meaning of the rule.

More evocative examples can clinch the point. Only by knowing what parks are for and by having in mind what this rule aims at achieving would one say that it prohibits automobiles from the park but not *baby strollers*, which easily fall within the definition of "vehicle." (Core meaning covers what is included in the rule's coverage as well as what is excluded.) No member of the community, no park enforcement officer, and no judge would even conceive that this rule prohibits baby strollers, which are a normal in parks.

Hart's argument can perhaps be saved by asserting that all conveyances with wheels (or tracks, etc.) are within the core meaning of the rule. The consequent prohibition of baby strollers and wheelchairs, then, does not involve ambiguity. These are just examples of unintended consequences clearly mandated by the rule. But this is not an accurate way of describing how rules are interpreted. It *goes without saying* that a baby stroller or a wheelchair is not prohibited by "No vehicles in the park"—no question about it. Assumptions about underlying purposes restrict, constrain, shape, and rank the possible meanings that occur to interpreters of a rule, even when not consciously considered. It is within the "core meaning" of this rule that automobiles are prohibited but baby strollers and wheelchairs are not because the implicitly understood purpose, not literal meaning alone, makes it so.

In a later work, Hart conceded that Fuller was correct to suggest that purposes can factor into interpretations of core meaning.[59] Schauer distances himself from Hart on this. He insists that formalism strictly precludes consideration of purpose when determining the core meaning of a rule.[60] Schauer describes a rule as "the *instantiation* of that rule's background justification,"[61] which has a meaning according to its terms apart from the purposes or justifications for the rule. "Hence, situating the concept of a rule at the point of divergence between instantiation and justification is premised on the meaning of an instantiation not being found *solely* in the instantiation's justification."[62]

Schauer places great weight on the fact that the results dictated by rules can diverge from the rule's purposes in given cases. If purpose dictates interpretation, presumably no gap between rule and purpose would arise, for the rule would always be interpreted in a way consistent with achievement of its purpose. "The divergence between rule and justification," Schauer writes, "a divergence I take to be crucial to understanding the idea of a rule, is possible only if formulated generalizations can have meanings different from the result that a direct application of the justification behind a rule would generate on a particular occasion."[63] This argument, however, only shows that purpose does not entirely *control* interpretation, which is *also* a function of literal meaning. It does not show that consideration of purpose has no role in interpretation. If purpose has no role in interpretation, if only literal meaning in isolation were considered (if we assume this is possible), the rule system would be dysfunctional. Rules as simple as "No vehicles in the park" would routinely (rather than occasionally) produce absurd consequences; every rule would have to be endlessly specified, crammed beyond capacity with terms and conditions, to account for every conceivable scenario.

Both literal meaning and consideration of purpose are intertwined, subconsciously and consciously, in interpretation. This holds for routine cases (typified fact situations and simple rules and facts) as well as complex cases, for determining core meaning as well as resolving ambiguities. The categorical distinction between rule and purpose that Schauer situates at the heart of formalism is unreal.

This argument is not just theoretical. It helps fill in earlier chapters about how social views and attitudes make their way into the law through judges, which is an essential component of balanced realism. At the basic level of language, social views come into law though the conventional meaning on which Schauer builds interpretation (interpretation of words in sentences, paragraphs, and full texts), for literal meaning is thoroughly informed by and is the product of the conventions of speakers within a community.[64] At another level social influences make their way into law through the *implicit* consideration of purpose in the interpretation and application of a rule without conscious thought. The infusion of social meaning and values also occurs when purposes are consciously contemplated by a judge. Consideration of purpose in these various ways occurs in the application of common law precedents, statutes, administrative regulations, and the Constitution, infusing the interpretation of law with social views and considerations at every stage.

Schauer's formalism presents legal rules as if they can be read as words on paper and placed on top of the facts, producing a result. In *theory*, perhaps, rules can be read solely though literal meaning—although the presence of multiple conventional meanings makes this questionable. But that is not how people interpret rules. To comply with Schauer's formalist strictures would require the strapping on of thought blinders that would make judges reason in an inhumanly stupid fashion. (Again, to clarify, Schauer describes this as theoretically entailed by formalism, without endorsing it.) Only a mechanical judge with no sense of context would think that baby strollers or wheelchairs fall within the meaning of "vehicles" and are therefore prohibited from the park. But judges do not reason mechanically. Legal rules are always understood by judges as social products with social purposes, which judges interpret through socially informed eyes and apply in particular social contexts.

This analysis helps address a potential confusion that overlaps with Schauer's artificial separation of the literal meaning of legal rules and their underlying purposes. Contemporary observers sometimes note, with an air of skepticism, that the fact that judges frequently agree in their interpretation of legal provisions does not in itself establish that the law at issue is determinate—rather the agreement may be the product of the shared background views of the judges that prompt them to see the law in similar ways. If this remark is offered to *explain* that shared social understandings help stabilize legal interpretation—as the historical jurists implied—then it is correct. That is the broader point of this discussion. If it is offered as a skeptical commentary about the law or the judges, however, as is often the case, then it is mistaken in so far as it suggests that legal interpretation can be conducted free from the influence of shared background social understandings. That idea is perpetuated by the false image of formalism. Legal interpretation is always socially informed. To be properly framed in a way that accounts for this, while retaining critical bite, the skeptical comment must be that the judges' shared legal interpretation is the product of social understandings that are not widespread within the community or are objectionable to significant elements of the community. This more precise formulation—which is frequently what the critics mean—narrows the objection to what is truly at issue.

The Artificial Separation of Rules and Rules of Thumb

A related claim Schauer makes in his account of formalism is that a judge who considers purposes in effect transforms a rule into a "rule of thumb." There are two kinds of "rules of thumb" for Schauer: those which are transparent to background justifications with no independent normative weight are not rules at all; those which create presumptions that must be overcome by weighty justifications, like common law precedents, have rule-like qualities and can function in a rule-like fashion (up to a point).[65]

Again Schauer makes a categorical analytical claim for matters that are fuzzier in actual practice. It is impossible for a judge to foreclose the possibility that a situation might arise that merits an exception to the application of a rule, situations that cannot be known in advance. In practice every rule comes with an unstated "but" or "unless" attached. The common adage, "There is an exception to every rule," attests to this. The potential defeasibility of all legal rules—even if a judge does not, in a given case, actually pierce the rule—means that all rules are tantamount to rules of thumb.[66] Hart suggested that this openness to unspecified exceptions is a general feature of rules—statutes and the common law included. He asserted, "A rule that ends with the word 'unless. . .' is still a rule."[67]

Schauer insists that Hart was wrong about this.[68] He insists that, as an analytical matter, the nature of rules dictates that they cannot be rules of thumb. A rule of thumb can have rule-like qualities but it is not a rule. "Thus," he summarizes, "formalism merges into rulesness, and both are inextricably intertwined with literalism, i.e., the willingness to make decisions according to the literal meaning of words or phrases or sentences or paragraphs on a printed page, even if the consequences of that decision seem either to frustrate the purpose behind those words or to diverge significantly from what the decisionmaker thinks—the rule aside—should be done."[69]

In contrast, Hart staked his position on "what rules actually are in any sphere of real life," including judging.[70] In real life, every rule is a (latent) rule of thumb. Situations that throw into question whether an applicable legal rule should be enforced can serve as prompts to the judge for the "but" to kick in—invoking the potential of all rules to be rules of thumb (even if not actually exercised). The judge will think deeply about whether the initial result can be avoided. The judge will be mindful of the duty to apply the law and the value of stare decisis in promoting stability and reliability. The judge will subconsciously or consciously weigh the purposes behind the rule, relevant social values, and any countervailing considerations thrown up by the situation at hand. The judge may search for or invent an exception, a fiction, an overriding principle, or find a way to distinguish away the application of the rule in an effort to avoid the rule.

This is a timeless problem, a source of endless debate among legal theorists.[71] It is impossible to determine or specify in advance when the latent potential of rules to be treated as rules of thumb should be exercised: no rule can be written to govern when a rule should give way. In these situations, advantages and costs, reasons for and reasons against, weigh on both sides. Judges disagree in their assessment of the burden to be overcome before a rule should give way, although most consider it extremely weighty, and they disagree over what counts as compelling considerations. At the bottom of these decisions lies, as Judge Wald wrote, "some sense of conscience or some core of personal beliefs."[72]

This familiar dilemma also blurs the distinction between rule-based and particularistic decision making. All legal decision making is particularistic because it is always done by individual judges in connection with specific questions raised in particular contexts. The inevitably particularistic setting of judging is what provokes complications in the interpretation and application of rules.

Schauer is well aware that the reality of judging is inconsistent with his account of formalism. He too has noted the earlier-described shift away from rule-bound decision making identified by other theorists, writing that "the current paradigm for adjudication in the American legal culture may already have departed from rule-bound decisionmaking."[73] "[T]his new jurisprudence treats what look like rules as continuously subject to molding in order best to maintain the purposes behind those rules in the face of a changing world."[74] Schauer sees positive benefits to this change, and he advocates that rules and precedent should have presumptive weight that can be overridden under compelling circumstances.[75] Thus, Schauer would appear to agree that the analytical requirements of formalism he specifies do not match contemporary judging in the U.S. legal system.

The critical analysis presented here presses harder to suggest that his analytical arguments are not illuminating because the model of judicial decision making he constructs, like Kennedy's mechanical rule application, not only is not an accurate description of judging but is not a viable account of judging for human judges. Their accounts of formalistic judging are conceivable only in a world of mechanical jurisprudence. If it is not possible to be a formalist, then thinking about rule-bound decisions in these terms, even as an analytical exercise, is counterproductive: it misleads by holding actual judging against an impossible standard.

Incompatibility of Formalism with Standards

There are additional reasons to doubt the relevance and value of Kennedy's and Schauer's accounts of "formalism." Open-ended standards have long been a part of the common law and statutes. Standards exist because rules can be inadequate to the kinds of judgments deemed necessary or desirable, particularly when the factors to be considered vary unpredictably or when fine-grained consideration is required.[76] Rules tend to be blind to variations in circumstances and obtuse about consequences. Standards overcome these disadvantages. Standards often allow the exercise of discretion by judges; they invite judges to pay attention to consequences and promote ends; they ask judges to balance competing social interests and values; they allow for context-specific judgments. The classic example of a standard is the century-old provision in the Sherman Antitrust Act that prohibits combinations "in restraint of trade."[77] What amounts to improper restraint is left for judges to work out.

Needless to say, standards are incompatible with Kennedy's and Schauer's analysis of formalism. Provisions that require determinations about "reasonableness" or "fairness," or the "best interests of the child" standard in custody cases, for example, either straddle or violate Kennedy's strict dichotomy between formal rule application and substantive decision making. Aware of this, Kennedy excludes these provisions with a shrug: his model of legal formality "is simply *not about them*."[78] The same misfit holds for Schauer's analysis. A standard is "transparent to background moral principles and requires particularistic decision-making" in the respects that rules are supposed to disallow.[79] Standards often require judges to consider the "totality of the circumstances."[80] The advantages of standards, the reasons they are preferred in certain contexts, follow from precisely the respects in which they are not completely rule-like;[81] accordingly, they cannot meet the requirements of formalism.[82]

Formalism Does Not Fit Common Law Judging

Common law systems are uniquely ill suited for Kennedy's and Schauer's formalism. Schauer was explicit about this. "There are things the common law undoubtedly refers to as 'rules,' " Schauer writes, "but if they are always subject to modification when the circumstances of some case appear to indicate the desirability of a modification, then the normative purchase is provided not by the supposed rule, but rather by whatever factors are used to determine whether a rule should be modified or applied as previously understood."[83] Common law rules become "encrusted" such that they operate like rules, so the system is substantially rule bound in the aggregate, but he concludes that the common law method involves "seeking case-specific optimization rather than rule-based stability."[84]

Judging in common law systems transgresses Kennedy's exclusive allocation of law-making authority to legislatures. *All lawyers know that judges make the common law.* This has been acknowledged for at least two centuries, as earlier chapters documented. Moved by considerations of policy, or by concerns about social or individual justice, common law judges have for hundreds of years developed and revised rules in the course of application.[85] Judges decide common law cases according to rule, but always with at least a glance at ends, prepared to make law if need be in compelling circumstances. Justice Scalia described the typical "mind-set" of the common law judge (with intentional overstatement) as, "What is the most desirable resolution of this case, and how can any impediments to the achievement of that result be evaded?"[86] Although judicial law making is piecemeal and glacial, the cumulative changes in the law effected by judges over time have been vast.

Judicial law making in connection with the common law, moreover, transgresses the formalist stricture specified by Kennedy and Schauer that judicial decisions must be based exclusively upon legal norms.[87] This closed legal realm can be read expansively to encompass the totality of authoritative legal materials, including constitutions, statutes, precedents, recognized legal principles, standards, and doctrines of interpretation. External factors can acquire legal status through affirmative legislative recognition. But judicial decisions, consistent with the dictates of formalism, cannot be based directly on factors outside this recognized legal realm.

Common law judges, however, have *always* accommodated the law to social circumstances.[88] A multitude of common law judges and jurists recounted in earlier chapters have declared that the consideration, subconsciously and consciously, by judges of social interests, customs, morals, and purposes is integral to the common law system of judging. Cardozo wrote that, when judges "are called upon to say how far existing rules are to be extended or restricted, they must let the welfare of society fix the path, its direction, and its distance."[89] Edward Levi argued in an influential midcentury book on legal reasoning that, by design, provisions exist throughout the law "in order to permit the infusion of new ideas."[90] This judicial attitude, jurists have observed, extends beyond common law interpretation to apply to statutes and the constitution as well. Some applaud and others bemoan it, but few jurists deny that it occurs, and few claim that outside factors can be entirely screened out from the judicial mind.

The permeation of law by outside factors and considerations—albeit always filtered through a legal lens—has been the lifeblood of the development and change of the common law over time. Unless one takes

James Carter's expansive position that these community norms are already in a sense "law" before being recognized as such by judges (which vastly expands the realm of law), or takes Ronald Dworkin's position that immanent political principles are a part of the "law" (which still leaves out social policies),[91] it must be conceded that judging in common law systems fails this requirement of formalism—and for worthy reasons.

The Emptiness of Formalism as Rule-Bound Decisions

In the various respects set forth above, judging in the United States does not fit the theoretical accounts of "formalism" produced by Kennedy and Schauer. Weber pressed several of the same points a century ago when he *contrasted* common law judging with formal legal rationality. A notion that manifestly ill fits the U.S. legal system has, nonetheless, come to assume prominence in the legal theory discourse. The story about the classical legal formalists was manufactured by critics to discredit courts, and now legal theorists are compounding this initial wrong turn by constructing, at high degrees of sophistication, contemporary theoretical understandings of formalism that have doubtful bearing on judging in the U.S. legal tradition.

It might be thought that "formalism" is still a relevant notion when stripped of the most demanding conditions attached by Kennedy and Schauer and restricted to the interpretation of statutes; this move sets to the side the common law, standards, provisions that require balancing or that rely upon judges to carry out legislative policies or fill in details—in combination, a substantial swath of the law—as hopelessly unformalistic. In his analysis of judging, Scalia in effect resorts to this bifurcation. He granted that common law decision making is not formalistic. He identified formalism with statutory and constitutional analysis[92] and criticized statutes with open-ended provisions as insufficiently rule bound (for being too much like common law judging).[93]

This paring back of the demands and scope of application of "formalism" does not preserve its theoretical relevance, however—it eliminates it. When trimmed and reduced to mean no more than "rule-bound decisions," "formalism" becomes *empty* and can be dispensed with. "Formalism," Schauer writes, is "merely rule-governed decision-making."[94] Larry Alexander defines formalism, like Schauer, as "strict adherence to the prescriptions of norms."[95] Sunstein defines formalism in terms of "rule bound law . . . constraining the discretion of judges in individual cases."[96] "[F]ormalism refers to a rule-bound decision-making strategy,"[97] writes Adrian Vermeule. "Long live formalism,"[98] proclaimed Scalia, celebrating the notion that rules should be applied according to their terms.

The only operative idea in these references to formalism is rule-bound decision making. Every statement that includes both terms— "rule-bound and formalistic,"[99] "formal legal rules"[100] —commits a redundancy. In every such sentence, the term formalism can be struck with no loss. The evidence for this comes from the theorists own work. Schauer published a lengthy philosophical book about rules that elaborates the very same points he raised in his prior exegesis of "formalism," yet he mentions the term formalism only a handful of times in passing, and it plays absolutely no role in his analysis.[101] Larry Alexander, whose theoretical views about formalism and rules are similar to Schauer's, coauthored a recent book (with Emily Sherwin) about legal rules that ranged across every important issue on the topic without once analyzing "formalism."[102]

A theoretical notion that can be deleted without any impact on the analysis is devoid of value. Even the assertions that formalism involves the "strict," "rigid," "inflexible," or "blind" application of rules adds nothing to the notion of rule-bound decision making. Those adjectives merely repeat what it means to apply a rule, appending an exclamation or registering a note of disapproval. Moreover, the emphasis misses the mark because, as the earlier discussion of rules as rules of thumb shows, in any given instance adherence to a rule at a deep level is not "blind" or "rigid" but a matter of an unexercised choice (often not conscious) in which the judge is not sufficiently compelled to set aside the application of the rule or to interpret it in a way that avoids the result the critic objects to.

Hart was right to be puzzled by the term. In the final analysis, the only distinctive meaning carried by "formalism" is the derogatory connotation it has traditionally conveyed.

The Realism of the "New Formalists"

The argument that "formalism" is an insult without distinctive theoretical meaning must be squared with the fact that in the past decade various theorists have announced allegiance to what is being called "new formalism." Prominent judges and legal theorists, including Justice Antonin Scalia, Judge Frank Easterbrook, Professor John Manning of Columbia, and Professor Lawrence Solum of Illinois, among others, self-identify or are tagged as modern-day formalists. The argument here is not that these jurists are espousing empty or irrelevant ideas; rather, the argument is that labeling their position "formalist" adds nothing distinctive[103] and is potentially misleading because these modern formalists accept the basic insights identified with balanced realism.

Judge Easterbrook, for example, emphasizes, " 'Plain meaning' as a way to understand language is silly. In interesting cases, meaning is not 'plain.' . . . *Hard questions have no right answers.* Let us not pretend that texts answer every question. Instead we must admit that there are gaps in statutes, as in the law in general."[104] Easterbrook recognizes, moreover, that social meanings and purposes necessarily play into interpretation. "Words take their meaning from contexts, of which there are many—other words, social and linguistic conventions, the problems the authors were addressing. Texts appeal to communities of listeners, and we use them purposively."[105]

A leading proponent of a "formalistic" approach to statutory interpretation, John Manning, offered a series of realistic assertions about contemporary formalism: "[M]odern formalists do not rely much on the-law-is-the-law styles of argument";[106] "modern formalists recognize that language is a social enterprise that yields meaning only in context. Hence, they routinely derive statutory meanings from extratextual sources, including unenacted materials such as cases or treatises that define terms of art or prescribe canons of construction."[107] "Modern formalists acknowledge that all texts require exposition when applied to specific factual situations, and hence that agencies and courts inevitably enjoy some delegated authority to specify the details of statutory meaning."[108] "Formalist Judges routinely use purpose to resolve ambiguity."[109] "If . . . judges must inevitably fill in the blanks of statutory interpretation," Manning allows pragmatically, "it does little violence to formalism to suggest that they design the resulting norms to fit sensibly within the web of structural relationships that the Constitution prescribes."[110]

A leading proponent of a formalistic approach to constitutional interpretation, Lawrence Solum, also stakes out a realistic position: "Formalism requires rule following. . . . But rule-following need not be mechanical in any literal sense of that word. The application of rules to particular facts may require sensitivity to context and purpose. . . . Formalists can take the purposes of rules into account in a variety of ways."[111] "[T]here is no reason for formalism to reject a practice of equity that refuses to apply a legal rule when it would lead to absurd consequences."[112] "A formalism that emphasizes fidelity to legal texts—constitutions, statutes, and precedents—cannot fairly be characterized as conceptualist, much less as relying upon some form of Platonism."[113] "Formalism can and should accept the proposition that more than one outcome in a case can be legally correct. And formalism

can and should accept the notion that the law sometimes confers discretionary authority on legal actors, including judges."[114] "The application of rules to particular situations necessarily involves practical judgment, and legal formalism does not seek to deny this."[115]

In the face of this considerable realism, one must ask, what is it about
their position that makes contemporary formalists distinctively "formalistic"? "The core idea of formalism is that the law (constitutions,
statutes, regulations, and precedent) provides rules and that these
rules can, do, and should provide a public standard for what is lawful
(or not)."[116] Beyond this general position, formalists focus on different
aspects and do not all agree among themselves. And the positions they
take do not owe anything specific to the notion of "formalism." The
loose cluster of positions identified with "formalism" are: they want
clear contractual terms to be enforced as written rather than be modified by courts;[117] they prefer the constraint and predictability of legal
rules over the openness of standards; they emphasize the text of legislation; they object to giving weight to legislative history in the interpretation of statutes; they would not permit purpose to trump the plain
meaning of statutory terms; they advocate adherence to precedent;
they argue that courts ought to defer to other institutional bodies (legislatures, administrative agencies, etc.) when the applicable legal provisions are vague or uncertain, or not rule-like; most argue that courts
should decide in accordance with clear rules even if the legally indicated outcome in a particular case would be unjust.

When this cluster of ideas is taken at the most general level, a broad
contrast among contemporary jurists can be drawn between those
identified as formalists and their opponents: formalists tend to emphasize the reasons why and ways in which legal rules, texts, and precedents can and should control; their opponents tend to emphasize the
limitations of legal rules. There are differences of attitude and emphasis. But these differences are neither deep enough nor sharp enough to
maintain the formalist-realist antithesis. Neither side adopts the complex of (exaggerated) beliefs typically associated, respectively, with formalism or realism.

Both sides—to draw out the key point that carries into the next
chapter—share a balanced realist view of judging. As just elaborated,
contemporary formalists accept the core positions realists espouse
about the openness of law and the limitations of human judges. The
U.S. legal culture has long been consummately realistic about these
matters. As the next chapter shows, realists accept that rules are often
clear and should be (and usually are) followed by judges. Both sides
share common ground that applies to the bulk of law and judging,

which could with equal fit be called "balanced realism" or "balanced formalism" (but for the negative connotations of the latter).

Disagreement between these camps breaks out over second-level issues that typically arise on the margins: what to do when the legal rules are vague or uncertain; whether rules or standards are preferable; whether certainty and predictability matter more than justice or equity; ; what should be done when statutory terms lead to an absurd or undesirable result; and so forth. What matters in these debates are theories about the proper role of judges in a democracy, normative disagreements about the place of justice in law, arguments over the institutional capabilities of judges, empirical disputes about the actual consequences of judicial decisions, arguments over efficiency or social utility, and other such considerations. The arguments raised on both sides of these issues, it is essential to recognize, do not draw on anything within or unique to the notions of formalism or realism. That is because "formalism" and "realism," in the end, are casual terms empty of theoretical content.

10

○ ○ ◉ ● ●

BEYOND THE FORMALIST-REALIST DIVIDE

Still Fighting (Nonexistent) Classical Formalists

How Judges Think, Judge Richard Posner's 2008 summa, is a sustained critique of the delusions of formalism. At the outset he substitutes "legalism" for the term formalism "because it carries less baggage,"[1] but the meaning remains unchanged. "Legalists decide cases by applying preexisting rules or, in some versions of legalism, by employing allegedly distinctive modes of legal reasoning, such as 'legal reasoning by analogy.' They do not legislate, do not exercise discretion other than in ministerial matters (such as scheduling), have no truck with policy, and do not look outside conventional legal texts—mainly statutes, constitutional provisions, and precedents (authoritative judicial decisions)—for guidance in deciding new cases. For legalists, the law is an autonomous domain of knowledge and technique."[2] Posner has relentlessly fought formalism for over two decades. In *Overcoming Law,* published a dozen years ago, his target was "the basic claim of the jurisprudential traditionalist" that law is autonomous: "that law has its own internal logic and therefore that when it changes it does so in response to the promptings of its inner nature, like a caterpillar turning into a moth, rather than in response to political and economic pressures."[3]

As preceding chapters have shown, for more than a century many prominent judges, law professors, and lawyers have many times said precisely the opposite—emphasizing the openness of law to social influences, social changes, and social needs, the uncertainty of law, and the inevitability that judges must occasionally make choices. Not a single notable jurist, past or present, is ever directly quoted for espousing the view that law is autonomous and judging is pure logical reasoning. In every mention of formalism, it is *always* critics who assert that most fellow jurists are formalists who foolishly believe in this wrongheaded vision of law. Judge Posner, the political scientists cited in chapter 7, as well as other avowed realists about judging, write as if the classical legal formalist phantom—never real to begin with—is still thriving and must be slain for us to finally see the light.

Set aside the question of historical accuracy: Who espouses this purported complex of formalist beliefs today? None of the lead ing "new formalists" described in the previous chapter embrace these ideas.

Posner identifies Scalia as *the* prime example.[4] But Scalia has never asserted the combination of positions Posner attributes to legalists/formalists. His basic position is that constitutional provisions and statutes should be interpreted in accordance with the meaning of their terms—as such, a mundane position (although execution is complicated, and his position leads in controversial directions). With respect to the common law, Scalia states unabashedly that judges "make the law," resolving policy issues in the process.[5] "Indeed, it is probably true that in these fields judicial lawmaking can be more freewheeling than ever," Scalia writes, "since the doctrine of *stare decisis* has appreciably eroded."[6] Scalia describes judges in common law cases as reasoning in much the pragmatic fashion that Posner urges that they should reason. Scalia's argument is that judges inappropriately usurp power accorded to legislators when they extend the common law method of judging to the realm of democratically produced statutes and the Constitution. He also regrets the use of broad standards and "totality of circumstances" and "balancing" tests, which grant discretion to judges and increase legal uncertainty.[7] But Scalia recognizes that open provisions have advantages, and he accepts that these "modes of analysis [will be] with us forever."[8] Judging from these positions, Scalia does not resemble the legalist Posner described.

Throughout his book, the deluded legalist serves as the foil for Posner's pragmatic view of judging.[9] He charges that law professors are the primary purveyors of a naive legalist understanding of judging.[10] In law schools: "The motivations and constraints operating on judges, and the judicial uncertainty that results, are ignored, as if judges were computers rather than limited human intellects navigating seas of uncertainty."[11] Legalism time and again is indicted by Posner for its foolish illusions. "Legalism treats law as an autonomous discipline,"[12] he repeats. Legalists believe that judging is purely a matter of "performing logical operations"; hence, it is not relevant desiderata for legalists "that judges are expected to have 'good judgment,' to be wise, experienced, mature; none are qualities requisite in a logician."[13] The deck is thus stacked against legalists, who hold a bevy of evidently daft positions:

> The ideal legalist decision is the product of a syllogism in which a rule of law supplies the major premise, the facts of the case supply the minor one, and the decision is the conclusion. The rule

might have to be extracted from a statute or a constitutional provision, but the legalist model comes complete with a set of rules of interpretation (the "canons of construction"), so that interpretation too becomes a rule-bound activity, purging judicial discretion. The legalist slogan is "the rule of law."[14]

The "legalist" jurist Posner cites for that last delusion is Brian Tamanaha (gulp).[15] Without belaboring the issue, although I have criticized his proposed pragmatic judging,[16] suffice it to say that I have never suggested the set of positions Posner pins on legalists. Nor has any other jurist who can be found. Judge Easterbrook, another formalist identified by Posner, advocates a textual approach: "sticking to lower levels of generality, preferring the language and structure of the law whenever possible over its legislative history and imputed [legislative] values."[17] Easterbrook believes that, in the interest of certainty and predictability, people (or their lawyers) should be able to rely upon the apparent meaning of legal provisions; and he believes that judicial resort to legislative history to search for intent encourages manipulation (via strategic insertions by staffers in the legislative record) and expands the discretion of judges.[18] Easterbrook holds these positions—debatable but hardly outlandish—without adopting any of the deluded formalist views Posner castigates; Easterbrook explicitly acknowledges, as indicated in the previous chapter, that meaning is often unclear, that social conventions infuse interpretation, that context and purpose matter, and that often there is "no right answer" to hard questions.[19]

The upshot of these observations is not the obvious point that Posner has constructed a straw man. It is to demonstrate that the tale about classical legal formalism continues to shape the debate over judging at the highest level. Posner is one of the nation's most influential judges as well as one of the most respected and prolific legal theorists. He is the Holmes of our age in more ways than one. What Posner says about judging carries heft. Political scientists who study judging will find in Posner's book abundant reinforcement for their conviction that modern jurists are still beguiled by the delusions of mechanical jurisprudence. "I am struck," he declares, "by how unrealistic are the conceptions of the judge held by most people, including practicing lawyers and eminent law professors, . . . —and even by some judges."[20]

The Formalism of Avowed Realists

Political scientists will also find an eminently quotable trove of skeptical-sounding statements about judging. To less than careful readers, Posner will sound like a modern-day Jerome Frank, the most extreme realist. "Because the materials of legalist decision making fail to generate acceptable answers to all the legal questions that American judges are required to decide, judges perforce have occasional—indeed rather frequent—recourse to other sources of judgment, *including their own political opinions or policy judgments, even their idiosyncrasies.* As a result, *law is shot through with politics* and with much else besides that does not fit a legalist model of decision making."[21] Judges are regularly confronted with "open areas" "in which the orthodox (the legalist) methods of analysis yield unsatisfactory and sometimes no conclusions, thereby allowing or even dictating that emotion, personality, policy intuitions, ideology, politics, background, and experience will determine a judge's decision."[22] In the conclusion: "So judging is political."[23]

Statements of this sort, scattered throughout the book, are like tossing red meat at the eager skeptics of judging—as Posner well knows. A political scientist reviewing the book enthused, with an air of vindication, that "this book by a highly regarded sitting judge confirms what social scientists . . . have demonstrated. Politics, ideology, and strategic concerns infuse judicial decisionmaking."[24]

Skeptics who take Posner's bait, however, are being fooled. Recall that more than a hundred years ago Judge Thomas Cooley—a purported formalist—acknowledged that disagreements about the interpretation and application of law "must always exist so long as there is variety in human minds, human standards, and human transactions."[25] Recall that Judge Lehman acknowledged in 1924 that law runs out and judges must make choices.[26] He added that "no thoughtful judge can fail to note that in conferences of the court, differences of opinion are based at least to some extent upon differences of viewpoint."[27] Recall that Judge Wald recently expressed a "ho-hum" reaction to judicial politics studies that found that "personal philosophies may well play a significant role in judging."[28] Judges have admitted many times over in the past hundred years, as conveyed throughout this book, that law runs out or supports contrary outcomes and that personal views can affect legal interpretations.

Judges also uniformly hasten to emphasize, however, that, notwithstanding the openness of law and the limitations of judges, their decisions are substantially determined by the law. And Judge Posner is no exception. After bluntly declaring (for maximum effect) that "judging is political," he soon tacks in the opposite direction: "But judging is not just personal and political. It is also impersonal and nonpolitical in the sense that many, *indeed most,* judicial decisions really are the product of a neutral application of rules not made up for the occasion to facts fairly found. Such decisions exemplify what is commonly called 'legal formalism,' though the word I prefer is 'legalism.' "[29]

Although easily overlooked beneath his blaring skeptical assertions, Posner has consistently said this for many years: "[T]he social interest in certainty of legal obligations requires the judge to stick pretty close to statutory text and judicial precedent in most cases and thus to behave, much of the time anyway, as a formalist."[30] Posner often repeats that a substantial proportion of time judges duly adhere to precedent because that is what their role demands.[31] Most judges, he says, strive to live up to the standards of judging to enhance their self-esteem and to earn the accolades and respect of their judicial colleagues and legal audiences.[32] A "willful" judge is a bad judge, according to the norms of judging, and judges aspire to be good judges.[33] "The business of judges is to enforce the law,"[34] Posner says, and that's what judges do.

Posner's statements about politics and ideology relate entirely to judging in the "open area,"[35] to the subset of cases with "legal uncertainty."[36] But "most cases are routine,"[37] he tells us, and the "routine cases are those that can be decided by legalist techniques."[38] Posner recognizes that the vast bulk of disputes never make it into court because the expected legal outcome is clear; most judicial decisions are not appealed "because the case is 'controlled' by precedent or clear statutory language."[39] One must wonder why Judge Posner thought it appropriate to pitch the book as an assault against prevailing legalist delusions when, by his own account, the legalist position is not a delusion at all for the mass of routine cases.

Stripping away the rhetorical excesses on both sides, the differences between Posner and his opponents play out on relatively narrow—albeit important—terrain. Legalists want judges to follow legal texts, precedents, and methods as far as they will go.[40] Posner similarly insists that pragmatic judges usually do, and should, follow texts and precedents when clear.[41] Both sides agree that this covers the bulk of cases.

Posner puts a different gloss on what comes to the same position. Legalists say judges are *obligated* to follow the law; Posner says judges should do what advances the social good, but he adds that society benefits from consistent interpretation of the legal rules and adherence to precedent. He acknowledges that "a pragmatist committed to judging a legal system by the results the system produced might think that the best results would be produced if the judges did not make pragmatic judgments but simply applied the rules."[42] Legalists say judges have a *duty* to set forth a reasoned, legally supported basis for their decision; with rascally delight, Posner says those are the "rules of the judicial game,"[43] though he admits that judges readily comply with these rules and obtain satisfaction in doing so.

When the law offers *no clear answer* or runs out—*that* is when matters get tricky, for legalists and pragmatists alike. As Posner recognizes, "Legalists acknowledge that their methods cannot close the deal every time."[44] Some jurists—Ronald Dworkin, for example—insist that a superior legal answer can always be determined,[45] so the judge must keep at it until the correct answer is worked out. But "legalists" do not necessarily agree with Dworkin. Whoever the label encompasses (by Posner's account, most in legal circles), "legalists" do not hold a uniform position on what a judge should do when no legal answer can be ranked stronger than others. Some "legalists" might well agree with Posner that if the law is truly uncertain—if no answer can be ranked superior in legal terms—the judge should decide in terms of what is best for the community.

As for *his* preferred method, Posner admits that pragmatism does not tell judges how to figure out what are the "best" ends for the community.[46] He also concedes that judges can only guess at the likely consequences of their decisions.[47] His final advice to a pragmatic judge offers scant guidance: "[T]here isn't too much more to say to the would-be pragmatic judge than make the most reasonable decision you can, all things considered."[48] Individual pragmatic judges will have different views of desirable social ends, and they will often lack reliable empirical information to make informed judgments about what decision will best advance those ends. The complexity and uncertainty involved in predicting the future consequences of decisions are immense. Opponents of pragmatic judging emphasize these flaws when objecting that Posner's preferred approach invites judges to engage in uncontrolled political decision making, contrary to their judicial role, a task for which they are ill equipped.[49]

The overarching point here is that the disagreement between Posner and his opponents mostly relates to the relatively small subset of legally uncertain cases (the precise proportion is unknown). For the bulk of cases there is substantial agreement about what judges *are doing*, as well as agreement about what they *should be* doing (with competing reasons for *why* they should be doing it). This is the rule-based aspect that balanced realism recognizes.

The Basic Tenets of Balanced Realism about Judging

Beneath the attacks on sham opponents that infect the discussion, a balanced realism is what most jurists have been saying about judging all along. It was expressed in Lieber's writings in the 1830s, in Cooley's in the 1890s, and in Cardozo's in the 1920s. It was the view of Pound and Llewellyn. It was the view expressed by many judges in the past hundred years, quoted throughout this book (including Posner and Scalia). It is in the recognition by Critical Legal Studies doyen Duncan Kennedy that "[j]udges are, to a significant extent, practically 'bound' by law and often, often, often declare and apply rules that they would never vote for it they were legislators."[50]

Legal rules and principles are irreducibly open and various problems unavoidably arise in connection with the interpretation and application of legal rules and precedents. Judges are unique individuals with bents, biases, and various strengths and limitations, as well as differences in moral and political views, and differing views of judging (beyond a common core). These aspects inherent to law, and to human judges, combine to create a zone of uncertainty and variation in judicial decision making. It has always been so. Nonetheless, legal rules frequently work and judges frequently render rule-bound decisions. All of this has been known for a long time. A few generalizations taken from previous chapters, particularly from judges, will draw out the basic insights of a balanced realist view.

Subconscious Bent of Judges Distinguished from Willful Judging

A balanced realism *expects* that the bents of judges will influence their decisions in various ways that are not conscious or deliberate. At a subconscious level, this occurs through what can be loosely called (without theoretical pretensions) *cognitive framing*, which relates to the categories of thought and perception through which cognition takes place, including language, concepts, ideas, and beliefs.[51] Cognitive framing accompanies, enables, and shapes thought and perception, triggering responses, influencing actions and decisions.[52] It is informed by social categories and is implanted and perpetuated through socialization.[53] This is not a flaw of human reasoning but a condition of thought that entails that there is no unmediated perception.

When judges perceive facts, interpret the law, and render judgments, they are influenced by cognitive framing in the same ways that all cognition is influenced.[54] Their thought processes operate through, and on the basis of, this deeply implanted social foundation. Training in legal language, categories, and knowledge, and participating in legal and judicial practices, also involve the transmission and implantation of cognitive framing,[55] a legal layer—which the legal realists identified among the factors that help stabilize the interpretation of legal rules.

No sharp line distinguishes cognitive framing from prejudices, which are often lodged at the level of cognitive framing.[56] The extent to which undesired effects of cognitive framing—which typically operates beneath awareness—can be counteracted is unclear and varies among individuals. It cannot be eliminated entirely, for cognitive framing is a condition of thought. In particular contexts, certain influences lodged at the cognitive level can, with effort and attention, be lessened, or at least brought to awareness.[57] For this to happen, the subconscious cognitive frame must be disrupted in some way.[58] Cardozo and Llewellyn (among others) suggested that the exchange of views on appellate panels, being confronted with an opposing position from a colleague, helps to offset the implicit personal bent of judges (an assertion consistent with the panel effects demonstrated by quantitative studies).

Think of cognitive frames as prescription sunglasses with different tints. Different judges have different prescriptions and different colors, which come in different shades of intensity. The lenses worn by all American judges share significant commonalities: that obtained from shared indoctrination into the legal tradition and shared indoctrination into the broader social community. These are legal conventions and social conventions, respectively, which shape meaning and interpretation. Because of these shared elements, despite having differently colored glasses and magnifications, judges often see much the same thing when looking at legal rules and fact situations. Owing to the differences in their respective cognitive lenses, however, they also sometimes perceive the law and facts at issue differently. Judges can be reminded, especially through exchanges with colleagues who disagree with their conclusions, that the glasses they wear have subtle effects on their perception, but for the most part they see through the lens without ever contemplating its influence.

Cognitive framing is distinct from willful judging—with a forthcoming caveat. Cognitive framing affects everyone and operates beneath consciousness. Willful judging, in contrast, is not ubiquitous and is not inevitable. The former influences a judge's *sincere*, noninstrumental interpretation of the law and facts; with the latter, a judge brings an instrumental attitude to the law and facts, marshaling both to achieve a desired end. The former judge genuinely works to arrive at the strongest legal interpretation; the latter judge is oriented toward achieving an objective regardless of whether it is the strongest legal interpretation. In the former mode, the law is seen as a guidepost toward the decision that the judge is obligated to follow, whereas in the latter the law mainly operates as a constraint that must be slipped if necessary. The caveat is that these two distinct modes of thought can shade into one another. Subconscious motivated reasoning—a phenomenon in which people see what they wish to see, or reason sincerely unaware of an underlying slant toward a preferred result—commingles willfulness with cognitive framing. But this mixed mode does not efface the general distinction.

From the outside, it is impossible to discern whether a particular decision is attributable to cognitive framing or willful judging.[59] They can produce the same result: a liberal judge, for example, may render a liberal decision either through sincere reasoning influenced by cognitive framing or through willful reasoning to achieve that end. Decisions produced either way look the same externally, supported by legal reasoning and citations to authority (the written opinion is an effort at producing the most persuasive legal justification, independent of which decisional orientation led to the conclusion). This is the ambiguity of judicial opinions described in chapter 4. The main check is an internal one: the judge's integrity and degree of commitment to engage in an unbiased search for the correct legal answer. There are also external checks against willful judging: legal decisions that do not meet the standards of acceptable legal analysis or that raise a strong suspicion of willful reasoning risk reversal by reviewing tribunals or condemnation from observers.

Judges deciding in a willful manner violate their judicial role obligations, while judges deciding in a manner that is shaped by cognitive framing or subconscious prejudices do not. Although the effect might be the same, and both will be objectionable from the losing party's perspective, balanced realism condemns the former but accepts the latter as an inherent aspect of human decision making that cannot be erased.

Purposes and Consequences

A balanced realism *expects* that when judges render legal decisions, except in the most routine cases, the purposes behind the applicable rules and the consequences of the decision will have a bearing. Rules are implicitly understood in terms of their underlying purposes and decisions are always made in concrete contexts with immediate results that cannot be screened out from the judge's mind. This does not mean that consideration of purpose or consequences dominates the interpretation of the rule or the decision made, nor is it necessarily conscious. The effect depends on the judge and the circumstances of the case. When a judge is especially concerned about ends (striving either to arrive at a desired end or to avoid an unpalatable one), the judge may engage in a mixed form of reasoning best described as rule-oriented instrumental rationality.[60] A judge who pays attention to consequence is not, by virtue of that alone, a willful judge; what matters is whether the judge's dominant orientation is to produce the correct (the strongest) legal decision or to reach a desired result.

Conflicts, Gaps, and Ambiguities in Law (Legal Uncertainty)

A balanced realism *expects* that uncertainties will inevitably arise in the interpretation and application of legal rules and principles. This is not about bad results or outcomes inconsistent with purposes—it is about uncertainties owing to gaps, conflicts, or ambiguities. Gaps will always exist because not everything can be anticipated or accounted for in advance; conflicts may arise between different bodies of rules; sometimes general rules can point to more than one outcome; and language is subject to ambiguity. This is controversial because the answer is not found in the standing law but rather is produced by the decision, and what is produced is essentially contestable.

The norms that surround the propriety of these judicial choices vary depending upon type of legal provision at issue. Judges have the greatest leeway when dealing with uncertainties in the common law, their traditional redoubt. But judges are under constant pressure from the view that law making is the preserve of democratically accountable bodies. This is especially confining for judges when dealing with uncertainties in legislative and constitutional interpretation. It is an unenviable bind: judges are not supposed to make the law, in theory, but when uncertainties arise the judge must make choices. And that is what they do.

The Significance of Legally Uncertain Cases

The region of legal uncertainty is where judges render decisions with the least legal guidance, and where judges' particular mix of legal and social views has the most leeway and impact—though still in a context thick with legal norms. This is why the political views of Supreme Court justices, who hear the highest proportion of legally uncertain cases, manifest a much stronger relationship with their legal decisions (although significantly short of a complete alignment) in comparison to lower court judges.

The proportion of legally uncertain cases is relatively small in relation to the mass of legal disputes and filed cases (uncertainty over the provable facts may have a greater impact on cases than legal uncertainty). Legal academics often emphasize the presence of legal uncertainty, but this gives a false impression of the whole. As critical theorist Duncan Kennedy observed (perhaps surprisingly, given the focus of critics on legal uncertainty), "[A] vast amount of energy goes into the fabrication of gaps, inconsistencies, and ambiguities where the 'real' objection is to the consequences of a formal system."[61] Legal academics also tend to see more legal uncertainty because their attention typically centers on appellate cases. At higher court levels, a greater proportion of cases is legally uncertain.

Because judges in legally uncertain cases have a greater capacity to mold the law in new or desired directions influenced by their views, these cases have an impact that exceeds their proportionately small numbers. For this reason, although political views come into play mainly at the margins in lower court judging (the bulk of cases are routine), this does not mean that their impact is marginal. The cumulative accretive impact of the multitude of individual decisions made in this fashion gives shape and direction to the outer edges of the law.

Bad Rules and Bad Results

A balanced realism *expects* that judges are sometimes confronted with what they consider "bad rules" or "bad results." The judge may consider a given legal rule unfair, unjust, unwise, or ill advised (not in the social interest, immoral, stupid, obsolete, inconsistent with surrounding legal rules, etc.), or overly broad or too narrow in relation to the desired objectives. Bad rules may produce bad results, but not all bad results are from bad rules. A sound rule can produce bad results owing to the particular circumstances of the case: when the application clashes with the purposes behind the rule, or the unique facts at hand make its application unfair, unjust, too harsh, or undesirable (measured in terms of either individual justice or the social good).

Judges draw from a variety of considerations, legal as well as extralegal, when making judgments that a rule is bad or a particular result is bad. Judges will not be uniform in their assessments, especially when their evaluation is influenced by their extralegal views. Some judges will be exercised by certain rules or results that other judges will find unobjectionable. When thinking about this problem, it must be kept in mind that with respect to many cases judges will not have strong feelings about the rules or results one way or the other.

Judges do not take a uniform position or follow the same course in such situations. They may initially wrestle with the legal rules and the facts to see if the rule can be interpreted in a way that is less objectionable, or if the bad result can be avoided. If that cannot be accomplished without doing violence to the law or facts, the judge faces a quandary. The standard approach with respect to statutes, although not universally adhered to, is that a judge should apply the law regardless of whether it is considered bad or produces bad results in a given case.[62] In connection with the common law, some judges are more prepared than others to step in and change an obsolete or socially detrimental precedent. Some judges give priority to doing justice over compliance with the law in cases of conflict between the two, while others take the opposition position. Even an avowed stickler for following the rules may, under compelling circumstances, depart from what the rules require.[63]

Situations like this highlight the latent rule of thumb potential of all rules.

Two Distinct Types of Hard Cases

What jurists refer to as "hard cases" usually fall into one of the two preceding categories: cases involving gaps, conflicts, or ambiguities in the law, and cases involving bad rules or bad results. It confuses matters to lump the two together under the same label because they raise distinct dilemmas. The former asks what a judge should do when the law is unclear; the latter asks what a judge should do when a clear law or its consequences is deemed objectionable. Both situations are "hard" in the sense that there is no easy course for the judge. They sometimes merge, for instance, when a bad result encourages a judge to see the law as less clear than initially thought, paving the way for a different result. But the distinction between these types of hard cases is generally marked. The former is continuous with legal analysis in which the judge engages in a difficult search for the correct legal answer, whereas the latter raises questions about the extent of the judge's obligation to follow the law.

What both types of hard cases share is an enhanced potential for the influence of the personal values of judges on law: in the former because legal uncertainty provides greater leeway for choice, and in the latter when the judge's values have been provoked by bad rules or bad results to a degree that affects the judge's legal decision.

Open Provisions

The common law and statutes contain a variety of standards like fairness and reasonableness, or provisions that require balancing, or that require judges (and juries) to make judgments. The judgments called for cannot be made in a rule-like fashion and are not determined by legal factors alone. Judges nonetheless will often agree in their judgments because they have undergone a similar training in the legal tradition and its values, and many share social views that span other differences. But judges (and juries) may also disagree in these judgments, particularly when they have different moral and political views and different perspectives on the facts.

The Infusion of Extralegal Factors and Considerations

A balanced realism *accepts* (indeed embraces) that social factors and considerations play into judicial decision making in various ways. At the most basic level, this occurs through language and cognitive framing, which are infused with social meanings and values. Owing to this shared social background substrate, every legal interpreter from the community immediately knows that "No vehicles in the park" does not exclude a baby stroller or wheelchair. Social factors and considerations come into play when judges implicitly or explicitly recur to the purposes behind legislation or common law rules in the course of interpretation or application.[64] Judges regularly contemplate social consequences when faced with a choice between two plausible interpretations of a statute, or between two alternative possible extensions of an existing line of precedent. Social considerations come into play when judges resolve conflicts, gaps, and ambiguities in the law, especially when techniques of legal analysis (canons of interpretation, coherence with other legal doctrine) prove insufficient. Social considerations also come into play when judges believe that the legal rules or results at hand are unjust or socially detrimental, or that a given rule is obsolete. Social considerations come into play in open standards that call for judgments.

Whether subconscious or conscious, unavoidable or resistible, invited or prohibited, implicit or explicit, social factors and considerations seep into the judicial interpretation and application of the common law, statutes, and the Constitution in the various ways set forth above. Judges are a sieve through which social factors filter. This is the role of politics in judging—although one must not forget that this process always operates through thick legal screens. And "politics" is a tendentious label for what amount to all-enveloping social influences. As the historical jurisprudents of the nineteenth century recognized, this manifold social influence on judging is as unavoidable as it is necessary.

Law is embedded within society, and society oozes into law though every pore. Although it has often been pinned on "formalists," the notion that law is autonomous from society is inconceivable, and no U.S. jurist of note has advocated it. The self-understanding of the common law tradition has always been that, via the medium of judges, law matches society. Now much of this is done through legislation. Law has its own internal language, concepts, practices, and imperatives that shape its operation and development, but the legislators, judges, and jurists who produce the law in the United States do so in connection with social values, social problems, social situations, social concerns, and social interests.

The Limitations of Human Judges

Balanced realism recognizes that the limitations of judges as human decision makers are unavoidable. Judges are not machines or computers. This has all been said many times, frequently by judges. Judges are subject to cognitive framing, they sometimes engage in motivated reasoning, and they have prejudices, predilections, and preferences that can subconsciously or consciously influence their legal decisions. Judges have different intellectual abilities, different masteries of legal knowledge, different capacities to engage in legal reasoning, different personality traits, different interests. They have differences in work ethic, differences in integrity and honesty, differences in commitment to the judicial role. They have different temperaments and differences in ability and willingness to engage in self-reflection and self-control. Some judges are wise and thoughtful, while others are less so. These human factors will always be a part of judging.

Judicial Decisions Determined by the Law

Notwithstanding all of the above, a balanced realism recognizes that judicial decisions frequently are consistent with and determined by the law. The preceding social factors come into play in the law within a context suffused with and structured by legal factors that lend it a legally governed rule-based quality. All judges and lawyers have been indoctrinated in legal principles, legal concepts, legal rules, legal standards, modes of legal interpretation, and modes of judging, inculcated in the course of legal education and legal practice. Upon ascending to the bench, judges also become immersed in existing judicial practices. This creates the thick meaning-infused context within which legal argumentation and judging take places. Deeply integrated with this legal layer is a shared social layer of language and cultural views upon which it sits. Llewellyn referred to legal indoctrination as the "law-spectacles" with which judges see and engage in the law.[65] An essential component of rule-bound judging is that judges internalize and act pursuant to the commitment to engage in the good-faith application of the law.[66]

The institutional context of judging blankets judges in multiple legal layers. Judges make legal decisions surrounded by colleagues, within a stable hierarchical institution, with the participation of and under the gaze of a legally trained audience of participants and observers.

Lawyers, law clerks, fellow judges, and legal academics engage with judges in working out legal answers and their implications in problematic situations. Appellate review adds a check against errors in interpretation or application. The engagement of other legally trained actors, particularly fellow judges oriented toward producing the correct legal answer, as Cardozo and others have argued,[67] helps hammer out a collective product that is distinctively legal in a way that transcends the views and desires of the individuals involved.

This reinforcing amalgamation of shared conscious orientation, shared legal indoctrination, shared judicial role orientation, shared social understandings, and shared institutional context stabilizes legal interpretation sufficiently for judges to see law and decide cases in much the same way most of the time regardless of differences in personal backgrounds, values, and preferences.[68] This is what the legal realists meant when they insisted that legal rules *in isolation* do not decide cases.

The Ongoing Construction of Law

A balanced realism understands that law is continuously being worked out by judges. Little conscious thought is required in typified situations or with respect to simple rules and facts. For anything more complex, however, in the various problematic situations described above, the aspect of law in-need-of-construction or filling out comes to the fore.

The story about formalism promotes the unrealistic image of self-applying legal rules; skeptical realism promotes the equally unrealistic opposite image of human judges pursuing their personal preferences beneath a veneer of legal rules. Informed by these extremes, it seems natural to interpret unsettled aspects of law or judging as indications of flaws or grounds for skepticism: dissenting opinions, splits among courts, judges changing their positions, negotiation or compromise on a panel, deferring to a majority in the interest of speaking with a single voice, or other actions beyond plain rule-application. If legal rules were perfectly preexistent and judges were calculating machines, these situations *would be* indications of flaws. But mechanical jurisprudence is impossible. It is a mistake, therefore, to think of these unavoidable aspects as flaws rather than as inherent conditions of law and judging.

A balanced realism holds that many corners of law are always in the making through judicial construction, in ways large and small, which does not defeat the broader enterprise of rule-bound judicial decision making. When evaluated in terms of what is possible, which takes the limitations of law and human judges as given, a system that manifests substantial uniformity in legal interpretations and decisions across judges is a highly successful legal system.

The Normative Disputes Will Continue

As the end of this exploration nears, there is disappointing news: the general recognition of balanced realism articulated in this book will not magically dissolve the many differences that now divide jurists in debates over judicial decision making. That is because disagreements over what should be done in problematic legal situations are driven by normative and empirical differences with solid arguments on all sides. Judge Richard Posner the avowed pragmatist and Judge Antonin Scalia the avowed textualist, for example, adopt contrasting stances on how judges should reason when confronted with legal uncertainty that are based on their contrasting views of the capacities of judges and the proper role of judges within a democracy.

Several of these debates trace as far back as Aristotle.[69] Some theorists and judges say the law must be applied as written regardless of an unjust outcome (to preserve certainty and predictability), whereas others say justice has primacy and the rule must give way. Some say obsolete or socially detrimental laws should be explicitly repudiated, or gutted through interpretation while maintaining the facade of compliance; others say that in a democracy legal change must come from legislatures. Some say that the purpose behind legislation trumps the text when the two are at odds; others take the opposite view. Some say that, when faced with a gap in the law, judges should match the community's values, or produce the welfare-enhancing outcome, or do what they think reasonable legislators would have done, or try to find the result that best fits surrounding legal rules and principles, or do what they think is right. Some distrust judges or see them as possessing limited capabilities and consequently want them to be restrained, whereas others place great hopes in judges as the vehicles of justice or positive social change. Abiding by rules has advantages and disadvantages; using standards, allowing judicial discretion, and engaging in particularistic decision making all have advantages and disadvantages. Disagreements arise on other aspects of law and judging as well. Each position on these various issues has something to commend it.

The position a judge holds on these disputed questions will have a direct impact on how that judge will decide a case when these issues arise. When standard legal analysis fails to provide the answer, Judge Posner and Justice Scalia will reason in quite different fashions. The latter will stick close to legal texts, while the former engages in a more broad-ranging analysis of the legal consequences of the decision.

Balanced realism will not resolve or lessen any of these real differences.

Nonetheless, a general recognition of balanced realism promises a change for the better. The two false extremes of this antithesis generate misunderstandings, misdirected efforts, and misleading statements about judging. No one thinks that law is autonomous and judging is mechanical deduction, and rare is the informed jurist who thinks that judges are engaged in the single-minded pursuit of their personal preferences. With these extreme positions set aside, the grounds of real normative and empirical disagreement will be more apparent and the discussion more focused and productive.

The Lesson of Balanced Realism

A final irony must be uncovered: although formalism is the villain that draws the most critical fire, the greater danger to the legal system today is posed not by excessive formalism but by excessive skepticism about judging. This excessive skepticism—often put forth in the name of "realism," but truly unrealistic—is unwarranted and corrosive. There is a vast difference in operation and consequences between a system that instructs judges to "Decide what you think right" and one that instructs judges to "Decide in accordance with the law." There is a vast difference between individual judges who decide cases in terms of the outcome they prefer, manipulating the legal rules to justify that outcome, and judges who to strive to produce the legally correct decision.

A prime source of contemporary skepticism about judging is the Supreme Court. The Supreme Court hears about one-tenth of 1 percent of federal court cases, a minuscule number winnowed and selected out from the massive total.[70] These are legally uncertain cases or cases that involve bad rules or bad results. They often have political salience. In virtually every case, the law is in need of construction. Legal guidance is limited. No higher tribunal reviews their decisions (though Congress can undo their statutory decisions). Inevitably, the personal views of justices will have an impact in a measurable proportion of their decisions.

To stop at this realization, however, misses much. Blanket assertions that judging on the U.S. Supreme Court is political obliterate the stark differences that follow from alternative decision-making orientations and institutional arrangements. This is evident if one examines the

Chinese system, where the Standing Committee of the National People's Congress has final authority to issue interpretations of the constitution and legislation, and where party committees review court decisions at various levels.[71] Or consider Iran, where judicial review of legislation and final interpretation of the constitution is conducted by the Guardian Council—staffed by cleric jurists—the same body that approves candidates for national office. The Chinese and Iranian institutions, both with controlling authority over legal interpretation, are "political" in a sense that does not apply to the U.S. Supreme Court. An extraordinary variety of courts and systems of judging exist around the world, some significantly more politically accountable or political in nature than others.[72]

Court observers have recognized for two centuries that the political views of justices come into play in Supreme Court decisions. Justices have admitted that they weigh consequences and are sometimes called upon to make what amounts to political decisions.[73] But this does not mean that judging on the Supreme Court can be reduced to political decision making. Over a third of Supreme Court decisions are unanimous despite political differences (36 percent from 1995 to 2005);[74] the justices' votes do not invariably line up with their personal views; and justices vary in the extent to which their decisions align with their political views. Quantitative studies show that justices' views about adherence to precedent and deference to Congress, as well as their general jurisprudential theory, have an impact on their decisions.[75] Law thus matters even in the most legally uncertain cases. As long as individual justices are genuinely oriented in their decision making to produce the correct legal answer, as long as their decisions must be justified in terms of conventionally acceptable legal reasoning and authority, this is legal decision making with political influences more so than political decision making with legal influences.

The greatest error committed in perceptions of judging, a mistake that fans unwarranted skepticism today, is to extrapolate from the U.S. Supreme Court to judging on other courts. The Supreme Court is a court unto itself. The factors identified above that enhance the potential influence of political views do not operate to the same extent on the lower federal courts (state high courts share some of these characteristics but not others).

Notwithstanding the multitude of differences in their surrounding circumstance, all judges on all courts in the United States share a core orientation. In rudimentary terms, it comes to this collection of ideas: apply the law, do not favor one side over the other, be fair; when the law is in doubt, strive to figure out the strongest legal answer; willful judging is inappropriate. This orientation holds across all levels of the judiciary across all types of cases. This is the most a rule-of-law system of judging can hope for—and it is enough.

What makes a system of judging effectively rule bound despite the limitations of law and human judgment is the commitment on the part of judges to render rule-bound decisions, even when (especially when) this is difficult to carry through. Judging is rule bound only if judges are committed to abide by the rules. If this commitment diminishes among the individuals who serve as judges, a less rule-bound system of judging will come about.

AFTERWORD

○ ○ ● ● ●

THESE CLOSING REFLECTIONS are an "afterword" in the full sense that the study of judging in this book is completed. I could not leave off, however, without saying a few words about a compelling question raised by this exploration. If the evidence and argument in this book are correct, we have collectively bought into a largely false story that became common currency in law and political science, with potentially harmful consequences.

How could this have happened? I ask not to condemn others who have been taken in by this story—for I believed it and repeated it as well—but in wonderment that it occurred on such a grand scale and lasted for so long. It is sobering to be reminded of the real effects, with much at stake, that false ideas can have when widely disseminated and taken as true.

A few contributing factors stand out.

Scholars centrally involved in the creation and entrenchment of the story about the formalists were driven by political motives. Several generations of progressive or leftist critics of courts (Pound, Frank, the Left in the 1960s and 1970s) constructed accounts of beliefs about judging that served their respective political agendas. The particular agenda of each generation differed, but across these differences they shared a critical, reformist orientation that was served by attacking aspects of rule-oriented judging. Allied implicitly by this orientation, later accounts built on elements of earlier ones—mechanical jurisprudence morphing into legal formalism—to become mutually reinforcing. Over time, as it became widely accepted, the political impetus behind this story receded from view.

Another contributing factor has been the tendency of histories and theories to be written in terms of canonical figures and stock narratives. The familiar string repeated many times here is: the formalists; Holmes; Pound; Cardozo; the realists; then us moderns (descendents of the realists). Stock narratives are constructed by scholars around easily identifiable positions, often represented by good and bad characters (iconoclasts and reactionaries). Canonical figures get close attention, while the mass of their contemporaries fade, no longer read or remembered, although many were as famous in their own day as the figures now considered canonical.

The citation practices of legal academics also contributed to the entrenchment of the formalist-realist story. Legal academics routinely support claims by citing an authoritative figure who made the same assertion. Pound claimed that judges believed in and reasoned in a mechanical fashion; others cited Pound for this proposition, and others in turn cited those who cited Pound, and so forth. A massive body of citations can be built in this manner to give the impression of solidly supported claims, but the whole rests on little more than the word of a handful of authoritative figures.

The stock narratives here were repeated again and again, permeating different realms of discourse (legal history, legal theory, political science, legal sociology, the entire legal culture), until they were simply taken as true. I was taught by my professors the stories about the formalists and realists, and in turn I have taught my students the same. Few of the many people who confidently repeated these stock narratives (including me) actually conducted an independent examination into its underlying basis, and those who did often limited their investigation to canonical figures (to Holmes, Pound, Cardozo, Frank, and Llewellyn). In the development and transmission of knowledge, we all rely heavily upon the work of others, especially on experts, who in this case (legal historians and legal theorists) appeared to agree about the basics of the story.

Experts are trained in standard narratives, which constitute knowledge within the field that all learn in the course of becoming an expert. This is how academic knowledge is reproduced. The experts often take the general stock narratives for granted, while doing research to shed new light on particular aspects.[1] Potentially disconfirming material they stumble across—like William Hammond's extraordinarily realistic 1881 observations about judging—is seen through the lens of the narrative. There is a natural tendency to explain away contrary evidence of this sort in a way that preserves the standard account: "That's just more proto-realism." The entrenched stock narrative thus enjoys a protective barrier against challenge.

A major factor that contributed to the spread and entrenchment of the formalist-realist divide is the seductive attraction of narratives constructed around polar opposites. Stark oppositions of this sort make a story more compelling and easier to repeat and grasp (legal history); they allow for sharper distinctions and analyses (legal theory); and they help build simplified models (quantitative studies). Legal historians, legal theorists, and political scientists may say they knew all along that matters were more complicated but nonetheless insist that the formalist-realist antithesis is justified because it is useful. Simplified oppositions can indeed be illuminating, if essentially correct, and if those who offer them constantly remind that they are oversimplifications. In this case, however, the formalist-realist divide is baseless historically and theoretically, and it distorts views of judging. *This* opposition obscures more than it clarifies. And those who invoke the formalist-realist divide keep talking about it as if it is fundamentally real, not an oversimplification.

Finally, the dynamics of interactions across academic disciplines have played a role. A lot of cross-fertilization takes place among legal theory, legal history, and political science. This healthy exchange expands the knowledge base of each and infuses each with fresh ideas. But there are costs as well. Distortions may occur when ideas are selectively extracted and implanted from one discipline to another. Political scientists, for example, relied upon an erroneous understanding of the legal realists to build their attitudinal model of judging. Another risk is that an error in one field may infect others; the error might be corrected in its field of origin even as it continues to spread elsewhere. In response to earlier drafts of this book, a few legal historians assured me that—although the conventional story about the formalist age has not been repudiated (and legal historians continue to repeat it)—most in the field have been aware for some time that it is flawed. That is no doubt news to people outside of legal history.

The above factors combined to produce and perpetuate the now-dominant formalist-realist divide. In hindsight it appears shockingly lacking in substance. It was a politically inspired story repeated innumerable times, given credibility by a string of citations to authoritative figures, resting on a wobbly, unsupported set of thin legs.

This is an unsettling image for anyone who believes, as I do, that scholars must strive to produce histories and theories that fit the facts without distortion. This is not the naive assertion that the political views of scholars do not matter, but an insistence that this political bent be disciplined by a commitment to be true to the evidence (the same is asked of judges with respect to their legal decisions). The enterprise of knowledge production depends upon adherence to these commitments.

Further reflections along these lines would be presumptuous. Readers must decide whether the standard account of the formalists and the realists is as comprehensively flawed as I believe. If I am right, in this instance our collective construction of knowledge went spectacularly amiss.

NOTES

○ ○ ● ● ●

CHAPTER ONE
INTRODUCTION

1. Chris Guthrie, Jeffrey J. Rachlinski, and Andrew J. Wistrich, "Blinking on the Bench: How Judges Decide Cases,"93 *Cornell L. Rev.* 1, 2 (2007).

2. Virginia A. Hettinger, Stefanie A. Lindquist, and Wendy L. Martinek, *Judging on a Collegial Court* (Charlottesville: Univ. of Virginia Press 2006) 30.

3. William M. Wiecek, *Liberty under Law: The Supreme Court in American Life* (Baltimore: John Hopkins Univ. Press 1988) 187.

4. Brian Leiter, "Positivism, Formalism, Realism,"99 *Colum. L. Rev.* 1138, 1145–46 (1999).

5. Id. 1147 n. 3.

6. Mathieu Deflem, *Sociology of Law: Visions of a Scholarly Tradition* (New York: Cambridge Univ. Press 2008) 98.

7. Maureen A. Flanagan, *America Reformed: Progressives and Progressivisms, 1890s–1920s* (New York: Oxford Univ. Press 2007) 121. Morton Keller repeats the same narrative in *America's Three Regimes: A New Political History* (New York: Oxford Univ. Press 2007) 158.

8. Mark Movsesian, "Rediscovering Williston,"62 *Wash. & Lee L. Rev.* 207, 210 (2005).

9. Richard A. Posner, *How Judges Think* (Cambridge, Mass.: Harvard Univ. Press 2008).

10. Daniel R. Pinello, "Linking Part to Judicial Ideology in American Courts: A Meta-Analysis,"20 *Just. Sys. J.* 219 (1999) (analyzing results of more than 100 separate empirical studies on judging).

11. See, e.g., David Charny, "New Formalism in Contract,"66 *U. Chi. L. Rev.* 842 (1999); Howard Erlanger, Bryant Garth, Elizabeth Mertz, and Jane Larson, "Is It Time for a New Legal Realism?" 2005 *Wisc. L. Rev.* 335 (2005).

12. The database is HeinOnline, at http:/HeinOnline.org.

13. An article with "formalism" in the title was published in 1934, but this is not counted because the term was invoked in a casual sense by way of contrast to "informal." Arthur E. Morgan, "Vitality and Formalism in Government,"13 *Social Forces* 1 (1934).

14. Grant Gilmore, "Security Law, Formalism, and Article 9,"47 *Neb. L. Rev.* 659 (1968).

15. A partial explanation for the increased quantity might be the growth in the number of journals, but a comparison suggests that this does not explain the entire increase. Articles with "legal positivism"(a leading contemporary theory of law) in the title go up only a bit over this period: four from 1968–79; ten from 1980–89; twelve from 1990–99; eleven from 2000–7.

16. In the 1930s there were eleven, in the 1940s there were seven, and in the 1950s there were sixteen. All of the numbers provided in this connection should be taken as approximate. "Realism" and "realist" have meanings invoked in legal contexts that are not related to legal realism. References that obviously invoked a different meaning were not included in the count.

17. Anthony J. Sebok, *Legal Positivism in American Jurisprudence* (Cambridge: Cambridge Univ. Press 1998) 57. Sebok raised serious questions about an aspect of the story.

18. William G. Hammond, "American Law Schools, Past and Future,"7 *Southern L. Rev.* 400, 412–13 (1881) (emphasis added).

19. See William P. LaPiana, "Jurisprudence of History and Truth,"23 *Rutgers L.J.* 519, 539–42, 555, 557 (1992); cf. David M. Rabban, "The Historiography of Late Nineteenth-Century American Legal History," 4 *Theoretical Inquiries in Law* 541, 567–78 (2003).

20. Benjamin N. Cardozo, *The Nature of the Judicial Process* (New Haven: Yale Univ. Press 1921) 128–29.

21. Karl N. Llewellyn, *The Common Law Tradition: Deciding Appeals* (Boston: Little Brown 1960) 53.

22. Id. 3–7, 19–35.

23. Id. 3.

CHAPTER TWO
THE MYTH ABOUT BELIEFS IN THE COMMON LAW

1. James C. Carter, "The Ideal and The Actual in the Law,"24 *American L. Rev.* 752 (1890).

2. Albert V. Dicey, *Law and Public Opinion in England during the Nineteenth Century* (London: Macmillan 1914 [1905]) 361–62 (emphasis added).

3. Jerome Frank, *Law and the Modern Mind* (New York: Tudor 1930).

4. Id. 9. I have retained the quotation marks where Frank placed them.

5. Id. 9.

6. Id. 32.

7. Henry Sumner Maine, *Ancient Law* (Tucson: Univ. of Arizona Press 1986 [1861]) 30 (emphasis added).

8. Frank, *Law and the Modern Mind*, 9.

9. Maine, *Ancient Law,* 31 (emphasis added).

10. John Stuart Mill, "Essay on Bentham," quoted in John F. Dillon, *Law and Jurisprudence of England and America* (Boston: Little Brown 1894) 335.

11. John M. Shirley, "The Future of Our Profession,"17 *American L. Rev.* 645, 659 (1883) (quoting James Fitzjames Stephen).

12. Maine, *Ancient Law,* 29–30.

13. Id. 30.

14. Id. 33.

15. Id.

16. Frank, *Law and the Modern Mind*, 55.

17. Joseph H. Beale, "The Necessity for a Study of Legal System,"1914 *AALS Proceedings* 31, 39 (1914).

18. Id. 44.

19. Joseph H. Beale, "The Development of Jurisprudence during the Past Century,"18 *Harv. L. Rev.* 271, 283 (1904).

20. See Anthony Sebok, *Legal Positivism in American Jurisprudence* (New York: Cambridge Univ. Press 1998) chap. 2.

21. Joseph H. Beale, "Juristic Law and Judicial Law,"*W.Va. L.Q.* 237, 248 (1931).

22. See *Lochner v. New York*, 198 U.S. 45, 76 (1905) (Holmes, J., dissenting).

23. Frank, *Law and the Modern Mind*, 10.

24. Id. 54.

25. Everett Abbott, *Justice and the Modern Law* (New York: Houghton Mifflin 1913) chap. 1.

26. Id. 8.

27. See Frank, *Law and the Modern Mind*, 326 n. 8, acknowledging his "immense debt" to Wurzel's article in his discussion of judging.

28. See Karl George Wurzel, "Methods of Juridical Thinking," in *Science of Legal Method* (Boston: Boston Book 1917) 286–428.

29. This can be confirmed by a search of the various HeinOnline electronic law journal catalogs.

30. See Karl Llewellyn, *The Common Law Tradition: Deciding Appeals* (Boston: Little Brown 1960) 40–41.

31. Grant Gilmore, *The Ages of American Law* (New Haven: Yale Univ. Press 1977) 12.

32. Id.

33. Id. 62.

34. "Written and Unwritten Systems of Law,"9 *Am. Jurist & L. Mag.* 5, 11 (1833) (emphasis added).

35. Edward M. Doe, "Codification,"5 *Western Jurist* 289, 289–90 (1871) (emphasis added).

36. Shirley, "The Future of Our Profession,"659 (emphasis added).

37. Munroe Smith, "State Statute and Common Law,"2 *Pol. Sci. Q.* 105, 121 (1887) (emphasis added).

38. Editors, "Current Topics,"29 *Albany L.J.* 481, 481 (1884) (quoting a Mr. Seymour) (emphasis added).

39. Emlin McClain, "Evolution of the Judicial Opinion,"36 *American L. Rev.* 801, 811 (1902) (emphasis added).

40. John S. Ewart, "What Is the Common Law?"4 *Colum. L. Rev.* 116, 125 (1904).

41. Hannis Taylor, "Legitimate Functions of Judge-Made Law,"17 *Green Bag* 557, 562 (1905) (emphasis added).

42. William Hornblower, "A Century of 'Judge-Made' Law,"7 *Colum. L. Rev.* 453 (1907).

43. Id. 473.

44. Gilmore, *Ages of American Law,* 15 (emphasis added).

45. William Rand, "Swift v. Tyson versus Gelpcke v. Dubuque,"8 *Harv. L. Rev.* 328, 330 (1894).

46. "Judicial Legislation,"1 *Albany L.J.* 105 (1870).

47. Albert J. Chapman, "Judicial Legislation,"6 *Western Jurist* 201 (1872).

48. Ezra R. Thayer, "Judicial Legislation: Its Legitimate Function in the Development of the Common Law,"5 *Harv. L. Rev.* 172 (1891).

49. J. C. Roberts, "Judicial Legislation,"10 *American Lawyer* 203 (1902).

50. A.H.F. Lefroy, "Judge-Made Law,"20 *L.Q. Rev.* 399 (1904).

51. Taylor, "Legitimate Functions of Judge-Made Law."

52. Hornblower, "A Century of 'Judge-Made' Law."

53. Morris R. Cohen, "The Process of Judicial Legislation,"48 *American L. Rev.* 161 (1914).

54. J. Newton Fiero, "A Practical View of Law Reform,"49 *Albany L.J.* 61, 62 (1894).

55. Thomas M. Cooley, "Another View of Codification,"2 *Colum. Jurist* 466, 465 (1886) (emphasis added).

56. Id. 465.

57. John F. Dillon, "Codification,"20 *American L. Rev.* 1, 32 (1886).

58. Dillon, *Laws and Jurisprudence of England and America*, 267–68 (emphasis added).

59. See, e.g., William P. LaPiana, "Jurisprudence of History and Truth,"23 *Rutgers L.J.* 519 (1992).

60. See Cooley, "Another View of Codification"; Dillon, *Laws and Jurisprudence of England and America*, Lectures XI, XII, and XIII.

61. A. M. Mackey, "Judge-Made Law,"2 *Okla. L.J.* 193, 197 (1903).

62. Le Baron Colt, "Law and Reasonableness,"37 *American L. Rev.* 657 (1903).

63. David P. Brewer, *The Nation's Safeguard*, quoted in G. Edward White, "Historicizing Judicial Scrutiny,"57 *S.C.L. Rev.* 1, 46 (2005).

64. *Osborn v. Bank of United States*, 22 U.S. (9 Wheaton) 736, 866 (1824) (Marshall, J.).

65. G. Edward White, *The American Judicial System: Profiles of Leading Judges* (New York: Oxford Univ. Press 2007) viii–ix.

66. Antonin Scalia, "Common Law Courts in a Civil-Law System: The Role of United States Federal Courts in Interpreting the Constitution and Laws," in Amy Gutmann, ed., *A Matter of Interpretation* (Princeton: Princeton Univ. Press 1997) 10.

67. An excellent historical study demonstrating awareness about the creativity of judging in the nineteenth century is Susanna L. Blumenthal, "Law and the Creative Mind,"74 *Chi. Kent L. Rev.* 151 (1998).

68. Cardozo, *The Nature of the Judicial Process*, 102.

69. Id. 136–37, 170.

70. Id. 108–9, 121.

71. Id. 175.

72. Gilmore, *Ages of American Law*, 77 (emphasis added).

73. Andrew L. Kaufman, *Cardozo* (Cambridge, Mass.: Harvard Univ. Press 1998) 217.

74. For positive reviews, see Nathan Isaacs, "Book Reviews,"20 *Mich. L. Rev.* 688 (1921); Rousseau Birch, "Book Reviews," 31 *Yale L.J.* 677 (1921); Charles M. Hough, "Book Reviews,"7 *Cornell L.Q.* 287 (1922); Francis E. Baker, 9 *A.B.A.J.* 34 (1923). Even in the most critical review, by Frank Johnston, "Books and Periodicals," 17 *Ill. L. Rev.* 152 (1922), the writer added, "With most of Judge Cardozo's conclusions . . . I fully agree." Id. 153. For positive reviews of Benjamin N. Cardozo, *The Growth of the Law* (New Haven: Yale Univ. Press 1924), see John B. Waite, "Book Reviews," 23 *Mich. L. Rev.* 682 (1925); A. Jacobs, "Book Reviews,"25 *Colum. L. Rev.* 121 (1925); George Wickersham, "Book Reviews," 34 *Yale L.J.* 917 (1925); Isaac Husik, "Book Reviews,"73 *U. Pa. L. Rev.* 327 (1925). For positive reviews of Benjamin N. Cardozo, *The Paradoxes of Legal Science* (New York: Columbia Univ. Press 1928), see Felix Frankfurter, "Book Reviews," 77 *U. Pa. L. Rev.* 436 (1929); George Roundtree, "Book Review,"7 *N.C.L. Rev.* 223 (1929); Bryant Smith, "Book Review," 7 *Tex. L. Rev.* (1929). Interestingly, two reviews with mildly critical comments came from legal realists, who chided Cardozo for not going far enough. See Max Radin, "Book Review, 10 *Cal. L. Rev.* 367 (1921); Walter Wheeler Cook, "Book Reviews," 38 *Yale L.J.* 404 (1929).

75. Judge Rousseau Burch, "Book Reviews,"31 *Yale L.J.* 677, 677 (1922) (emphasis added).

76. Id. 680.

77. Francis E. Baker, "Book Review,"9 *A.B.A.J.* 34, 34 (1923).

78. Charles M. Hough, "Book Reviews,"7 *Cornell L. Rev.* 287, 288 (1922).

79. Id. 289.

80. Harlan F. Stone, "Book Reviews,"22 *Colum. L. Rev.* 382, 385 (1922).

81. Simeon E. Baldwin, "Education for the Bar in the United States,"9 *Am. Pol. Sci. Rev.* 437, 447 (1915) (emphasis added).

82. Simeon E. Baldwin, *The American Judiciary* (New York: Century 1905) 74.

83. Munroe Smith, "State Statute and Common Law,"3 *Pol. Sci. Q.* 136, 142–43 (1888).

84. Id. 143.

85. Id. (emphasis added).

86. Id.

87. Id. 143 n. 1.

88. James C. Carter, *Law: Its Origin, Growth and Function* (New York: Putnam 1907) 86–87.

89. Id. 193.

90. Christopher Tiedeman, "Dictum and Decision,"6 *Colum. L. T.* 35, 35 (1892).

91. Id.

92. Id.

93. Thomas Ewing, "Codification,"41 *Albany L.J.* 439, 440 (1890).

94. Hough, "Book Reviews,"287.

95. As Morton Horwitz observed, "The single most influential representative of orthodox lawyer's legal history is the writing of Roscoe Pound." Morton Horwitz, "The Conservative Tradition in the Writing of American Legal History," 17 *Am. J. Legal Hist.* 275, 276 (1973).

96. Roscoe Pound, "Courts and Legislation,"7 *Am. Pol. Sci. Rev.* 361, 375 (emphasis added); Roscoe Pound, *The Formative Era of American Law* (Boston: Little Brown 1938) 110–11.

97. Oliver Wendell Holmes, "The Path of the Law,"10 *Harv. L. Rev.* 457, 465 (1897).

98. Id.

99. An excellent explication of Weber's work is Anthony T. Kronman, *Max Weber* (Stanford: Stanford Univ. Press 1983) chap. 4.

100. Max Weber, *Economy and Society,* ed. Guenther Roth and Claus Wittich (Berkeley: Univ. Ca. Press 1978) 657–58.

101. Id. 656.

102. Id. 787.

103. Id. 784–808, 852–59, 889–92.

104. Frederick Pollock, *The Genius of the Common Law* (New York: AMS Press 1967 [1911]) 27.

105. James Bryce, "The Influence of National Character and Historical Environment on the Development of the Common Law,"19 *Green Bag* 569, 571 (1907).

CHAPTER THREE
THE MYTH ABOUT "MECHANICAL JURISPRUDENCE"

1. Roscoe Pound, "Mechanical Jurisprudence,"8 *Colum. L. Rev.* 605, 605 (1908).

2. Id.

3. Id. 606.

4. Id. 611–12.

5. Id. 607–13.

6. Although he mentions both cases, Pound emphasizes *Adair* more than *Lochner*; I have taken the liberty of reversing this emphasis because *Lochner* stands out more today.

7. Id. 616.

8. Id. 622.

9. See, e.g., Pound, "Mechanical Jurisprudence,"606 n. 6, 607 n. 9; 610. It should also be noted that the protests of American sociologists Pound avers to in the final sentence is a lament in a three-page book review about the invalidation of laws by courts that cite old precedents. C. H. Henderson, "Reviews," 11 *Am. J. Soc.* 846, 847 (1906).

10. Blackstone, *Commentaries,* II, 2, quoted in Daniel J. Boorstin, *The Mysterious Science of Law: An Essay on Blackstone's Commentaries* (Chicago: Univ. Chicago Press 1996) 20.

11. David Dudley Field, "Magnitude and Importance of Legal Science"(1859), reprinted in Stephen B. Presser and Jamil S. Zainaldin, *Law and Jurisprudence in American History,* 5th ed. (St. Paul, Minn.: West 2000) 740.

12. Daniel Mayes, "Whether Law Is a Science,"9 *Am. Jurist & L. Mag.* 349 (1833).

13. A. P. Sprague, "The New Science of Law,"1 *L. Mag. & Rev. Q. Dig.* 648 (1876).

14. Edward Lindsey, "The Need for a Science of Law,"48 *American L. Rev.* 714 (1914).

15. Huntington Cairns, *The Theory of Legal Science* (New York: Augustus Kelly 1969 [1941]) 3.

16. Anonymous, "Nature and Method of Legal Studies,"3 *U.S. L. Mag.* 31, 31 (1851).

17. Langdell, quoted in C. Edward White, "The Impact of Legal Science on Tort Law,"78 *Colum. L. Rev.* 213, 220 (1978).

18. William A. Keener, "Methods of Legal Education,"1 *Yale L.J.* 143, 144 (1892); William A. Keener, "The Inductive Method in Legal Education," 28 *American L. Rev.* 709, 710 (1894).

19. Editors, "Is the Law a Philosophy, a Science, or an Art?"10 *Albany L.J.* 371, 371 (1874).

20. Fitzjames Steven, quoted in id. 371.

21. Henry C. White, "Three Views of Practice,"2 *Yale L.J.* 1, 6 (1892).

22. Elihu Root, "Address of the President,"41 *Reports of the American Bar Assoc.* 355, 364 (1916).

23. Editors, "Is Law a Science?"2 *Univ. L. Rev.* 257, 257 (1895).

24. Harlan Fiske Stone, "The Importance of Actual Experience at the Bar as a Preparation for Teaching Law,"3 *Am. L. School Rev.* 205, 207 (1911–15).

25. Other examples are P. H. Kaiser, "Logic and the Law,"1 *W. Res. L.J.* 181 (1895); Nicholas F. Lucas, "Logic and Law," 3 *Marq. L. Rev.* 210 (1918).

26. Anonymous, "Legal Dialectics,"5 *Albany L.J.* 293, 293 (1872). Munroe Smith made a similar statement in a footnote, without elaboration, although he also made very realistic comments about precedent. Munroe Smith, "State Statute and Common Law," 2 *Pol. Sci. Q.* 105, 143 n. 1 (1887).

27. Walter Wheeler Cook, "Scientific Method and the Law,"13 *A.B.A.J.* 303, 307 (1927).

28. John M. Zane, "German Legal Philosophy,"16 *Mich. L. Rev.* 287, 337–38, 345–48 (1918).

29. Austin Abbott, "Existing Questions on Legal Education,"3 *Yale L.J.* 1, 2 (1893).

30. Jabez Fox, "Law and Logic,"14 *Harv. L. Rev.* 39, 42 (1900).

31. Id. 43.

32. J. B. Thayer, "Law and Logic,"14 *Harv. L. Rev.* 139, 142 (1900).

33. Jabez Fox, "Law and Morals,"1 *Boston L. School Mag.* 1, 6 (1897).

34. Id.

35. Wilbur Larremore, "Judicial Legislation in New York,"14 *Yale L.J.* 312, 312 (1904).

36. Id. 314.

37. Id. 318 (emphasis added).

38. Edward B. Whitney, "The Doctrine of Stare Decisis,"3 *Mich. L. Rev.* 89 (1904).

39. Id. 94–95.

40. Id. 100 (emphasis added).

41. Emlin McClain, "The Evolution of the Judicial Opinion,"36 *American L. Rev.* 801, 814 (1902). Like McClain, Whitney also noted that some judges decided in an overly rule-bound fashion while others reasoned freely.

42. Id. 818.

43. Henry Craft, "The Judiciary—What It Is, and What It Should Be,"1 *Memphis L.J.* 15, 24 (1878).

44. Id.

45. Thomas Ewing, "Codification,"41 *Albany L.J.* 439, 440 (1890).

46. Id.

47. Uriah M. Rose, "American Bar Association,"64 *Albany L.J.* 333, 336 (1902).

48. Albert R. Savage, "Some Sore Spots,"7 *Maine L. Rev.* 29, 37 (1913).

49. Elihu Root, "Address of the President,"41 *Reports of the American Bar Assoc.* 355, 364 (1916).

50. Oscar Fellows, "The Multiplicity of Reported Decisions,"6 *Maine L. Rev.* 263, 264 (1912).

51. Frederick N. Judson, "The Progress of the Law in the United States,"23 *Green Bag* 560, 567 (1911).

52. Id. 560.

53. James Bryce, The Methods and Conditions of Legislation in Our Time, 8 *Colum. L. Rev.* 157, 157 (1908).

54. Id.

55. See Thomas M. Cooley, "The Uncertainty of Law,"22 *American L. Rev.* 347 (1888).

56. Seymour D. Thompson, "More Justice and Less Technicality,"23 *American L. Rev.* 22, 44 (1889).

57. Editors, "Current Topics,"39 *Albany L.J.* 221, 222 (1889).

58. Cooley, "The Uncertainty of Law,"350.

59. John F. Dillon, "Codification,"20 *American L. Rev.* 29, 36 (1886).

60. Id.

61. Charles P. Sherman, "One Code for all the United States the Only Remedy to Cure American Law of Its Confusion and Uncertainty,"25 *Green Bag* 460, 460 (1913).

62. Ernst Freund, "Constitutional Labor Legislation,"4 *Ill. L. Rev.* 609, 620 (1910).

63. Pound, "Mechanical Jurisprudence,"617–20.

64. Id. 621.

65. Pound, "Mechanical Jurisprudence,"620.

66. John Henry Wigmore, "Scientific Books in Evidence,"26 *American L. Rev.* 390, 402 (1892).

67. Roscoe Pound, *Interpretations of Legal History* (London: Cambridge Univ. Press 1923) 34.

68. Frederick Pollock, "A Plea for Historical Interpretation,"39 *L.Q. Rev.* 163, 164–66 (1923). Pollock was reviewing Pound's *Interpretations of Legal History,* which elaborated on the same arguments Pound articulated in "Mechanical Jurisprudence."

69. Id. 165.

70. Mayes, "Whether Law Is a Science?"355.

71. See William Green, "Stare Decisis,"14 *American L. Rev.* 609 (1880).

72. Chancellor Kent, *Commentaries*, quoted in H. Campbell Black, "The Principle of Stare Decisis,"34 *Am. L. Reg.* 745 (1886).

73. Parker, J., quoted in Green, "Stare Decisis,"641.

74. For several nineteenth-century quotations indicating this understanding, see H. Campbell Black, "The Doctrine of Stare Decisis,"23 *Bar* 312 (1916).

75. Oliver W. Holmes, "Law in Science and Science in Law,"12 *Harv. L. Rev.* 443, 460 (1899).

76. *Leavitt v. Blatchford*, 17 N.Y. 521, quoted in Green, "Stare Decisis,"635.

77. Editors, "Stare Decisis,"6 *Albany L.J.* 329, 329 (1872) (emphasis added).

78. Black, "The Doctrine of Stare Decisis,"748.

79. Editors, "The Scientific Basis of Law,"7 *Albany L.J.* 321, 321 (1873).

80. Christopher G. Tiedeman, "The Income Tax Decisions as an Object Lesson in Constitutional Construction,"6 *Annals of Am. Acad. of Pol. & Soc. Sci.* 72, 72 (1895).

81. Id.

82. Christopher Tiedeman, "Dictum and Decision,"6 *Colum. L. T.* 35, 35–36 (1892).

83. Editors, "Stare Decisis,"6 *Albany L.J.* 329, 329 (1872).

84. Editors, "Current Topics,"31 *Albany L.J.* 281, 281 (1885).

85. Munroe Smith, "State Statute and Common Law,"2 *Pol. Sci. Q.* 105, 121 (1887).

86. Wilbur Larremore, "Stare Decisis and Contractual Rights,"22 *Harv. L. Rev.* 182 (1908).

87. W. M. Lile, "Some Views on the Rule of Stare Decisis,"4 *Va. L. Rev.* 95, 106 (1916).

88. Roscoe Pound, "Spurious Interpretation,"7 *Colum. L. Rev.* 379, 384 (1907).

89. Eugene V. Rostow, "American Legal Realism and the Sense of the Profession,"34 *Rocky Mountain L. Rev.* 123, 127 (1961).

90. This discussion draws from several sources, particularly Alan Trachtenberg, *The Incorporation of America: Culture and Society in the Gilded Age* (New York: Hill and Wang 2007); Elizabeth Sanders, *Roots of Reform: Farmers, Workers, and the American State, 1877–1917* (Chicago: Univ. of Chicago Press 1999); Rebecca Edwards, *New Spirits: Americans in the Gilded Age, 1865–1905* (New York: Oxford Univ. Press 2006); Maureen A. Flanagan, *America Reformed: Progressives and Progressivisms, 1890s–1920s* (New York: Oxford Univ. Press 2007); Jack Beatty, *Age of Betrayal: The Triumph of Money in America, 1865–1900* (New York: Knopf 2007).

91. Henry Carter Adams, "Economics and Jurisprudence,"8 *Science* 15, 17–18 (1886).

92. Tiedeman, "Dictum and Decision,"36, noting the "strong tendency to socialism" evident in the preceding decades.

93. Joseph H. Beale, "The Development of Jurisprudence during the Past Century,"18 *Harv. L. Rev.* 271, 274 (1904).

94. See Albert V. Dicey, *Law and Opinion in England during the Nineteenth Century* (London: Macmillan 1914 [1905]).

95. Leonard C. Crouch, "Judicial Tendencies of the Court of Appeals during the Incumbency of Chief Judge Hiscock,"12 *Cornell L.Q.* 137, 142 (1927) (emphasis added).

96. Id. 141–42 (emphasis added).

97. Id. 142.

98. Id. 140.

99. Id. 147–52.

CHAPTER FOUR
THE HOLES IN THE STORY ABOUT LEGAL FORMALISM

1. The early Roman law system also had a formulary system, but will not be discussed here. See G.S., "Forms of Action,"12 *Am. L. Reg.* 705 (1864).

2. See Frederick W. Maitland, *The Forms of Action at Common Law* (Cambridge: Cambridge Univ. Press 1958 [1909]) 1.

3. For an excellent introduction to the system, see Alison Reppy, "The Development of the Common-Law Forms of Action,"22 *Brooklyn L. Rev.* 179 (1956).

4. Maitland, *Forms of Action*, 5.

5. See Frederick W. Maitland and Frederick Pollock, *The History of English Law*, vol. 2, 2nd ed. (Cambridge: Cambridge Univ. Press 1899) chap. 9; Reppy, "Development of the Common Law Forms of Action,"202–6.

6. Maitland, *The Forms of Action at Common Law*, 1–7; G.S., "Forms of Action,"713.

7. Frederick Pollock, *The Genius of the Common Law* (New York: AMS Press 1967 [1911]) 15.

8. Id. 14–15.

9. Maitland and Pollock, *History of English Law*, 563.

10. Id.

11. Id.

12. G.S. "Forms of Action,"712, 713–14.

13. See Maitland, *The Forms of Action at Common Law*, Lecture V.

14. A.K.R. Kiralfy, *Potter's Outlines of English Legal History*, 5th ed. (London: Sweet & Maxwell 1958) 33–35.

15. Maitland, *Forms of Action at Common Law*, 59.

16. Id. 71.

17. For a series of examples of such common fictions, see Pollock, *The Genius of the Common Law*, 30–31.

18. Maitland, *Forms of Action at Common Law*, 79.

19. See Kiralfy, *Potter's Outlines of English Legal History*, 37–38.

20. John P. Salmond, "Observations on Trover and Conversion,"21 *L.Q. Rev.* 43, 43 (1905).

21. G.S., "Forms of Action,"713.

22. "Formula,"*Webster's Revised Unabridged Dictionary*, http://dictionary .reference.com/browse/formula.

23. Anonymous, "Legal Education,"6 *Law Mag. Q. Rev. Juris.* 175, 175 (1847).

24. Henry C. White, "Three Views of Practice,"2 *Yale L.J.* 1, 6 (1892).

25. Robert Gordon notes that by 1830 the orthodox bar had come to express a general reaction against the "excessive technicality and artificiality of law and procedure." Robert W. Gordon, "Book Review: American Codification Movement, a Study of Antebellum Legal Reform," 36 *Vand. L. Rev.* 431, 454 (1983).

26. "Recent American Decisions: *Page v. Dennison*,"5 *American L. Rev.* 476 (1857) ("ignorant and slavish formalism") (dissenting opinion of Lowrie, J.).

27. William G. Hammond, "The Legal Profession—Its Past—Its Present—Its Duty,"9 *W. Jurist* 1, 8 (1875) (emphasis added).

28. Anonymous, "Reform in Legal Education,"10 *American L. Rev.* 626, 626 (1876).

29. S.S.P. Patterson, "Law Reform," 13 *Va. L.J.* 460, 466 (1889).

30. John Henry Wigmore, "Scientific Books in Evidence,"26 *American L. Rev.* 390, 402 (1892).

31. Id.

32. Alex Thomson, "The Historical and Philosophical Methods in Jurisprudence,"7 *Juridical Rev.* 66, 70, 69 (1895).

33. See Lex (pseudonym), "The English Law Courts,"7 *Green Bag* 418, 419 (1895).

34. Edward Jenks, "On the Early History of Negotiable Instruments,"9 *L.Q. Rev.* 70, 76 (1893).

35. See "Written and Unwritten Systems of Law,"9 *Am. Jurist & L. Mag.* 5 (1833) (discussing this).

36. Jeremy Bentham, *Legal Fictions*, appendix A, in C. K. Ogden, *Bentham's Theory of Fictions* (New York: Harcourt, Brace 1932) 141.

37. Id. 149.

38. Anonymous, "Legal Fictions,"25 *Am. Jurist & L. Mag.* 69, 73 (1841).

39. See id. 76.

40. See Charles M. Campbell, "The Necessity and Importance of the Study of Common Law Procedure,"5 *American Lawyer* 207, 208 (1897).

41. Henry Sumner Maine, *Ancient Law* (Tucson: Univ. Arizona Press 1986 [1861]) 29–31.

42. See, e.g., Anonymous, "Legal Fictions"; Oliver R. Mitchell, "The Fictions of the Law: Have They Proved Useful or Detrimental to Its Growth," 7 *Harv. L. Rev.* 249 (1893); Clifford Thorn, "Correction of the Law,"33 *American L. Rev.* 522 (1899); Simeon Baldwin, "A Legal Fiction with Its Wings Clipped," 41 *American L. Rev.* 38 (1907); Sidney T. Miller, "The Reasons for Some Legal Fictions,"8 *Mich. L. Rev.* 623 (1908).

43. See LeBaron B. Colt, "Law and Reasonableness,"37 *American L. Rev.* 657 (1903); William Seton Gordon, "Judiciary Law," 43 *Albany L.J.* 165 (1891).

44. Editors, "Legal Reform,"1 *Albany L.J.* 291, 291 (1870).

45. See Jeremiah Smith, "Surviving Fictions II,"27 *Yale L.J.* 317, 320 (1917); Jeremiah Smith, "Surviving Fictions," 27 *Yale L.J.* 147 (1917).

46. See Brian Bix, *Jurisprudence: Theory and Context* (Durham, N.C.: Carolina Academic Press 2004) 178–200.

47. An account of this understanding of law can be found in Thomas C. Grey, "Langdell's Orthodoxy,"45 *U. Pitt. L. Rev.* 1 (1983).

48. See William Wiecek, *The Lost World of Classical Legal Thought* (New York: Oxford Univ. Press 1998) 3. Wiecek acknowledges that this label is used synonymously with "legal formalism," which is the label he used in his previous book, *Liberty under Law* (Baltimore: John Hopkins Univ. Press 1988) chap. 5 "The Formalist Era, 1873–1937."

49. An excellent philosophical exploration of this type of formalism is Duncan Kennedy, "Legal Formality,"2 *J. Legal Stud.* 351 (1973).

50. See Roscoe Pound, "Liberty of Contract,"18 *Yale L.J.* 454, 469–70 (1909).

51. Daniel Mayes, "Whether Law Is a Science,"9 *Am. Jurist & L. Mag.* 349, 354 (1833).

52. Id. 356.

53. Id.

54. See Charles E. Carpenter, "Court Decisions and the Common Law,"17 *Colum. L. Rev.* 593 (1917).

55. See A.W.B. Simpson, "Legal Iconoclasts and Legal Ideals,"58 *U. Cin. L. Rev.* 819, 837 (1990) ("Thus legal scientists did not in the least maintain that courts and judges did not fall into error; it was this very concession which made it impossible for them to identify 'the law' with legal decisions").

56. Anonymous comments from *United States Law Journal* of 1822, quoted by Simeon E. Baldwin, "The United States Law Journal of 1822,"4 *A.B.A.J.* 37, 40 (1918).

57. George H. Smith, "Of the Certainty of the Law and the Uncertainty of Judicial Decisions,"23 *American L. Rev.* 699 (1889).

58. Simpson, "Legal Iconoclasts and Legal Ideals,"837.

59. A balanced view of this can be found in Morris Cohen, "The Place of Logic in the Law,"29 *Harv. L. Rev.* 622 (1916).

60. Following Gilmore, Thomas Grey identifies Langdell as *the* classical formalist. See Thomas C. Grey, "Modern American Legal Thought,"106 *Yale L.J.* 493 (1996).

61. Christopher Columbus Langdell, preface to *Selection of Cases on the Law of Contracts*, reprinted in Stephen B. Presser and Jamil S. Zainaldin, *Law and Jurisprudence in American Legal History*, 5th ed. (St. Paul, Minn.: West 2000) 746–48.

62. Oliver Wendell Holmes, "Book Review,"14 *American L. Rev.* 233, 234 (1880).

63. Grey, "Modern American Legal Thought,"493.

64. Id. 496.

65. See Langdell quote, in M .H. Hoeflich, "Law and Geometry: Legal Science from Leibniz to Langdell,"30 *Am. J. Legal Hist.* 95, 120 (1986) (Langdell asserted that the library is the workshop for the jurist in the same sense that the garden is for the botanist).

66. See Edward White, "Impact of Legal Science on Tort Law,"78 *Colum. L. Rev.* 213, 220–25 (1978).

67. For an argument that the formalism of Langdell has been exaggerated, see Robert Gordon, "The Elusive Transformation,"6 *Yale J.I.. & Human.,* 137, 156 (1994).

68. Grey, "Modern American Legal Thought,"499.

69. Samuel Williston, *Life and Law: An Autobiography* (Boston: Little Brown 1941) 209.

70. Id.

71. Samuel Williston, "Change in the Law,"69 *U.S. L. Rev.* 237 (1935).

72. See Bruce A. Kimball, "Langdell on Contracts and Legal Reasoning: Correcting the Holmesian Caricature,"25 *Law & Hist. Rev.* 345 (2007); Bruce A. Kimball, "The Langdell Problem: Historicizing the Century of Historiography, 1906–2000," 22 *Law & Hist. Rev.* 277 (2004).

73. Kimball, "Langdell on Contracts and Legal Reasoning,"374–75.

74. Grey, "Langdell's Orthodoxy,"13.

75. Id. 11 n. 33.

76. Frederick Pollock, "The Vocation of the Common Law,"3 *American Lawyer* 301, 302 (1895).

77. Id.

78. Marcia Speziale, "Langdell's Concept of Law as Science: The Beginning of Anti-Formalism in American Legal Theory,"5 *Vt. L. Rev.* 1 (1980).

79. Morton Horwitz, "The Rise of Legal Formalism,"19 *Am. J. Leg. Hist.* 251, 252 (1975); see also Grey, "Langdell's Orthodoxy," 9–10 (connecting these two senses of legal formalism).

80. See William P. LaPiana, "Jurisprudence of History and Truth,"23 *Rutgers L.J.* 519, 557 (1992). LaPiana raises a few hesitations about this proposition after setting it out, although he holds to it. While legal historians regularly invoke the term formalism, they do not all mean the same thing by it, and often they do not carefully define it, which generates a lot of confusion.

81. Irving Lehman, "Influence of the Universities on Judicial Decision,"10 *Cornell L.Q.* 1 (1924) 3.

82. William G. Hammond, "American Law Schools, Past and Future,"7 *Southern L. Rev.* 400, 412–13 (1881).

83. Thomas M. Cooley, "Another View of Codification,"2 *Colum. Jurist* 466, 465 (1886).

84. Id.

85. Id.

86. Id.

87. Quoted without identification in Henry C. Merwin, "Style in Judicial Opinion,"9 *Green Bag* 521, 521 (1897).

88. Id. 523.

89. Id. 525.

90. Id. 524.

91. John H. Wigmore, "The Qualities of Current Judicial Decisions,"9 *Ill. L. Rev.* 529, 531 (1915).

92. Walter F. Pratt, "Rhetorical Styles on the Fuller Court,"24 *Am. J. Legal Hist.* 189 (1980).

93. John Dewey, "Logical Method and the Law,"10 *Cornell L.Q.* 17, 24 (1924).

94. Id. 25.

95. See Roscoe Pound, "Do We Need a Philosophy of Law?"5 *Colum. L. Rev.* 342, 345–47 (1905).

96. Id. 63.

97. Duncan Kennedy, "Toward an Historical Understanding of Legal Consciousness: The Case of Classical Legal Thought in America, 1850–1940,"3 *Research in Law and Soc.* 3 (1980).

98. Lawrence Friedman, *A History of American Law*, 2nd ed. (New York: Touchstone 1985) 384.

99. Jerome Frank, *Law and the Modern Mind* (New York: Tudor 1930) 137–38.

100. Karl Llewellyn, *The Common Law Tradition: Deciding Appeals* (Boston: Little Brown 1960) 40.

101. Karl Llewellyn, *Cases and Materials on the Law of Sales* (1930), quoted in N.E.H. Hull, *Roscoe Pound and Karl Llewellyn* (Chicago: Univ. Chicago Press 1997) 178.

102. Morton Horwitz, *The Transformation of American Law, 1780–1860* (Cambridge, Mass.: Harvard Univ. Press 1977) 10, 254; Morton J. Horwitz, *The Rise of Legal Formalism*, 19 *Am. J. Legal Hist.* 251, 264 (1975) ("For the paramount social condition that is necessary for legal formalism to flourish in a society is for the powerful groups in that society to have a great interest in disguising and suppressing the inevitably political and redistributive functions of law"). Robert Gordon described the conventional view (without endorsing it) of the period as follows: "[A]fter the Civil War, the law suffered a deterioration into sterile formalism, or 'mechanical jurisprudence,' which served to mask its deployment as a tool of reactionary social views." Robert W. Gordon, "Commentary: John W. Johnson, Creativity and Adaptation: A Reassessment of American Jurisprudence, 1801–1857 and 1908–1940,"7 *Rutgers-Camden L.J.* 648, 648 (1976). This formulation leaves open the question whether the judges were actually reasoning in a formalistic fashion or merely writing their opinions to give it that appearance, though it suggests the latter.

103. Robert Cover, *Justice Accused: Antislavery and the Judicial Process* (New Haven: Yale Univ. Press 1975) 235.

104. Id. 233–34.

105. Grant Gilmore, *Ages of American Law* (New Haven: Yale Univ. Press 1977) 42.

106. Cover, *Justice Accused*, 235.

107. See Max Weber, *Economy and Society*, vol. 2 (Berkeley: Univ. of Calif. Press 1978) 880–900. Llewellyn mentioned Weber's influence in a 1930 article, "Realistic Jurisprudence—The Next Step,"30 *Colum. L. Rev.* 431, 456 (1930), but did not discuss formalism.

108. Karl Llewellyn, "On the Good, the True, the Beautiful in Law,"9 *U. Chi. L. Rev.* 224 (1942).

109. Morton White, *Social Thought in America: The Revolt against Formalism*, 2nd ed. (Boston: Beacon Press 1957 [1949]) 11.

110. Llewellyn, *Common Law Tradition*, 38.

111. Grant Gilmore, "Legal Realism: Its Cause and Cure,"70 *Yale L.J.* 1037, 1038 (1961).

112. Wilfrid E. Rumble, *American Legal Realism Skepticism, Reform, and the Judicial Process* (Ithaca, N.Y.: Cornell Univ. Press 1968).

113. In two superb works on legal realism, published in 1969 and 1973, Edward Purcell used the term "legalistic formalism" to describe reasoning at the time. Purcell had read White's book and takes up similar themes relating to the influence of pragmatism on American thought. See Edward Purcell, "American Jurisprudence between the Wars: Legal Realism and the Crisis of Democratic Theory," 75 *Am. Hist. Rev.* 424 (1969); Edward A. Purcell, *The Crisis of Democratic Theory: Scientific Naturalism and the Problem of Value* (Lexington: Univ. of Kentucky Press 1973).

114. Grant Gilmore, "The Age of Anxiety,"84 *Yale L.J.* 1022 (1975).

115. Horwitz, "The Rise of Legal Formalism."

116. Duncan Kennedy, "Legal Formality,"2 *J. Legal Stud.* 351 (1973). Although circulated among historians and theorists at the time, Duncan Kennedy's influential book on this topic was not published until 2006. Duncan Kennedy, *The Rise and Fall of Classical Legal Thought* (Washington, D.C.: Beard Books 2006); a piece of this was published at the time in Duncan Kennedy, "Toward an Historical Understanding of Legal Consciousness: The Case of Classical Legal Thought in America, 1850–1940," 3 *Research in Law and Soc.* 3 (1980).

117. William E. Nelson, "The Impact of the Antislavery Movement upon Styles of Judicial Reasoning in Nineteenth Century America,"87 *Harv. L. Rev.* 513 (1974).

118. Cover, *Justice Accused.*

119. Brian Z. Tamanaha, *Law as a Means to an End: Threat to the Rule of Law* (New York: Cambridge Univ. Press 2006) chap. 6.

120. Editors, "With the Editors,"83 *Harv. L. Rev.* 31 (1970).

121. Id. xi.

122. Gilmore, *Ages of American Law,* 108.

123. Grant Gilmore, "Formalism and the Law of Negotiable Instruments,"13 *Creighton L. Rev.* 441 (1979) (emphasis added).

124. Friedman, *A History of American Law,* 623. Raising another set of doubts about the image of the formalist age, Susanna Blumenthal published a superb historical study that argues that throughout the nineteenth century the creative aspects of judging were well understood. Susanna L. Blumenthal, "Law and the Creative Mind."74 *Chi.-Kent L. Rev.* 151 (1998).

125. One exception among legal theorists is Anthony Sebok, who raised doubts in his book *Legal Positivism in American Jurisprudence* (New York: Cambridge Univ. Press 1998) chap. 3. Historian Robert Gordon has also expressed various doubts about the story of the legal formalists; see Gordon, "The Elusive Transformation"; Gordon, "Book Review." A new generation of historians has begun to challenge various aspects of the story. Bruce Kimball has contested the formalist image of Langdell, as mentioned earlier. Lewis Grossman challenges the portrayal of James Carter in "Langdell Upside-Down: James

Coolidge Carter and the Anti-classical Jurisprudence of Anticodification,"19 *Yale J.L. & Human.* 149 (2007).

126. Stephen A. Siegel, "John Chipman Gray and the Moral Basis of Classical Legal Thought,"86 *Iowa L. Rev.* 1513, 1514 (2001).

127. Grey, *Modern American Legal Thought,* 503.

128. Id. 512.

CHAPTER FIVE
REALISM BEFORE THE LEGAL REALISTS

1. Brian Leiter, *Naturalizing Jurisprudence: Essays on American Legal Realism and Naturalism in Legal Philosophy* (Oxford: Oxford Univ. Press 2007) 1.

2. Hannoch Dagan, "The Realist Conception of Law,"57 *U. Toronto L.J.* 607, 607 (2007).

3. See William P. LaPiana, "Jurisprudence of History and Truth,"23 *Rutgers L.J.* 519, 539–42, 555, 557 (1992); cf. David M. Rabban, "The Historiography of Late Nineteenth-Century American Legal History," 4 *Theoretical Inquiries in Law* 541, 567–78 (2003).

4. Laura Kalman, *Legal Realism at Yale, 1927–1960* (Chapel Hill: Univ. North Carolina Press 1986) 231.

5. John Henry Schlegel, *American Legal Realism and Social Science* (Chapel Hill: Univ. of North Carolina Press 1995) 1–2 (emphasis added).

6. Historian Thomas Grey makes this claim, in Thomas C. Grey, "Modern American Legal Thought,"106 *Yale L.J.* 493, 502 (1996).

7. The link between the legal realists and the New Deal is drawn in broad terms in G. Edward White, "From Sociological Jurisprudence to Realism: Jurisprudence and Social Change in Early Twentieth Century America,"58 *Va. L. Rev.* 999 (1972).

8. Alan Brinkley, *The End of Reform: New Deal Liberalism in Recession and War* (New York: Vintage Books 1995) 3.

9. Karl Llewellyn, "A Realistic Jurisprudence—The Next Step,"30 *Colum. L. Rev.* 431 (1930).

10. See N.E.H. Hull, *Roscoe Pound and Karl Llewellyn: Searching for an American Jurisprudence* (Chicago: Univ. Chicago Press 1997) chap. 4.

11. Roscoe Pound, "The Call for a Realist Jurisprudence,"44 *Harv. L. Rev.* 697 (1931).

12. Karl Llewellyn, "Some Realism about Realism—Responding to Dean Pound,"44 *Harv. L. Rev.* 1222 (1931).

13. Hull, *Roscoe Pound and Karl Llewellyn,* 202–20.

14. The various lists are reproduced as the appendix in id. 342–46.

15. Id. 215.

16. Id. 207, 208 (quoting responses from Corbin and Yntema).

17. Leon Green, "Innocent Misrepresentation,"19 *Va. L. Rev.* 242, 247, 250–51 (1933).

18. Llewellyn, "Some Realism about Realism,"1226 n. 18.

19. Id. 1234.

20. Morton Horwitz, *Transformation of American Law, 1870–1960* (New York: Oxford Univ. Press 1992) 171.

21. Benjamin Cardozo, *The Nature of the Judicial Process* (New Haven: Yale Univ. Press 1921) 128.

22. Felix Frankfurter, "Hours of Law and Realism in Constitutional Law,"29 *Harv. L. Rev.* 353 (1916).

23. Robert Summers, *Instrumentalism and American Legal Theory* (Ithaca, N.Y.: Cornell Univ. Press 1982).

24. Schlegel, *American Legal Realism and Social Science.*

25. See Kalman, *Legal Realism at Yale.*

26. See Horwitz, *Transformation of American Law, 1870–1960.*

27. The main internal divide relates to the social scientific vein of realism, which some heartily endorsed and engaged in, and others took less seriously. See Schlegel, *American Legal Realism.*

28. William Draper Lewis, the dean of the University of Pennsylvania Law School and later Director of the American Law Institute, was a strong progressive critic of the courts, and advocated introducing social science into legal academia, but has not been considered a realist by anyone. See William Draper Lewis, "The Social Sciences as the Basis of Legal Education,"61 *U. Pa. L. Rev.* 531 (1913). Also not recognized as a realist, Harvard Law professor Albert Kales published a highly skeptical critique of the Supreme Court. See Albert Kales, " 'Due Process' The Inarticulate Major Premise and the Adamson Act," 26 *Yale L.J.* 519 (1917). Also not on the list of realists were Robert Eugene Cushman, Charles G. Haines, and Max Lerner, who published realistic reformist articles on judging in law reviews. See Robert E. Cushman, "The Social and Economic Interpretation of the Fourteenth Amendment,"20 *Mich. L. Rev.* 737 (1922); Charles Grove Haines, "General Observations on the Effects of Personal Political and Economic Influences in the Decisions of Judges," 17 *Ill. L. Rev.* 96 (1922); Max Lerner, "The Supreme Court and American Capitalism,"42 *Yale L.J.* 668 (1933).

29. Walter F. Murphy and C. Herman Pritchett, *Courts, Judges, and Politics*, 3rd ed. (New York: Random House 1979) 6.

30. Llewellyn, "Some Realism about Realism,"1233–34.

31. Id. 1256.

32. Karl Llewellyn, *The Common Law Tradition: Deciding Appeals* (Boston: Little Brown 1960) 510.

33. See Horwitz, *Transformation of American Law, 1870–1960*, chap. 6; Summers, *Instrumentalism and American Legal Theory.*

34. The ages and matriculation dates of the realists can be found in Schlegel, *American Legal Realism*, 264–69, bibliographic appendix.

35. President Roosevelt, "Message to Congress," December 8, 1908, quoted in Cardozo, *Nature of the Judicial Process*, 171.

36. See, e.g., Editors, "The Adoption of the Recall in California,"23 *Green Bag* 634 (1911).

37. See William Draper Lewis, "The Recall of Judicial Decisions,"3 *Proc. of the Academy of Political Science* 37 (1913); Munroe Smith, "The Development of

American Constitutional Law," 3 *Proc. of the Academy of Political Science* 52 (1913).

38. W. F. Dodd, "The Growth of Judicial Power,"24 *Pol. Sci. Q.* 193, 198 (1909); W. F. Dodd, "The Recall and the Political Responsibility of Judges," 10 *Mich. L. Rev.* 79, 87 (1911).

39. Robert L. Owen, "The Right of Election and Recall of Federal Judges,"9 *Maine L. Rev.* 82, 93 (1911).

40. H. T. Walsh, "The Recall of Judges,"10 *Okla. L.J.* 349, 354 (1912).

41. Joseph Bingham, "What Is Law?"11 *Mich. L. Rev.* 109, 113 n. 32 (1912).

42. Felix Frankfurter, "The Zeitgeist and the Judiciary," in Archibald MacLeish, ed., *Law and Politics: Occasional Papers of Felix Frankfurter, 1913–1938* (New York: Harcourt Brace 1939) 6. This speech was delivered in 1912 and published in 1913.

43. Gilbert E. Roe, *Our Judicial Oligarchy* (New York: Huebosch 1912) chaps. 1–5.

44. Gustavus Myers, *History of the Supreme Court of the United States* (New York: Burt Franklin 1912).

45. Theodore Schroeder, "Social Justice and the Courts,"22 *Yale L.J.* 19, 26 (1912).

46. Id. 26–27.

47. John Henry Wigmore, *The Judicial Function, in Science of the Legal Method: Select Essays by Various Authors* (Boston: Boston Book 1917) xl, xxx.

48. Thomas Reed Powell, "The Logic and Rhetoric of Constitutional Law,"15 *J. of Phil., Psy. and Scientific Methods* 645, 646 (1918).

49. Id. 648.

50. Id. 652.

51. Theodore Schroeder, "The Psychologic Study of Judicial Decisions,"6 *Cal. L. Rev.* 89, 93 (1918).

52. Wendell Phillips Stafford, "Imagination in the Law,"53 *American L. Rev.* 648 (1919) 647–48.

53. Id. 658.

54. Id. 654.

55. Karl N. Llewellyn, "Remarks on the Theory of Appellate Decision and the Rules or Canons about How Statutes Are to Be Construed,"3 *Vand. L. Rev.* 395 (1950).

56. Ernst Freund, "Interpretation of Statutes,"U. Pa. L. Rev. 207, 215 (1917).

57. Id. 217.

58. Id. 231.

59. Id.

60. Munroe Smith, "State Statute and Common Law,"2 *Pol. Sci. Q.* 105, 121 (1887).

61. Id. 122–23.

62. Id. 130.

63. Id.

64. Sylvester Pennoyer, "The Case of *Marbury v. Madison*,"30 *American L. Rev.* 188, 202 (1896).

65. John C. Gray, "Some Definitions and Questions in Jurisprudence,"6 *Harv. L. Rev.* 21, 33 (1892).

66. Walter D. Coles, "Politics and the Supreme Court of the United States,"27 *American L. Rev.* 182, 205 (1893).

67. Id. 182.

68. Id. 190.

69. John F. Dillon, "Our Law,"3 *The Counsellor* 99, 103 (1894).

70. 156 U.S. 1 (1895).

71. 157 U.S. 429 (1895).

72. Alan Furman Westin, "The Supreme Court, the Populist Movement and the Campaign of 1896,"15 *J. of Politics* 3, 32 (1953) (Judge Shiras changed his mind); Camm Patterson, "The Judicial Usurpation of Power," 10 *Va. L. Reg.* 855 (1905).

73. 158 U.S. 564 (1895).

74. The outrage provoked by this trio of cases is described in Westin, "The Supreme Court, the Populist Movement and the Campaign of 1896"; Charles Warren, *The Supreme Court in United States History* (Boston: Little Brown 1922) 421–26.

75. Seymour D. Thompson, "Government by Lawyers,"30 *American L. Rev.* 672, 685 (1896).

76. Reprinted in Warren, *Supreme Court in United States History,* supra 426.

77. Examples of these statements can be found in Westin, "The Supreme Court, the Populist Movement and the Campaign of 1896."

78. *Hepburn v. Griswold*, 8 Wall 603, 638 (1870) (Miller, J., dissenting).

79. The Legal Tender Act was held invalid in *Hepburn v. Griswold*, 8 Wall 603 (1870), but held valid the following year in *Knox v. Lee*, 12 Wall 457 (1871). In the interim, a seat was added to the Court, and Justice Grier resigned, allowing President Grant to appoint Justice William Strong and Justice Joseph P. Bradley, both of whom voted to uphold the Act.

80. Editors, *The Nation*, April 27, 1871, 281.

81. See Sidney Ratner, "Was the Supreme Court Packed by President Grant,"50 *Pol. Sci. Q.* 343, 348, 351 (1935).

82. Id. 353.

83. Anonymous, "The Civil Code of the State of New York: Relations of Judge-Made Law to a Code,"2 *Albany L.J.* 450, 451 (1870).

84. Id.

85. Eli K. Price, "An Obituary Notice of Chief Justice John Meredith Read,"14 *Proc. of the American Philosophical Society* 271, 273 (1874).

86. Oliver Wendell Holmes, "Book Review,"14 *American L. Rev.* 233, 234 (1880).

87. Editors, "The Scientific Basis of Law,"7 *Albany L.J.* 321, 321 (1873).

88. Id. 321.

89. Id. 321 (emphasis added).

90. Anonymous, "Forensic Eloquence,"7 *Albany L.J.* 7, 7 (1973).

91. C. B. Labatt, "State Regulation of the Contract of Employment,"27 *American L. Rev.* 857, 864, 872 (1893). There are several reasons to believe that Holmes had read this article: this was the leading law review of the day;

Holmes worked for the journal early in his career and contributed a number of articles to it over time; the author discusses a Massachusetts Supreme Court case that Holmes participated in, and he singled Holmes out for praise.

92. Id. 864.

93. Id. 872.

94. Id. 867.

95. Id. 869.

96. Christopher G. Tiedeman, "The Doctrine of Stare Decisis,"3 *University L. Rev.* 11, 19–20 (1896) (emphasis added). Not surprisingly, given these views, Tiedeman was considered at the time as something of a skeptic of judging. See Alan H. Monroe, "The Supreme Court and the Constitution," 18 *Am. Pol. Sci. Rev.* 737, 745 (1924).

97. Christopher G. Tiedeman, "Dictum and Decision,"6 *Colum. L. Times* 35 (1892).

98. Max Radin, "The Theory of Judicial Decisions: Or How Judges Think,"11 *A.B.A.J.* 357, 362 (1925).

99. Karl N. Llewellyn, *The Bramble Bush: On Our Law and Its Study* (New York: Oceana 1951) 68.

100. Frederick Pollock, "The Science of Case Law," reprinted in Frederick Pollock, *Jurisprudence and Legal Essays* (New York: St. Martin's Press 1961) 170.

101. Id. 178.

102. Tiedeman, "Doctrine of Stare Decisis,"20.

103. Jerome Frank, *Law and the Modern Mind* (New York: Tudor 1936 [1930]) 125.

104. Karl Llewellyn, "Law and the Modern Mind: A Symposium,"31 *Colum. L. Rev.* 82, 83–84 (1931).

105. Frank, *Law and the Modern Mind*, 125.

106. Thomas M. Cooley, "Another View of Codification,"2 *Colum. Jurist* 466, 465 (1886).

107. Christopher Tiedeman, "Methods of Legal Education,"1 *Yale L.J.* 150, 152 (1892).

108. Llewellyn, *Bramble Bush*, 62.

109. Walter Wheeler Cook, "Book Review,"38 *Yale L.J.* 405, 406 (1929).

110. Seymour D. Thompson, "More Justice and Less Technicality,"23 *American L. Rev.* 22, 48 (1889).

111. Frank, *Law and the Modern Mind*, 148.

112. Llewellyn, *Bramble Bush*, 62.

113. Id. 71.

114. W. G. Hammond, "American Law Schools, Past and Future,"7 *Southern L. Rev.* 400, 412–13 (1881).

115. Munroe Smith, "State Statute and Common Law,"2 *Pol. Sci. Q.* 105, 121 (1887).

116. Llewellyn, *Bramble Bush*, 38.

117. Hammond, "American Law Schools," 412–13.

118. William O. Douglas, "Stare Decisis,"*Essays in Jurisprudence from the Columbia Law Review* (New York: Columbia Univ. Press 1963) 19, quoted in Wil-

fred E. Rumble, *American Legal Realism: Skepticism, Reform, and the Judicial Process* (Ithaca, N.Y.: Cornell Univ. Press 1968) 56.

119. Frank, *Law and the Modern Mind*, 101.

120. Id. 135.

121. Hammond, "American Law Schools,"412–13.

122. Christopher G. Tiedeman, "Silver Free Coinage and the Legal Tender Decisions,"9 *Annals of the American Academy of Political and Social Science* 198, 205 (1897).

123. Wilbur Larremore, "Judicial Legislation in New York,"14 *Yale L.J.* 312, 318 (1904).

124. John F. Dillon, *Law and Jurisprudence of England and America* (Boston: Little Brown 1894) 19.

125. Id. 13 n. 1.

126. Id. 19.

127. Radin, "Theory of Judicial Decisions,"357.

128. Id.

129. Id. 358.

130. Walter Wheeler Cook, "An Unpublished Chapter,"37 *Ill. L. Rev.* 418, 419 (1943).

131. Id. 421.

132. Id. 422.

133. Radin, "Theory of Judicial Decisions,"359.

134. See Herman Oliphant, "A Return to Stare Decisis,"14 *A.B.A.J.* 71 (1928).

135. See Leiter, *Naturalizing Jurisprudence*, 21–25.

136. James C. Carter, "The Provinces of the Written and Unwritten Law,"24 *American L. Rev.* 1, 15 (1890); see also James C. Carter, *Law: Its Origin, Growth and Function* (New York: De Capo Press 1974 [1907]) 69.

137. Carter, "Provinces of the Written and Unwritten Law,"15.

138. Id.

139. Carter, *Law*, 279.

140. Max Radin, "Legal Realism,"31 *Colum. L. Rev.* 824, 824 (1931).

141. Tiedeman, "The Doctrine of Stare Decisis,"19.

142. Tiedeman, "Dictum and Decision,"36.

143. Id. 35–36.

144. Coles, "Politics and the Supreme Court of the United States,"190.

145. Consistent with the argument here, Lewis Grossman recently argued that there are strong parallels between the work of James Carter and the legal realists. Lewis A. Grossman, "Langdell Upside-Down: James Coolidge Carter and the Anticlassical Jurisprudence of Anticodification,"19 *Yale J.L. & Human.* 149 (2007). There are important differences in our argument. Grossman links Carter's realism to his anticodification position, whereas I have linked it to the general position held by historical jurists. This matters because several historical jurists, most prominently John Dillon, advocated codification, but still held the same realist views. Another important difference is that Grossman continues to privilege the legal realists by calling Carter a "pre-realist," whereas I argue that realism about judging was in place before the legal realists.

146. See William P. LaPiana, "Jurisprudence of History and Truth,"23 *Rutgers L.J.* 519, 557 (1992). LaPiana recognizes that the historical jurists, Tiedeman especially, wrote things that were inconsistent with this proposition, although he asserts it nonetheless. My argument is that is it wrong to identify historical jurists with any version of formalism—unless one (arbitrarily) equates formalism with belief in liberty and the public-private distinction. In the latter usage, formalism amounts to a pejorative label applied to conservatives.

147. Leon Green, "My Philosophy of Law,"3 *Lawyers Guild Rev.* 10, 12 (1940).

148. Leon Green, "The Law Must Respond to the Environment,"47 *Texas L. Rev.* 1327 (1969).

149. Llewellyn, *Bramble Bush*, 59.

150. Id. 59–60.

151. Carter, *Law,* 129–30.

152. James C. Carter, "The Ideal and Actual in the Law,"24 *American L. Rev.* 752, 769 (1890).

153. Carter, *Law,* 327.

154. Carter, "Ideal and Actual in the Law,"773.

155. Carter, *Law,* 334.

156. Id. 335.

157. Dillon, *Law and Jurisprudence of England and America,* 13 n. 1.

158. Id. 381.

159. Tiedeman, "Doctrine of Stare Decisis,"19.

160. Llewellyn, "Some Realism about Realism,"1236.

161. Carter, "Ideal and Actual in the Law,"773.

162. Llewellyn, "Some Realism about Realism,"1236.

163. William G. Hammond, "The Legal Profession—Its Past—Its Present—Its Duty,"9 *W. Jurist* 1, 12 (1875).

164. Carter, "Ideal and Actual in the Law,"773.

165. Llewellyn, "Some Realism about Realism,"1236.

166. Id. 1237.

167. Carter, *Law,* 73.

168. Hammond, "The Legal Profession,"12.

169. Carter, *Law,* 329.

170. Frank, *Law and the Modern Mind,* 120.

171. Id. 281.

172. Dillon, *Law and Jurisprudence of England and America,* 19.

173. Benjamin N. Cardozo, *The Growth of the Law* (New Haven: Yale Univ. Press 1924) 103–4.

174. Frankfurter, "The Zeitgeist and the Judiciary,"7.

175. See Brian Z. Tamanaha, *A General Jurisprudence of Law and Society* (Oxford: Oxford Univ. Press 2001) 89–96.

176. See Clyde E. Jacobs, *Law Writers and the Courts: The Influence of Thomas M. Cooley, Christopher G. Tiedeman, and John F. Dillon upon American Constitutional Law* (Berkeley: Univ. Calif. Press 1954).

177. Quoted in Alan Jones, "Thomas M. Cooley and 'Laissez-Faire Constitutionalism': A Reconsideration,"53 *Am. J. Legal Hist.* 751, 753 (1967).

178. In addition their texts cited earlier, these various positions can be found in Morton Keller, *Affairs of State: Public Life in Late Nineteenth Century America* (Cambridge, Mass.: Harvard Univ. Press 1977) 187, 344–46, 400, 410, 452, 521. See Louise A. Halper, "Christopher G. Tiedeman, 'Laissez-Faire Constitutionalism' and the Dilemmas of Small-Scale Property in the Gilded Age,"51 *Ohio St. L.J.* 1349 (1990).

179. As Hull points out, none of the realists were political conservatives, though not all of them advocated political reform. Hull, *Roscoe Pound and Karl Llewellyn*, 203.

CHAPTER SIX
A RECONSTRUCTION OF LEGAL REALISM

1. See Albert H. Putney, "Five to Four Constitutional Law Decisions,"24 *Yale L.J.* (1914); Robert Eugene Cushman, "Constitutional Decisions by a Bare Majority of the Court," 19 *Mich. L. Rev.* 771 (1921).

2. Chief Justice Vaughan, *Bushell's Case*, 6 How. St. Tr. 999, 1006, 1012 (1670), quoted in Edmond Cahn, "Jurisprudence,"1952 *Ann. Surv. Am. L.* 765, 769 (1952).

3. Robert Rantoul, *Oration at Scituate* (1836), reprinted in Kermit L. Hall, William Wiecek, and Paul Finkelstein, eds., *American Legal History*, 2nd ed. (New York: Oxford Univ. Press 1996) 318.

4. C. S. Davies, "Constitutional Law,"46 *North American Rev.* 126, 153, 154 (1838).

5. Anonymous, "Political Regeneration,"11 *Am. Monthly Mag.* 297, 299 (1838).

6. Id. 300 (emphasis added).

7. See generally Michael Herz, "Rediscovering Francis Lieber: An Afterward and Introduction,"16 *Cardozo L. Rev.* 2135 (1995).

8. Francis Lieber, *Legal and Political Hermeneutics, or Principles of Interpretation and Construction in Law and Politics* (Boston: Little Brown 1839) 40.

9. Id. 230. This passage was taken from Greenleaf's "Introductory Lecture," published in 1 *Law Reporter* (1838).

10. Id. 236–37.

11. Paul D. Carrington, "William Gardiner Hammond and the Lieber Revival,"16 *Cardozo L. Rev.* 2135, 2144 (1995).

12. See M. H. Hoeflich and Ronald D. Rotunda, "Simon Greenleaf on Desuetude and Judge-Made Law: An Unpublished Letter to Francis Lieber,"10 *Const. Comment* 93, 94 n. 11, 101 n. 32.

13. Jerome Frank, *Law and the Modern Mind* (New York: Tudor 1936 [1930]) chaps. 13, 14.

14. Holmes, quoted in Louis Menand, *The Metaphysical Club: A Story of Ideas in America* (New York: Farrar, Straus 2001) 213.

15. *Baldwin v. Missouri*, 281 U.S. 586, 595 (1930) (Holmes, J., dissenting).

16. Id.

17. Frederick Schauer, *Playing by the Rules: A Philosophical Examination of Rule-Based Decision-Making in Law and in Life* (Oxford: Clarendon Press 1997) 192.

18. Karl Llewellyn, "On the Good, the True, the Beautiful in Law,"9 *U. Chi. L. Rev.* 224, 264 (1042).

19. Id. 250.

20. Eugene V. Rostow, "American Legal Realism and the Sense of the Profession,"34 *Rocky Mountain L. Rev.* 123, 132 (1961).

21. Jerome Frank, *Courts on Trial: Myth and Reality in American Justice* (Princeton: Princeton Univ. Press 1949) 2.

22. Most of the biographical details mentioned in this paragraph can be found in John Henry Schlegel, *American Legal Realism and Social Science* (Chapel Hill: Univ. of North Carolina Press 1995) 263–69.

23. See Karl Llewellyn, "On What Is Wrong with So-called Legal Education,"35 *Colum. L. Rev.* 651 (1935).

24. See Jerome Frank, "Why Not a Clinical Lawyer School?"81 *U. Pa. L. Rev.* 907 (1933).

25. Rostow, "American Legal Realism and the Sense of the Profession,"131.

26. Walter Wheeler Cook, "The Logical and Legal Basis of the Conflict of Law,"33 *Yale L.J.* 457, 487 (1924).

27. Walter Wheeler Cook, "Unpublished Chapter of the Logical and Legal Bases of the Conflict of Laws,"37 *Ill. L. Rev.* 418, 421 (1943).

28. Karl N. Llewellyn, *The Bramble Bush: On Our Law and Its Study* (New York: Oceana 1951) 73.

29. Karl Llewellyn, *The Common Law Tradition: Deciding Appeals* (Boston: Little Brown 1960) 45.

30. Id. 19–20.

31. Id. 20–21.

32. Id. 21–25.

33. Id. 26.

34. Id. 45–51.

35. Morris Cohen, "The Place of Logic in the Law,"29 *Harv. L. Rev.* 622, 638 (1916).

36. Herman Oliphant, "A Return to Stare Decisis,"14 *A.B.A.J.* 71, 159 (1928).

37. Felix S. Cohen, "Transcendental Knowledge and the Functional Approach,"35 *Colum. L. Rev.* 809, 843 (1935).

38. Id 845.

39. Id. 843.

40. Felix S. Cohen, "Field Theory and Judicial Logic,"59 *Yale L.J.* 238, 251 (1950).

41. Brian Leiter labels this the "Frankification of Realism"—the tendency to wrongly see realism in terms of Frank's unrepresentative position. Brian Leiter, *Naturalizing Jurisprudence: Essays on American Legal Realism and Naturalism in Legal Philosophy* (Oxford: Oxford Univ. Press 2007) 17.

42. Karl Llewellyn, "Some Realism about Realism—Responding to Dean Pound,"44 *Harv. L. Rev.* 1222, 1230 (1931).

43. Id. 1242–43.

44. Karl Llewellyn, "Law and the Modern Mind: A Symposium,"31 *Colum. L. Rev.* 82, 87 (1931).

45. Id.

46. Cohen, "Transcendental Nonsense,"849; Cohen, "Field Theory and Judicial Logic," 248.

47. Jerome Frank, *Law and the Modern Mind* (New York: Tudor 1936 [1930]) 131.

48. Id.

49. Frank, *Courts on Trial*, 286.

50. *In re J.P. Linahan, Inc.*, 138 F.2d 650, 652 (1943). Frank wrote the unanimous opinion for a three-judge panel, which included Judge Learned Hand, another judge with a realistic view of the law. Frank made the same point in a later publication: "It is well, too, that a judge be himself aware of his own human foibles and prejudices; he will then be better able to master them." Jerome Frank, "The Cult of the Robe," *Saturday Review of Literature,* October 13, 1945, 12.

51. Jerome Frank, "Cardozo and the Upper Court Myth,"13 *Law & Contemp. Probs.* 369, 373 (1948), citing a passage from Benjamin Cardozo, *The Growth of the Law* (New Haven: Yale Univ. Press 1924) 60.

52. Id.

53. See Jerome Frank, "Modern and Ancient Legal Pragmatism—John Dewey & Co. vs. Aristotle,"25 *Notre Dame Lawyer* 460 (1950).

54. William Twining, *Karl Llewellyn and the Realist Movement* (London: Weidenfeld and Nicholson 1973).

55. William Twining, "Talk about Realism,"60 *N.Y.U. L. Rev.* 329, 350 (1985).

56. Llewellyn, *Bramble Bush, 7.*

57. Id. 8–10.

58. Thurman Arnold, "Judge Jerome Frank,"24 *U. Chi. L. Rev.* 633, 635 (1957).

59. Id. 635.

60. Id.

61. A challenge to the credibility of this narrative can be found in William Novak, "The Myth of the Weak American State,"*Am. Hist. Rev.*, forthcoming.

62. Edward McWhinney, "Judge Jerome Frank and Legal Realism: An Appraisal,"3 *New York L. Forum* 113, 116.

63. Editor, 10 *Science* 2, 2 (1887).

64. Frederick N. Judson, "The Progress of the Law in the United States,"23 *Green Bag* 560, 560 (1911).

65. William B. Shaw, "Social and Economic Legislation of the States in 1890,"5 *Quar. J. of Econ.* 385, 385 (1891).

66. William B. Shaw, "Social and Economic Legislation of the States in 1891,"6 *Quar. J. of Econ.* 227, 232 (1892); William B. Shaw, "Social and Economic Legislation of the States in 1894," 9 *Quar. J. of Econ.* 195, 195 (1895).

67. Shaw, "Social and Economic Legislation of the States in 1891,"227.

68. William B. Shaw, "Social and Economic Legislation of the States in 1893,"8 *Quar. J. of Econ.* 230, 237 (1894).

69. Morton Keller, *Affairs of State: Public Life in Late Nineteenth Century America* (Cambridge, Mass.: Harvard Univ. Press 1977) 407.

70. Charles Warren, "A Bulwark to the State Police Power—The United States Supreme Court,"8 *Colum. L. Rev.* 667, 695 (1913).

71. Charles Warren, "The Progressiveness of the United States Supreme Court,"13 *Colum. L. Rev.* 294, 309 (1913).

72. *People v. Lochner,* 177 N.Y. 145 (1904).

73. A historical study confirms Warren's argument that a high proportion of state statues survived challenge. Michael J. Phillips, "The Progressiveness of the Lochner Court,"75 *Den. L. Rev.* 453 (1998).

74. Munroe Smith, "The Development of American Constitutional Law,"3 *Proc. of the Academy of Political Science* 52, 63 (1913).

75. Ernst Freund, "Constitutional Limitations and Labor Legislation,"4 *Ill. L. Rev.* 609, 610 (1910).

76. Id.

77. See Novak, "The Myth of the Weak American State." An superb account of this is Keller's *Affairs of State*. See Richard R. John, "Ruling Passions: Political Economy in Nineteenth-Century America," 18 *J. of Policy Hist.* 1 (2006) (noting that historians no longer accept the myth of nineteenth-century laissez-faire).

78. Christopher G. Tiedeman, "Dictum and Decision,"6 *Colum. L. Times* 35, 36 (1892) 36. In a convincing study that details the great amount of regulation in the early nineteenth century, much of it local, William Novak shows that the nineteenth century was not a golden age of laissez-faire, although this has often been repeated. William Novak, *The People's Welfare: Law and Regulation in the Nineteenth Century* (Chapel Hill: University of North Carolina Press 1996).

79. Joseph H. Beale, "The Development of Jurisprudence during the Past Century,"18 *Harv. L. Rev.* 271, 282 (1904).

80. See Sidney Webb, "The Difficulties of Individualism,"1 *Econ. J.* 360 (1891).

81. Thomas Whittaker, "Individualism and State Action,"13 *Mind* 52, 52 (1888).

82. Leonard C. Crouch, "Judicial Tendencies of the Court of Appeals during the Incumbency of Chief Judge Hiscock,"12 *Cornell L.Q.* 137, 147–52 (1927).

83. Letter from John Henry Wigmore to William Howard Taft, January 28, 1914, quoted and summarized in Daniel R. Ernst, "The Critical Tradition in the Writing of American Legal History,"102 *Yale L.J.* 1019, 1019–20 (1993).

84. Edwin R. Keedy, "The Decline of Traditionalism and Individualism,"65 *U. Pa. L. Rev.* 764, 764 (1917).

85. Id. 766.

86. Robert Eugene Cushman, "The Social and Economic Interpretation of the Fourteenth Amendment,"20 *Mich. L. Rev.* 737, 763 (1922).

87. Cardozo, *The Growth of the Law,* supra 127. Frederick Pollock also wrote that the law had begun to change in these respects in the late nineteenth century. See Frederick Pollock, *The Genius of the Common Law* (New York: AMS Press 1967 [1911]) chap. 7.

88. See William Draper Lewis, "Social Sciences as the Basis of Legal Education,"61 *U. Pa. L. Rev.* 531 (1913).

89. William Draper Lewis, "The Possibility of New Legal Observations,"45 *Am. L. Reg.* 1, 6 (1897).

90. LeBaron Colt, "Law and Reasonableness,"17 *American L. Rev.* 657, 674 (1903).

91. Id.

92. Id. 670, 673.

93. Id.

94. Charles F. Amidon, "The Nation and the Constitution,"19 *Green Bag* 594, 598 (1907).

95. Id. 599.

96. Id.

97. See, e.g., Ernst Freund, "Interpretation of Statutes,"*U. Pa. L. Rev.* 207, 215 (1917); Samuel Williston, "Change in the Law," 69 *U.S. L. Rev.* 237 (1935); John Henry Wigmore, "The Qualities of Current Judicial Decisions,"9 *Ill. L. Rev.* 529 (1915); John Henry Wigmore, "Problems of the Law's Evolution," 4 *Va. L. Rev.* 247 (1917); John Henry Wigmore, "Problems of the Law's Mechanism in America,"4 *Va. L. Rev.* 337 (1917); Harlan F. Stone, "Some Phases of Legal Education," 5 *Am. L. Sch. Rev.* 389 (1924); Harlan F. Stone, "Fifty Year's Work of the United States Supreme Court,"14 *A.B.A.J.* 428 (1928). See also Cardozo, *The Growth of the Law*, 14–16, noting the reformist work of several of these thinkers, and others.

98. Thomas C. Grey, "Modern American Legal Thought,"106 *Yale L.J.* 493, 499 (1996).

99. See Mark L. Movsesian, "Rediscovering Williston,"62 *Wash. & Lee L. Rev.* 207, 270–73 (2005) (revealing the pragmatic strains of Williston's position).

100. Samuel Williston, *Life and Law: An Autobiography* (Boston: Little Brown 1941) 214.

101. Id.

102. Id. 215.

103. William W. Fisher, Morton Horwitz, and Thomas A. Reed, *American Legal Realism* (New York: Oxford Univ. Press 1993) 51.

104. Pound to Llewellyn, April 9, 1931, quoted in N.E.H. Hull, *Roscoe Pound and Karl Llewellyn: Searching for an American Jurisprudence* (Chicago: Univ. Chicago Press 1997) 215.

105. Llewellyn, "Some Realism about Realism,"1234.

106. See G. Edward White, *Tort Law in America* (New York: Oxford Univ. Press 2003).

107. See Hull, *Roscoe Pound and Karl Llewellyn*, 345.

108. Llewellyn, "Some Realism about Realism,"1256.

109. See Edward A. Purcell, *The Crisis of Democratic Theory: Scientific Naturalism and the Problem of Value* (Lexington: Univ. of Kentucky Press 1973) chaps. 8 and 9.

110. See Brian Z. Tamanaha, *Law as a Means to an End: Threat to the Rule of Law* (New York: Cambridge Univ. Press 2006) chap. 4. This chapter describes the rise of realism and instrumental thinking about law. Although the general transformation toward an increasingly instrumental view of law took place,

the time frame of the analysis now appears to be incorrect, as I did not know at the time that realism was in place much earlier than I had identified.

111. See Hull, *Roscoe Pound and Karl Llewellyn*, 344.

112. See Robert M. Hutchins, "The Autobiography of an Ex-Law Student," 7 *Am. L. Sch. Rev.* 1051 (1934). Thurman Arnold also later expressed doubt about the fruits of the social science initiative, Arnold, "Judge Jerome Frank," 641–42.

113. See Lon Fuller, "American Legal Realism,"82 *U. Pa. L. Rev.* 429 (1934); John Dickinson, "Legal Rules: Their Function in the Process of Decision," 79 *U. Pa. L. Rev.* 833 (1931); John Dickinson, "The Problem of the Unprovided Case,"81 *U. Pa. L. Rev.* 115 (1932); Hermann Kantorowicz, "Some Rationalism about Realism," 43 *Yale L.J.* 1240 (1934).

114. Roscoe Pound, "The Call for a Realist Jurisprudence,"44 *Harv. L. Rev.* 697, 707 (1931).

115. Llewellyn, *Bramble Bush*, 7–10.

116. Another remarkable example of early realism about judging can be found in a 1812 work urging the reform of common law crimes, John Goodenow, *Historical Sketches of the Principles and Maxims of American Jurisprudence* (New York: Arno Press 1972 [1812]).

117. See Lawrence Friedman, *A History of American Law*, 2nd ed. (New York: Simon & Schuster 1985) part. 3.

118. See Tamanaha, *Law as a Means to an End*, chap. 5.

119. Id. chaps. 6 and 7.

120. Id. chaps. 10 and 13.

121. Lieber, *Legal and Political Hermeneutics*, 40.

122. See Tamanaha, *Law as a Means to an End*, chap. 10.

123. Arnold, "Judge Jerome Frank,"635.

CHAPTER SEVEN
THE SLANT IN THE "JUDICIAL POLITICS" FIELD

1. See Walter F. Murphy and C. Hermann Pritchett, *Courts, Judges, and Politics: An Introduction to the Judicial Process* (New York: Random House 1979 [1961]) chap. 1 "Political Jurisprudence."

2. Martin Shapiro, "Political Jurisprudence,"52 *Kentucky L.J.* 294, 296 (1964).

3. Nancy Maveety, "The Study of Judicial Behavior and the Discipline of Political Science," in Nancy Maveety, ed., *The Pioneers of Judicial Behavior* (Ann Arbor: Univ. Michigan Press 2003) 3. The more neutral label "law and courts" is also used, though "judicial politics" appears to be favored.

4. Barry Friedman, "Taking Law Seriously,"4 *Perspectives on Politics* 261, 262 (2006).

5. See Maveety, "The Study of Judicial Behavior and the Discipline of Political Science,"10, describing the claims of the quantitative research on judging.

6. Marc C. Miller, "Introduction: The Study of Judicial Politics," in Mark C. Miller, ed., *Exploring Judicial Politics* (New York: Oxford Univ. Press 2009) 4 .

7. Murphy and Pritchett, *Courts, Judges, and Politics*, 4–7.

8. Maveety, "The Study of Judicial Behavior and the Discipline of Political Science,"2.

9. Id.

10. Id. 8.

11. Charles Grove Haines, "General Observations on the Effects of Personal Political and Economic Influences in the Decisions of Judges,"17 *Ill. L. Rev.* 96 (1922) 97–98.

12. Haines referred mainly to a collection of the works by German "free legal decision" thinkers (with a contribution from Pound). See *Science of the Legal Method* (Boston: Boston Book 1917).

13. Robert Eugene Cushman, "The Social and Economic Interpretation of the Fourteenth Amendment,"20 *Mich. L. Rev.* 737, 741–43 (1922).

14. Id. 744 (emphasis added).

15. Id. 744 n. 21, quoting Roscoe Pound, "Courts and Legislation,"7 *Am. Pol. Sci. Rev.* 361, 364 (1913) (emphasis added).

16. Edward S. Corwin, "The Supreme Court and the Fourteenth Amendment,"7 *Mich. L. Rev.* 643, 643 (1909) (emphasis added).

17. Id. 659–72.

18. C. Herman Pritchett, "The Development of Judicial Research," in Joel B. Grossman and Joseph Tanenhaus, eds., *Frontiers of Judicial Research* (New York: John Wiley & Sons 1969) 27.

19. Id. 28.

20. Pritchett, "The Development of Judicial Research,"29.

21. Walter D. Coles, "Politics and the Supreme Court of the United States,"27 *American L. Rev.* 182, 207 (1893).

22. See Jeffrey A. Segal and Harold J. Spaeth, *The Supreme Court and the Attitudinal Model Revisited* (New York: Cambridge Univ. Press 2002).

23. Lee Epstein and Jeffrey A. Segal, *Advice and Consent* (New York: Oxford Univ. Press 2005) 135.

24. Pritchett, "The Development of Judicial Research,"29 (emphasis added).

25. Murphy and Pritchett, *Courts, Judges, and Politics,* 7 (emphasis added).

26. Karl Llewellyn, *The Common Law Tradition: Deciding Appeals* (Boston: Little Brown 1960) 3.

27. Jeffery A. Segal, Harold J. Spaeth, and Sara C. Benesh, *The Supreme Court in the American Legal System* (New York: Cambridge Univ. Press 2005) 16.

28. Id. 22.

29. Id. 21.

30. For a detailed account of these competing models, see Tracey E. George, "Developing a Positive Theory of Decision Making on the U.S. Court of Appeals,"58 *Ohio St. L.J.* 1635 (1998).

31. Jason J. Czarnezki and William K. Ford, "The Phantom of Philosophy? An Empirical Investigation of Legal Interpretation,"65 *Md. L. Rev.* 841, 843 (2006).

32. Lawrence Baum, "C. Herman Pritchett: Innovator with an Ambiguous Legacy," in Maveety, *Pioneers of Judicial Behavior*, 60.

33. Baum has reservations about the attitudinal model, so his characterizations of the models in the field do not fully match his own preferred approach.

See Lawrence Baum, *The Puzzle of Judicial Behavior* (Ann Arbor: Univ. of Michigan Press 1997).

34. Virginia Hettinger, Stefanie A. Lindquist, and Wendy L. Martinez, *Judging on a Collegial Court: Influences on Federal Appellate Court Decision Making* (Charlottesville: Univ. Virginia Press 2006) 31.

35. H. R. Glick, *Courts, Politics, and Justice* (New York: McGraw Hill 1983) 243.

36. Lee Epstein and Jack Knight, "Toward a Strategic Revolution in Judicial Politics: A Look Back, a Look Ahead,"53 *Pol. Research Q.* 625, 628 (2000).

37. James L. Gibson, "Judges' Role Orientations, Attitudes, and Decisions: An Interactive Model,"72 *Am. Pol. Sci. Rev.* 911, 912 (1978).

38. Lee Epstein and Jack Knight, *The Choices Justices Make* (Washington, D.C.: Congressional Quarterly Press 1998) xii.

39. James L. Gibson, "From Simplicity to Complexity: The Development of Theory in the Study of Judicial Behavior,"5 *Political Behavior* 7, 9 (1983).

40. Judicial politics scholars might assert that they know the attitudinal model is overly simplified, that of course judging is more complex; nonetheless, they would argue, it is still useful for the purposes of testing. My argument is that even as a simplified model it suffers from distortion.

41. Epstein and Knight, "Toward a Strategic Revolution in Judicial Politics,"652.

42. Id. 630.

43. See Lawrence Baum, *Courts and Their Audiences* (Princeton: Princeton Univ. Press 2006) 6. Baum is critical of the strategic model and notes that it need not be linked in this way to political preferences.

44. David E. Klein, *Making Law in the United States Court of Appeals* (New York: Cambridge Univ. Press 2002) 11–12 (emphasis added).

45. Frank B. Cross, "Political Science and the New Legal Realism: A Case of Unfortunate Interdisciplinary Ignorance,"92 *Nw. U. L. Rev.* 251, 326 (1997).

46. Klein, *Making Law in the United States Courts of Appeal*, 11–12.

47. Baum, *Courts and Their Audiences*, 7.

48. This reasoning is laid out in Baum, *The Puzzle of Judicial Behavior*, 119.

49. Baum notes that this view of judging is unrealistic, id. 14–21.

50. Id. 102.

51. Two political scientists have told me privately that quantitative scholars of judging are marginalized within political science, not the institutionalists. A recent collection, however, claims that "behavioralism became the dominant paradigm in both political science in general and in the specific study of judicial politics." Miller, "Introduction," 5. It is hard for an outsider to know which position is correct. What is clear is that within the subfield of quantitative studies the law has heretofore not been taken seriously.

52. A persistent critic of prevailing approaches is Howard Gillman, "What's Law Got to Do with It? Judicial Behavioralists Test the 'Legal Model' of Judicial Decision Making,"26 *Law & Social Inquiry* 465 (2001). For a collection about this work, see Howard Gillman and Cornel W. Clayton, eds., *Supreme Court Decision-Making: New Institutional Approaches* (Chicago: Univ. of Chicago Press 1999).

53. Maveety, "The Study of Judicial Behavior,"29 (emphasis added).

54. Until the past decade, researchers did not systematically test directly for adherence to precedent or other legal factors. See Gibson, "From Simplicity to Complexity."

55. Lee Epstein and Gary King, "The Rules of Inference,"69 *U. Chi. L. Rev.* 1, 10 (2002).

56. See P. Brace and M. G. Hall, "Studying Courts Comparatively: The View from the American States,"48 *Pol. Research Q.* 5 (1995); Donald R. Songer and Susan Haire, "Integrating Alternative Approaches to the Study of Judicial Voting: Obscenity Cases in the U.S. Courts of Appeals," 36 *Am. J. of Pol. Sci.* 963 (1992).

57. Shapiro, "Political Jurisprudence,"318.

58. See Miller, "Introduction,"5.

59. Epstein and Segal, *Advice and Consent*, 3.

60. C. Herman Pritchett, "Divisions of Opinion among Justices of the U.S. Supreme Court, 1939–1941,"35 *Am. Pol. Sci. Rev.* 890, 890 (1941) (emphasis added).

61. Epstein and Segal, *Advice and Consent*, 3 (emphasis added).

62. As a matter of standard practice, the authors use "justice" when they mean to refer only to the Supreme Court.

63. See Hettinger, Lindquist, and Martinek, *Judge on a Collegial Court*, 47.

64. Cass R. Sunstein, David Schkade, Lisa M. Ellman, and Andres Sawicki, *Are Judges Political* (Washington, D.C.: Brookings Inst. Press 2006) 5. Epstein and Segal cite an earlier version of this same study; *Advice and Consent*, 127 n. 12.

65. Epstein and Segal, *Advice and Consent*, 128.

66. Id. 129.

67. Martin Shapiro, "Judges as Liars,"17 *Harv. J. L. & Pub. Policy* 155, 155 (1994).

68. Id. 156.

69. Id. 155 nn. 3, 4. The first quote is from Antonin Scalia, "The Rule of Law as a Law of Rules,"56 *U. Chicago L. Rev.* 1175, 1176–77 (1989); the second quote is from *James B. Bean Distilling Co. v. Georgia*, 111 S.Ct. 2439, 2451 (1991) (Scalia, J., concurring).

70. Antonin Scalia, "Common Law Court in a Civil Law System," in Amy Gutmann, ed., *A Matter of Interpretation* (Princeton: Princeton Univ. Press 1997) 6, 9, 12.

71. Klein, *Making Law in the United States Court of Appeals*, 138.

72. Baum, *The Puzzle of Judicial Behavior*, 19.

73. Frank Cross, *Decision Making in the U.S. Courts of Appeal* (Stanford: Stanford Univ. Press 2007) 1477, 1465–67.

74. Richard Posner, *The Problems of Jurisprudence* (Cambridge, Mass.: Harvard Univ. Press 1990) 189.

75. Richard Posner, *How Judges Think* (Cambridge, Mass.: Harvard Univ. Press 2008) 2.

76. Walter V. Schaefer, "Precedent and Policy,"54 *U. Chi. L. Rev.* 3, 4–5 (1966). Although this was published in 1966, he gave the speech in 1955.

77. Id. 5.

78. John Dewey, "Logical Method and the Law,"10 *Cornell L.Q.* 17, 22 (1924).

79. Another early articulation of this distinction (though not citing Dewey) can be found in Karl Llewellyn, "Some Realism about Realism—Responding to Dean Pound,"44 *Harv. L. Rev.* 1222 (1931): "viewing them [opinions] no longer as mirroring the process of deciding cases, but rather as trained lawyers' arguments made by the judges (after the decision has been reached), intended to make the decision seem plausible, legally decent, regally right, to make it seem, indeed, legally inevitable." Id. 1238–39.

80. Schaefer, "Precedent and Policy,"9.

81. Benjamin N. Cardozo, *The Nature of the Judicial Process* (New Haven: Yale Univ. Press 1921) 112.

82. Id. 98–141.

83. Id. 105.

84. Id. 105–6.

85. Id. 108.

86. Id. 108–10.

87. Id. 110–11.

88. Id. 110.

89. Id. 106 (emphasis added).

90. Frank Harris Hiscock, "Progressiveness of New York Law,"9 *Cornell L.Q.* 371, 376 (1924).

91. Id 381.

92. Id. 374.

93. Irving Lehman, "The Influence of the Universities on Judicial Decisions,"10 *Cornell L.Q.* 1 (1924).

94. Id. 2–3.

95. Id. 6.

96. Id. 12.

97. Cuthbert W. Pound, "Constitutional Aspects of American Administrative Law,"9 *A.B.A.J.* 409, 411 (1923).

98. Cuthbert W. Pound, "Defective Law—Its Cause and Remedy,"*Bulletin*, New York State Bar Association, September 1929, 279, 281.

99. Id. 283.

100. Id. 282. Compare this with Llewellyn's statement: "What these officials [judges] do about disputes is, to my mind, the law itself." Karl N. Llewellyn, *The Bramble Bush: On Our Law and Its Study* (New York: Oceana 1951) 12.

101. Horace Stern, "Book Review,"51 *Harv. L. Rev.* 178, 179 (1937).

102. Id. 181.

103. See William E. Leuchtenburg, *The Supreme Court Reborn: The Constitutional Revolution in the Age of Roosevelt* (New York: Oxford Univ. Press 1995).

104. Bernard L. Shientag, *The Personality of the Judge (and the Part It Plays in the Administration of Justice)* (New York: Association of the Bar of the City of New York 1944) 73.

105. Id. 51.

106. Id. 56.

107. Amistead D. Dobie, "A Judge Judges Judges,"1951 *Wash. U.L.W.* 471, 480 (1951).

108. Id. 479.

109. Charles E. Wyzanski, "A Trial Judge's Freedom and Responsibility,"65 *Harv. L. Rev.* 1281, 1282 (1952).

110. Leon Yankwich, "The Art of Being a Judge,"105 *U. Pa. L. Rev.* 374, 375 (1957).

111. Id. 377.

112. Id. 377–78.

113. Id. 382.

114. Calvert Magruder, "The Trials and Tribulations of an Intermediate Appellate Court,"44 *Cornell L.Q.* 1, 5 (1958).

115. Id. 11.

116. Albert Tate, "The Judge as a Person,"19 *La. L. Rev.* 438 (1959).

117. Id. 439.

118. Albert Tate, " 'Policy' in Judicial Decisions,"20 *La. L. Rev.* 62, 62 (1959).

119. Tate, "The Judge as a Person,"440.

120. Id.

121. Tate, " 'Policy' in Judicial Decisions,"68.

122. Id. 69.

123. Henry J. Friendly, "Reactions of a Lawyer—Newly Become Judge,"71 *Yale L.J.* 218, 231 (1961).

124. Roger J. Traynor, "La Rude Vita, La Dolce Giustizia; Or Hard Cases Can Make Good Law,"29 *U. Chi. L. Rev.* 223 (1962). Traynor made similar statements in an earlier article, Roger Traynor, "Some Open Questions on the Work of State Appellate Courts," 24 *U. Chi. L. Rev.* 211 (1957).

125. Traynor, "Law Rude Vita, La Dolce Giustizia,"229–30.

126. Id. 224.

127. Id. 234.

128. Id.

129. Charles E. Clark, "The Limits of Judicial Objectivity,"12 *American L. Rev.* 1, 4 (1963).

130. Id. 12.

131. Id. 10.

132. Schaefer, "Precedent and Policy,"4.

133. Id.

134. Id. 7.

135. Id.

136. Id. 6.

137. Id. 12.

138. Id. 14.

139. Id. 22.

140. Pritchett, "The Development of Judicial Research,"31.

CHAPTER EIGHT
WHAT QUANTITATIVE STUDIES OF JUDGING HAVE FOUND

1. An excellent recent study demonstrates the effect of legal factors. See Michael A. Bailey and Forrest Maltzman, "Does Legal Doctrine Matter? Un-

packing Law and Policy Preferences on the U.S. Supreme Court,"102 *Am. Pol. Sci. Rev.* 369 (2008).

2. Id. 381; see also Mark J. Richards and Herbert Kritzer, "Jurisprudential Regimes in Supreme Court Decision Making,"96 *Am. Pol. Sci. Rev.* 305 (2002).

3. Richard A. Posner, "A Political Court,"119 *Harv. L. Rev.* 32 (2005).

4. A powerful argument that the Supreme Court has less of an impact than is typically thought can be found in Frederick Schauer, "Foreword: The Court's Agenda and the Nation's,"120 *Harv. L. Rev.* 4 (2006).

5. Frank Cross, *Decision Making in the U.S. Court of Appeals* (Stanford: Stanford Univ. Press 2007) 2.

6. Jeffery A. Segal, Harold J. Spaeth, and Sara C. Benesh, *The Supreme Court in the American Legal System* (New York: Cambridge Univ. Press 2005) 196.

7. Id. 171.

8. Cross, *Decision Making in the U.S Court of Appeals*, 2.

9. Daniel R. Pinello, "Linking Part to Judicial Ideology in American Courts: A Meta-Analysis,"20 *Just. Sys. J.* 219 (1999).

10. See Laura Langer, *Judicial Review in State Supreme Courts* (Albany: SUNY Press 2002).

11. Kenneth N. Vines, "The Judicial Role in the American States," in Joel B. Grossman and Joseph Tanenhaus, eds., *Frontiers of Judicial Research* (New York: John Wiley & Sons 1969) 474–77. Vines studied the high courts in Louisiana, Pennsylvania, Massachusetts, and New Jersey.

12. Id. 478–82.

13. Id. 481.

14. John T. Wold, "Political Orientations, Social Backgrounds, and Role Perceptions of State Supreme Court Judges,"27 *Western Pol. Q.* 239, 240 (1974). Wold studied the high courts in Delaware, Maryland, New York, and Virginia.

15. Id. 246–47.

16. Id. 240.

17. J. Woodford Howard, "Role Perceptions and Behavior in Three U.S. Courts of Appeals,"39 *J. of Politics* 916, 191 (1977).

18. Id. 920.

19. Id. 918.

20. Id. 924.

21. Id. 928.

22. Id. 930.

23. Id. 931–34.

24. Id. 937–38.

25. William Kitchen, *Federal District Judges* (Baltimore: Collage Press 1978), summarized in C. K. Rowland and Robert A. Carp, *Politics and Judgment in Federal District Courts* (Lawrence: Univ. Press of Kansas 1996) 6.

26. See John M. Scheb, Thomas, D. Ungs, and Allison L. Hayes, "Judicial Role Orientations, Attitudes and Decision Making: A Research Note,"42 *Western Pol. Q.* 427 (1989); James L. Gibson, "Judges' Role Orientations, Attitudes and Decisions: An Interactive Model," 72 *Am. Pol. Sci. Rev.* 911 (1978).

27. These results are tabulated in David E. Klein, *Making Law in the United States Court of Appeals* (New York: Cambridge Univ. Press 2002) 22.

28. Id. 40–41.

29. Id. 46.

30. Id. 81–85.

31. Id. 141.

32. Id. 141–42.

33. See Harry T. Edwards, "The Effects of Collegiality on Judicial Decision Making,"151 *U. Pa. L. Rev.* 1369 (2002); Harry T. Edwards, "Collegiality and Decision Making on the D.C. Circuit," 84 *Va. L. Rev.* 1335 (1999); Collins J. Seitz, "Collegiality and the Court of Appeals,"75 *Judicature* 26 (1991).

34. Virginia Hettinger, Stefanie A. Lindquist, and Wendy L. Martinek, *Judging on a Collegial Court: Influences on Federal Appellate Court Decision Making* (Charlottesville: Univ. Virginia Press 2006) 47.

35. Id. 63–64.

36. Id. 64. Chief judges, freshman judges, and district court judges sitting on a panel by designation are all less likely to dissent, although this did not show with respect to concurrences.

37. Id. 67.

38. Id. chap. 4. Klein's study also raised doubts about the applicability of the strategic model. Klein, *Making Law in the United States Courts of Appeals*, 127.

39. Id. 97.

40. Id. 91.

41. Id. 98–99, 117–19.

42. Id. 195.

43. One of the authors of this study also produced a recent study that showed there was some correlation between ideology and the rate of reversal. The authors suggest that this different finding is explained by the fact that the other study was limited only to civil rights cases, which perhaps have a greater ideological charge. Hettinger, Lindquist, and Martinek, *Judging on a Collegial Court*, 118. The other study is Susan B. Haire, Stephanie A. Lindquist, and Donald R. Songer, "Appellate Court Supervision in the Federal Judiciary: A Hierarchical Perspective,"37 *Law & Soc. Rev.* 143 (2003). A much less elaborate 1993 study of the D.C. Circuit, widely thought at the time to be a highly political court, also found that rates of reversal *did not* link up with ideology: Eva M. Rodriguez, "Report Card for Federal Trial Bench," *Legal Times*, 16, no. 22, October 18, 1993, 1.

44. Cross, *Decision Making in the U.S. Court of Appeals*, 38.

45. Id. 67.

46. Id. 103–8.

47. Id. 92.

48. Id. chap. 4.

49. Id. chap. 5.

50. Id. chap. 6.

51. Id. 228.

52. Id. 229.

53. Id.

54. Jason J. Czarnezki and William K. Ford, "The Phantom of Philosophy? An Empirical Investigation of Legal Interpretation,"65 *Md. L. Rev.* 841, 883 (2006).

55. See Donald R. Songer and Reginald S. Sheehan, "Supreme Court Impact on Compliance and Outcomes: Miranda and New York Times in the United States Court of Appeals,"43 *Western Pol. Q.* 297 (1990).

56. The Supreme Court did not review the determinations of state law in any of the 697 cases covered in the twenty-eight-year period examined in the study; see Donald R. Songer, Martha Humphries Ginn, and Tammy A. Sarver, "Do Judges Follow the Law When There Is No Fear of Reversal?"24 *Just. Sys. J.* 137, 142 (2003).

57. Id. 148–51.

58. Id. 151–54.

59. Robert A. Carp and C. K. Rowland, *Policymaking and Politics in the Federal District Courts* (Knoxville: Univ. of Tennessee Press 1983) chap. 7.

60. Id. 165.

61. C. K. Rowland and Robert A. Carp, *Politics and Judgment in Federal District Courts* (Lawrence: Univ. Press of Kansas 1996) 31–45.

62. Id. 49.

63. Id. chap. 6.

64. Id. 159.

65. Id. chap. 7.

66. See Charles A. Johnson, "Law, Politics, and Judicial Decision Making: Lower Federal Court Uses of Supreme Court Decisions,"21 *Law & Soc. Rev.* 325 (1987).

67. Orley Ashenfelter, Theodore Eisenberg, and Stewart J. Schwab, "Politics and the Judiciary: The Influence of Judicial Background on Case Outcomes,"24 *J. Leg. Stud.* 257, 281 (1995).

68. Joseph L. Smith, "Patterns and Consequences of Judicial Reversals: Theoretical Considerations and Data from a District Court,"27 *Just. Syst. J.* 29, 38 (2006).

69. Id. 37.

70. Id. 39–43.

71. Gregory C. Sisk and Michael Heise, "Judges and Ideology: Public and Academic Debates about Statistical Measures,"99 *Nw. U. L. Rev.* 743, 743 (2005); see also Pauline T. Kim, "Lower Court Discretion," 82 *N.Y.U.L. Rev.* 383 (2007).

72. See Richard L. Revesz, "Environmental Regulation, Ideology, and the D.C. Circuit,"83 *Va. L. Rev.* 1717 (1997); Kevin Clermont and Theodore Eisenberg, "Litigation Realities," 88 *Cornell L. Rev.* 19 (2002).

73. See Christina L. Boyd, Lee Epstein, and Andrew D. Marin, "Untangling the Causal Effects of Sex on Judging,"(2008), http://ssrn.com.abstract=1001748. See also Donald R. Songer, Sue Davis, and Susan Haire, "A Reappraisal of Diversification in the Federal Courts: Gender Effects in the Courts of Appeals," 56 *J. of Politics* 425 (1994), finding no gender effects in obscenity and search and seizure cases, but effects in employment discrimination cases.

74. See Adam B. Cox and Thomas J. Miles, "Judging the Voting Rights Act,"108 *Colum. L. Rev.* 1, 24 (2008). The authors also found that African Ameri-

can judges voted for liability at about twice the rate of white judges, but the sample of judges and cases was small. Id. 30.

75. Lawrence Baum suggests the same in *The Puzzle of Judicial Behavior* (Ann Arbor: Univ. of Michigan Press 1997) 8–11.

76. Revesz, "Environmental Regulation, Ideology, and the D.C. Circuit."

77. William S. Jordon, "Judges, Ideology, and Policy in the Administrative State: Lessons from a Decade of Hard Look Remands of EPA Rules,"53 *Admin. L. Rev.* 45 (2001).

78. A critical exploration of these issues is Harry T. Edwards and Michael A. Livermore, "Pitfalls of Empirical Studies That Attempt to Understand the Factors Affecting Appellate Decisionmaking,"*Duke Law Journal* (forthcoming).

79. An excellent elaboration of both problems can be found in Joshua B. Fischman and David S. Law, "What Is Judicial Ideology, and How Should We Measure It?"29 *Wash. U. J. Law & Policy* (forthcoming), http://ssrn.com/abstract=1121228.

80. See, e.g., Ashenfelter, Eisenberg, and Schwab, "Politics and the Judiciary,"273–74.

81. For the latest elaboration of this, see Lee Epstein, Andrew D. Martin, Jeffrey A. Segal, and Chad Westerland, "The Judicial Common Space,"23 *J. Law, Econ., & Org.* 303 (2007).

82. Several of these objections are elaborated in Edwards and Livermore, "Pitfalls of Empirical Studies That Attempt to Understand the Factors Affecting Appellate Decisionmaking."

83. See Anna Harvey, "What Makes a Judgment 'Liberal'? Coding Bias in the United States Supreme Court Judicial Database," June 15, 2008, http://ssrn.com/abstract=1120970.

84. In a recent study, William Landes and Richard Posner had to recode certain cases in the federal appellate court database. See William M. Landes and Richard A. Posner, "Rational Judicial Behavior: A Statistical Study," John M. Olin L. & Econ. Working Paper No. 404, 2008.

85. Fischman and Law, "What Is Judicial Ideology?"4.

86. Songer and Haire, "Integrating Alternative Approaches to the Study of Judicial Voting,"964.

87. See Patricia M. Wald, "Thoughts on Decisionmaking,"87 *W.Va. L. Rev.* 1, 10 (1984); Richard Posner, *How Judges Think* (Cambridge, Mass.: Harvard Univ. Press 2008) 51.

88. Jon O. Newman, "Between Legal Realism and Neutral Principles: The Legitimacy of Institutional Values,"72 *Cal. L. Rev.* 200, 204 n. 8 (1984).

89. Barry Friedman, "Taking Law Seriously,"4 *Perspectives on Politics* 261, 271 (2006).

90. Newman, "Between Legal Realism and Neutral Principles: The Legitimacy of Institutional Values,"204.

91. Alex Kozinski, "What I Ate for Breakfast and Other Mysteries of Judicial Decision Making,"26 *Loy.L.A.L. Rev.* 993, 994 (1992). Although Kozinski takes a hard line on strictly following the law when it is clear, he admits that on occasion his personal views have influenced his decisions. See Emily Bazelon,

"The Big Kozinski," *Legal Affairs*, http://www.legalaffairs.org/issues/January-February-2004/feature_bazelon.

92. Kozinski, "What I Ate for Breakfast and Other Mysteries of Judicial Decision Making,"996.

93. Id. 997.

94. Id.

95. Id.

96. Edwards, "The Effects of Collegiality on Judicial Decision Making,"1648.

97. Harry T. Edwards, "The Judicial Function and the Elusive Goal of Principled Decisionmaking,"1991 *Wisc. L. Rev.* 837, 854 (1991).

98. Patricia M. Wald, "A Response to Tiller and Cross,"99 *Colum L. Rev.* 235, 236 (1999) (emphasis added).

99. Id. 250.

100. Patricia M. Wald, "Some Thoughts on Judging as Gleaned from One Hundred Years of the Harvard Law Review and Other Great Books,"100 *Harv. L. Rev.* 887, 895 (1987).

101. Patricia M. Wald, "Changing Course: The Use of Precedent in the District of Columbia Circuit,"34 *Clev. St. L. Rev.* 477, 481 (1986).

102. Id. 490.

103. Patricia M. Wald, "Thoughts on Decisionmaking,"87 *W.Va. L. Rev.* 1, 12 (1984).

104. Newman, "Between Legal Realism and Neutral Principles,"204.

105. Kozinski, "What I Ate for Breakfast and Other Mysteries of Judicial Decisionmaking,"994, 997.

106. Wald, "A Response to Tiller and Cross,"236 n. 6.

107. Edwards, "The Judicial Function and the Elusive Goal of Principled Decisionmaking,"857.

108. Posner, *How Judges Think*, 51.

109. Id.

110. Id. 46.

111. See Stephen T. Ziliak and Deirdre N. McCloskey, *The Cult of Statistical Significance* (Ann Arbor: Univ. Mich. Press 2008) introduction.

112. See Id. introduction and chap. 3.

113. Id. 5.

114. The identification of the 1-in-20 figure as the threshold is arbitrary, initially proposed by a leading theorist as a "convenient" marking point for confidence in the result, which then became entrenched in statistical analysis. Id. 45–47.

115. Ziliak and McCloskey point out that the question of *whether* is rarely at issue in scientific inquires. Ziliak and McCloskey, *The Cult of Statistical Significance*, 50–53. This is one of those rare situations, but only because of the *false* story about formalist beliefs in mechanical judging. When this false story is exposed, the whether question immediately becomes a nonissue, as is almost always the case.

116. Hettinger, Lindquist, and Martinek, *Judging on a Collegial Court*, 16 (emphasis added).

117. Id. 65–66.

118. Id. 70 (emphasis added).

119. Id.

120. Id. 33.

121. Id. 110 (emphasis added).

122. Frank Cross's study of appellate court decision making is exemplary in addressing the actual significance of his findings in the context of the total body of judicial decisions.

123. Cass R. Sunstein, David Schkade, Lisa M. Ellman, and Andres Sawicki, *Are Judges Political* (Washington, D.C.: Brookings Inst. Press 2006) 11.

124. David A. Schkade and Cass Sunstein, "Judging by Where You Sit,"*New York Times*, June 11, 2003, A 31.

125. Id. 10–11.

126. Id.

127. Sunstein et al., *Are Judges Political?*, 155 n. 20.

128. See "U.S. Court, Judicial Business of the United States Courts, U.S. Courts of Appeals—Types of Opinions or Orders Filed in Cases Terminated on the Merits after Oral Argument of Submission on Briefs," http://www .uscourts.gov. Circuits vary in their publication rates, but the average of opinions *not* published for all federal circuits in 2000 was 79.8 percent; 2001, 80.4 percent; 2002, 80.5 percent; 2003, 79.9 percent; 2004, 81 percent; 2005, 81.6 percent; 2006, 84.1 percent; 2007, 83.5 percent.

129. Charles R. Wilson, "How Opinions Are Developed in the United States Court of Appeals for the Eleventh Circuit,"32 *Stetson L. Rev.* 247, 253–57 (2003); Segal, Spaeth, and Benesh, *The Supreme Court in the American Legal System*, 223–26.

130. Sunstein et al., *Are Judges Political?,* 18.

131. Wald, "A Response to Tiller and Cross,"246.

132. The data were taken from the Clerk's Office of the D.C. Circuit, reported in Edwards, "Effects of Collegiality on Judicial Decision Making,"1658.

133. Sunstein et al., *Are Judges Political?*, 11.

134. Id. 129.

135. See Sisk and Heise, *Judges and Ideology,* 578.

136. Sunstein et al., *Are Judges Political?*, 13.

137. Id. 12.

138. Id. 5.

139. Thomas J. Miles and Cass R. Sunstein, "The New Legal Realism,"11, http://ssrn.com/abstract_id=1070283.

140. See H.L.A. Hart, *The Concept of Law* (Oxford: Clarendon Press 1961) 135.

141. Alvin Rubin, "Views From the Lower Court,"23 *UCLS L. Rev.* 448, 453–454 (1976).

142. A study showing that ideological influences have a greater impact on judicial decision making in connection with standards than rules is Adam B. Cox and Thomas J. Miles, "Transformation of the Voting Rights Jurisprudence,"75 *U. Chi. L. Rev.* (forthcoming).

143. Wald, "A Response to Tiller and Cross,"237.

144. Id. 237.

145. Edwards, "The Judicial Function and the Elusive Goal of Principled Decisionmaking,"851.

146. A study that looked at these cases, finding no evidence that the political views of judges influenced outcomes, is Ashenfelter, Eisenberg, and Schwab, *Politics and the Judiciary*.

147. Posner, *How Judges Think*, 44–45.

148. *Bush v. Gore*, 531 U.S. 98 (2000).

149. See Stephen J. Ware, "Money, Politics and Judicial Decisions: A Case Study of Arbitration Law in Alabama,"15 *J.L. & Pol.* 645, 686 (1999).

150. Stanley Sporkin, quoted in Rodriquez, "Report Card for Federal Trial Bench,"19. Rodriquez suggests that Sporkin's view is shared by other district judges in this circuit. At the time, the D.C. Circuit was reputed to be the most politically infused federal appellate court.

151. Edwards, "The Effects of Collegiality on Judicial Decision Making,"1648.

152. See Nancy Scherer, *Scoring Points: Politicians, Activists, and the Lower Federal Court Appointment Process* (Stanford, Calif.: Stanford Univ. Press 2005) part 1.

153. For an overview of the literature on judicial appointments, see Brian Z. Tamanaha, *Law as a Means to an End: Threat to the Rule of Law* (Cambridge: Cambridge Univ. Press 2006) chap. 10.

154. See Scherer, *Scoring Points*.

155. Id. 194.

156. Cross, *Decision Making in the U.S. Court of Appeals*, 56.

157. Posner, *How Judges Think*, 21.

158. Id.

159. This extrapolation is made merely for the purposes of a simple illustration. Liberal judges also vote in a conservative direction more often than liberal, so the liberal vote would have to shift a greater amount in the liberal direction to reach as high as the current conservative vote.

160. See Tamanaha, *Law as a Means to an End*, 185–88.

161. See Wald, "A Response to Tiller and Cross"; Emerson H. Tiller and Frank B. Cross, "A Modest Reply to Judge Wald," 99 *Colum L. Rev.* 262 (1999); Richard L. Revesz, "Ideology, Collegiality, and the D.C. Circuit: A Reply to Chief Judge Harry T. Edwards,"85 *Va. L. Rev.* 805 (1999); Harry T. Edwards and Linda Elliott, "Beware of Numbers (and Unsupported Claims of Judicial Bias)," 80 *Wash. U. L.Q.* 723 (2002); Kevin M. Clermont and Theodore Eisenberg, "Judge Harry Edwards: A Case in Point!"80 *Wash. U. L.Q.* 1275 (2002).

162. Kozinski, "What I Ate for Breakfast and Other Mysteries of Judicial Decision Making,"999, 998.

163. Edwards, "The Judicial Function and the Elusive Goal of Principled Decisionmaking,"855.

CHAPTER NINE
THE EMPTINESS OF "FORMALISM" IN LEGAL THEORY

1. H.L.A. Hart, "Positivism and the Separation of Law and Morals,"71 *Harv. L. Rev.* 593, 610 (1958).

2. Id.

3. H.L.A. Hart, *The Concept of Law* (Oxford: Clarendon Press 1961) chap. 7.

4. Id. 249, note to p. 126.

5. Cass R. Sunstein, "Must Formalism Be Defended Empirically?"66 *U. Chi. L. Rev.* 636 (1999).

6. Richard H. Pildes, "Forms of Formalism,"66 *U. Chi. L. Rev.* 607, 608–9 (1999).

7. Brian Leiter, "Positivism, Formalism, Realism,"99 *Colum. L. Rev.* 1138, 1145–46 (1999).

8. Sunstein, "Must Formalism Be Defended Empirically?"638–39.

9. A leading source of the view that classical legal formalists thought this way is Thomas C. Grey, "Langdell's Orthodoxy,"45 *U. Pitt. L. Rev.* 1, 6–8 (1983). Previous chapters have argued that this is a problematic interpretation of Langdell, and, more importantly, that these views were not widely accepted.

10. Duncan Kennedy, *A Critique of Adjudication (fin de siècle)* (Cambridge, Mass.: Harvard Univ. Press 1997) 105.

11. See Brian Z. Tamanaha, *Law as a Means to an End: Threat to the Rule of Law* (New York: Cambridge Univ. Press 2006).

12. Duncan Kennedy, "Legal Formalism," in Neil J. Smelser and Paul B. Baltes, eds., *Encyclopedia of the Social & Behavioral Sciences*, vol. 13 (New York: Elsevier 2001) 8634.

13. Pildes, "Forms of Formalism,"607.

14. Frederick Schauer, "Formalism,"97 *Yale L.J.* 509, 510 (1988).

15. Id. 538.

16. Benjamin N. Cardozo, *The Nature of the Judicial Process* (New Haven: Yale Univ. Press 1921) 66 (emphasis added).

17. *Boumediene v. United States*, 128 S. Ct, 2229, 2267 (2008), (emphasis added). The court was quoting an earlier negative reference to the term in *Jones v. Cunningham*, 371 U.S. 236, 243 (1963).

18. A recent example of the difficulty of keeping apart an analysis of formalism as just meaning "rule bound" from the story about the classical legal formalists is Paul N. Cox, "An Interpretation and (Partial) Defense of Legal Formalism," 36 *Ind. L. Rev.* 57 (2003).

19. An entirely different approach to the topic is taken by Ernest Weinrib, who constructs "formalism" in terms of the immanent rationality of law. Ernest J. Weinrib, "Legal Formalism: On the Immanent Rationality of Law," 97 *Yale L.J.* 949 (1988); Ernest J. Weinrib, "The Jurisprudence of Legal Formalism,"16 *Harv. J.L. & Pub. Pol'y* 583 (1993). His theory has received little sustained attention from theorists and will not be discussed here. As Joseph Raz observed, Weinrib's position is better labeled "essentialist" than "formalist"; Weinrib chose the label formalism mainly for "the pleasure of casting himself in the devil's role." Joseph Raz, "Formalism and the Rule of Law," in Robert George, ed., *Natural Law Theory* (Oxford: Clarendon Press 1992) 336 n. 1.

20. Duncan Kennedy, "Legal Formality,"2 *J. Leg. Stud.* 351, 355–59 (1973).

21. Id. 356–57.

22. Id. 358.

23. Id. 359.

24. Id. 359.

25. Id. 378.

26. Id. 364.

27. Id. 370–75.

28. Id. 374.

29. Id. 377.

30. Another leading contributor to Critical Legal Studies, Roberto M. Unger, who also was influenced by Weber, set out a similar argument about the relationship between legal formalism and liberalism in Roberto M. Unger, *Knowledge and Politics* (New York: Free Press 1975).

31. John Manning, "Constitutional Structure and Statutory Formalism,"66 *U. Chi. L. Rev.* 685, 694 (1999).

32. See Brian Z. Tamanaha, *On the Rule of Law: History, Politics, Theory* (New York: Cambridge Univ. Press 2004) chap. 7.

33. Schauer, "Formalism,"510.

34. Id. 514, 535. Schauer adopts Hart's argument that rules have a core of certain meaning and a "penumbra of doubt," or fringe of vagueness or open texture. Hart, *The Concept of Law*, chap. 7, 119–20.

35. Schauer, "Formalism,"534–35.

36. Id. 534–35.

37. Id. 535.

38. Id. 538–44.

39. Frederick Schauer, *Playing by the Rules: A Philosophical Examination of Rule Based Decision Making in Law and Life* (Oxford: Clarendon Press 1991) 137–66.

40. Schauer, "Formalism,"544.

41. Id. 544.

42. Even a strict legal positivist view of law does not deny that judges consider social factors; legal positivism merely insists that these factors do not have "legal" status until they have been recognized by legal institutions.

43. A more extensive discussion of this can be found in Brian Z. Tamanaha, *Realistic Socio-Legal Theory: Pragmatism and a Social Theory of Law* (Oxford: Clarendon Press 1997) 236–40.

44. Philippe Nonet and Philip Selznick, *Law and Society in Transition: Toward Responsive Law* (New York: Octagon Books 1978).

45. Patrick S. Atiyah, "From Principles to Pragmatism: Changes in the Function of the Judicial Process and the Law,"65 *Iowa L. Rev.* 1249 (1980).

46. Roberto M. Unger, *Law in Modern Society* (New York: Free Press 1976) 192–200.

47. Abraham Chayes, "The Role of the Judge in Public Law Litigation,"89 *Harv. L. Rev.* 1281 (1976).

48. Id 1303.

49. In a superb overview and analysis of the relationship between rules and discretion, Carl E. Schneider persuasively argues that rules that do not allow some scope for judicial discretion are rare. Carl E. Schneider, "Discretion and Rules: A Lawyer's View," in Keith Hawkins, ed., *The Uses of Discretion* (Oxford: Clarendon Press 1992) 47–88.

50. H.L.A. Hart, "Positivism and the Separation of Law and Morals,"71 *Harv. L. Rev.* 593, 607 (1958).

51. Id. 607–8.

52. Hart, "Positivism and the Separation of Law and Morals,"606–8.

53. Lon L. Fuller, "Positivism and Fidelity to Law—A Reply to Professor Hart,"71 *Harv. L. Rev.* 630, 661–69 (1958).

54. Id. 663.

55. An excellent recent overview of this debate is Frederick Schauer, "A Critical Guide to Vehicles in the Park,"83 *NYU L. Rev.* 1109 (2008).

56. Hart, "Positivism and the Separation of Law and Morals,"610–11.

57. See http://dictionary.reference.com/browse/vehicle.

58. Hart, "Positivism and the Separation of Law and Morals,"607.

59. See Schauer, "A Critical Guide to Vehicles in the Park,"1129–31. Hart made this concession in H.L.A. Hart, *Essays in Jurisprudence and Philosophy* (Oxford: Clarendon Press 1983) 7–8.

60. Schauer, *Playing by the Rules*, 53–62.

61. Id. 54.

62. Id. 55 (emphasis added).

63. Id. 61.

64. A simple example: the phrase "I love football" evokes entirely different images depending upon one's community. Americans think of an oval-shaped ball with two pointed ends (a prolate spheroid) that is carried and thrown, while people from most of the rest of the world think of a round ball that is kicked.

65. Schauer, *Playing by the Rules*, 196–206.

66. Kennedy makes a variation of this point when he argues that judges are responsible for the decision even when they follow a rule or precedent because it was possible for them not to. Kennedy, "Legal Formality,"383–95.

67. Hart, *Concept of Law*, 136.

68. Schauer, "A Critical Guide to Vehicles in the Park,"1128.

69. Schauer, "Formalism,"538.

70. Hart, *Concept of Law*, 136.

71. The standard example is *Riggs v. Palmer*, 115 N.Y. 506 (1889), where the Court invoked a principle to defeat the literal application of a statute that would have allowed a murderer to inherit the estate of his victim.

72. Patricia Wald, "A Response to Tiller and Cross,"99 *Colum L. Rev.* 235, 36 (1999).

73. Frederick Schauer, "The Jurisprudence of Reasons,"85 *Mich. L. Rev.* 847, 847 (1987).

74. Id.

75. Schauer, *Playing by the Rules*, 196–206.

76. For a discussion of discretion in standards, see Hart, *Concept of Law*, 127–31.

77. 15 U.S.C. Section 1 (2006).

78. Kennedy, "Legal Formality,"356 n. 11.

79. Larry Alexander and Emily Sherwin, *The Rule of Rules: Morality, Rules, and the Dilemmas of Law* (Durham, N.C.: Duke Univ. Press 2001) 30.

80. Antonin Scalia, "The Rule of Law as a Law of Rules,"56 *U. Chi. L. Rev.* 1175, 1186–87 (1989).

81. See Larry Alexander, " 'With Me, It's All or Nuthin': Formalism in Law and Morality,"66 *U. Chi. L. Rev.* 530, 542–46 (1999) (standards not rule-like).

82. Standards can become more rule-like if they are interpreted in a way that narrows down the considerations. Frederick Schauer, "The Failure of the Common Law,"36 *Ariz. St. L.J.* 765 (2004); Frederick Schauer, "The Convergence of Rules and Standards," 2003 *N.Z.L. Rev.* 303 (2003).

83. Schauer, *Playing by the Rules,* 177; see also Frederick Schauer, "Is the Common Law Law?"77 *Cal. L. Rev.* 455 (1989).

84. Schauer, *Playing by the Rules,* 180–81.

85. Id. 174–81.

86. Antonin Scalia, "Common Law Courts in a Civil Law System," in Amy Gutmann, ed., *A Matter of Interpretation* (Princeton: Princeton Univ. Press 1997) 13.

87. For a discussion of this, see Schauer, "Formalism,"535–38.

88. See Melvin A. Eisenberg, *The Nature of the Common Law* (Cambridge, Mass.: Harvard Univ. Press 1988).

89. Cardozo, *The Nature of the Judicial Process,* 67.

90. Edward Levi, *An Introduction to Legal Reasoning* (Chicago: Univ. of Chicago Press 1949) 4.

91. See Ronald Dworkin, *Law's Empire* (Cambridge, Mass.: Harvard Univ. Press 1986).

92. See Scalia, "Common Law Court in a Civil Law System."

93. See Antonin Scalia, "The Rule of Law as a Law of Rules,"56 *U. Chi. Rev.* 1175 (1989).

94. Id. 537.

95. Alexander, "With Me, It's All or Nuthin',"531 n. 2.

96. Sunstein, "Must Formalism Be Defended Empirically?"638.

97. Adrian Vermeule, *Judging under Uncertainty: An Institutional Theory of Judging* (Cambridge, Mass.: Harvard Univ. Press 2006) 5.

98. Scalia, "Common Law Court in a Civil Law System,"25.

99. Sunstein, "Must Formalism Be Defended Empirically?"636.

100. Alexander, "With Me, It's All or Nuthin',"554.

101. Schauer, *Playing by the Rules,* 170, 214.

102. The term "formal rules" is used once, but with no additional meaning beyond just "rules." Alexander and Sherwin, *The Rule of Rules,* 168.

103. Although Scalia and Easterbrook have been labeled formalists by others, neither identify themselves as "formalists."

104. Frank H. Easterbrook, "Text, History, and Structure in Statutory Interpretation,"17 *Harv. J.L. & Pub. Pol'y* 61, 67–68 (1994).

105. Id. 61.

106. John Manning, "Constitutional Structure and Statutory Formalism,"66 *U. Chi. L. Rev.* 685, 685 (1999).

107. Id. 688.

108. Id. 688–89.

109. Id. Id. 693.

110. Id.

111. Lawrence B. Solum, "The Supreme Court in Bondage: Formalism and the Future of Unenumerated Rights,"9 *U. Pa. J. Const. L.* 155, 177–72 (2006).

112. Id. 173.

113. Id. 173–74.

114. Id. 174.

115. Id. 175.

116. Id. 169–70.

117. See Robert E. Scott, "The Case for Formalism in Relational Contract,"94 *Nw. U. L. Rev.* 847 (2000).

Chapter Ten
Beyond the Formalist-Realist Divide

1. Richard Posner, *How Judges Think* (Cambridge, Mass.: Harvard Univ. Press 2008) 7. For another recent attack against formalism by a judge, see E. W. Thomas, *The Judicial Process: Realism, Pragmatism, Practical Reasoning and Principles* (Cambridge: Cambridge Univ. Press 2005) ("It is the lingering judicial commitment to formalism that explains why so much judicial reasoning is still legalistic, strained, or mechanical." Id. xix).

2. Posner, *How Judges Think*, 7–8. There is no question that Posner means formalism when he says legalism. At the end of this passage, Posner quotes a summary description of the "legal formalists" by Thomas C. Grey, "Judicial Review and Legal Pragmatism," 38 *Wake Forest L. Rev.* 473, 478 (2003). In the index to his book, the "Formalism" entry says "See Legalism."

3. Richard Posner, *Overcoming Law* (Cambridge, Mass.: Harvard Univ. Press 1995) 17.

4. Posner, *How Judges Think*, 8 n. 16.

5. Antonin Scalia, "Common Law Courts in a Civil Law System: The Role of United States Federal Courts in Interpreting the Constitutional and Law," in Amy Gutmann, ed., *A Matter of Interpretation* (Princeton: Princeton Univ. Press 1997) 6, 9, 12.

6. Id. 12.

7. Antonin Scalia, "The Rule of Law as a Law of Rules,"*U. Chi. L. Rev.* 1175 (1989).

8. Id. 1187.

9. Posner, *How Judges Think*, chap. 1.

10. Id. chap. 8, especially 219–21.

11. Id. 377.

12. Id. 42.

13. Id.

14. Id. 41.

15. At the end of the final sentence quoted, Poser cites my *Law as a Means to an End: Threat to the Rule of Law* (New York: Cambridge Univ. Press 2006) 227–31 (2006), and "How an Instrumental View of Law Corrodes the Rule of Law,"56 *DePaul L. Rev.* 469 (2007).

16. See Tamanaha, *Law as a Means to an End*, chap. 13.

17. Frank H. Easterbrook, "Text, History, and Structure in Statutory Interpretation,"17 *Harv. J.L. & Pub. Pol'y* 61, 64 (1994).

18. Id. 62–64.

19. See id. 61, 64, 67–68.

20. Posner, *How Judges Think*, 2.

21. Id. 9.

22. Id. 11.

23. Id. 369.

24. Mark Kessler, "Review of How Judges Think," *Law and Politics Book Review*, http://www.bsos.umd.edu/gvpt/lpbr/reviews/2008/08/how-judges-think.html.

25. Posner, *How Judges Think*, 369.

26. Irving Lehman, "The Influence of the Universities on Judicial Decisions,"10 *Cornell L.Q.* 1 (1924).

27. Id. 6.

28. Patricia Wald, "A Response to Tiller and Cross,"99 *Colum L. Rev.* 235, 236 (1999) (emphasis added).

29. Id. 370 (emphasis added).

30. Richard A. Posner, *The Problematics of Moral and Legal Theory* (Cambridge, Mass.: Harvard Univ. Press 1999) 209.

31. Posner, *How Judges Think*,. 45, 61, 71, 125, 145.

32. Id. 61, 71.

33. Id. 112.

34. Id. 213.

35. Id. 15.

36. Id. 11, 82.

37. Id. 46.

38. Id. 76, 373.

39. Id. 44–45.

40. See Tamanaha, *Law as a Means to an End*, chap. 13.

41. Posner, *How Judges Think*, 253.

42. Posner, *Problematics of Moral and Legal Theory*, 241.

43. Posner, *How Judges Think*, 253.

44. Id. 47, identifying Tamanaha.

45. Ronald Dworkin, *Justice in Robes* (Cambridge, Mass.: Harvard Univ. Press 2006) 41–43.

46. Posner, *How Judges Think*, 240, 253.

47. Id. 334.

48. Richard A. Posner, *Law, Pragmatism, and Democracy* (Cambridge, Mass.: Harvard Univ. Press 2003) 64.

49. Dworkin, *Justice in Robes*, 84–104; Tamanaha, *Law as a Means to an End*, chap. 13.

50. Duncan Kennedy, *A Critique of Adjudication (fin de siècle)* (Cambridge, Mass.: Harvard Univ. Press (1997) 275.

51. See generally Gregory L. Murphy, *The Big Book of Concepts* (Cambridge, Mass.: MIT Press 2002).

52. A large body of psychological research shows that perception, actions, and decisions are influenced by subconscious processes. See John A. Bargh and Tanya L. Chartrand, "The Unbearable Automaticity of Being,"54 *American Psychologist* 462 (1999); Jonathan Haidt, "The Emotional Dog and Its Rational Tail: A Social Intuitionist Approach to Moral Judgment," 108 *Psychological Rev.* 814 (2001).

53. See Alfred Schutz, *The Problem of Social Reality* (The Hague: Martinus Nijhoff 1962); Alfred Schutz, *The Phenomenology of the Social World* (Evanston, Ill.: Northwestern Univ. Press 1967); George Herbert Mead, *Mind, Self, and Society* (Chicago: Univ. of Chicago Press 1934).

54. For an excellent exploration of the effect of cognitive framing (what they call "value-motivated cognition"), see Dan M. Kahan, David A. Hoffman, and Donald Braman, "Whose Eyes Are You Going to Believe? *Scott v. Harris* and the Perils of Cognitive Illiberalism," 122 *Harv. L. Rev.* 837 (2009).

55. An account of this is contained in Brian Z. Tamanaha, *Realistic Socio-Legal Theory: Pragmatism and a Society Theory of Law* (Oxford: Clarendon Press 1997).

56. See Charles R. Lawrence, "The Id, the Ego and Equal Protection; Reckoning with Racism,"39 *Stan. L. Rev.* 317 (1987).

57. See Kahan, Hoffman, and Braman, "Whose Eyes Are You Going to Believe."

58. See Bargh and Chartrand, "The Unbearable Automaticity of Being,"473–76; Haidt, "The Emotional Dog and Its Rational Tail," 820, 822.

59. For a more elaborate discussion of the differences between these modes of decision making and their implications, see Tamanaha, *Law as a Means to an End*, 241–45.

60. See Tamanaha, *Realistic Socio-Legal Theory*, 240–42.

61. Duncan Kennedy, "Legal Formality,"2 *J. Leg. Stud.* 351, 376 n. 41 (1973).

62. For a thoughtful exploration of these issues, see Douglas Edlin, *Judges and Unjust Laws: Common Law Constitutionalism and the Foundations of Judicial Review* (Ann Arbor: Univ. of Michigan Press 2008). Edlin takes the position that judges should not follow an unjust law.

63. An avowed "formalist," Judge Alex Kozinski, admitted in an interview that he would not have applied procedural bars in a death penalty case if he thought the defendant was innocent, and he admitted that in a case he was moved by compassion to depart from what the mandatory sentencing rules required. See Emily Bazelon, "The Big Kozinski," *Legal Affairs*, http://www.legalaffairs.org/issues/January-February-2004/featyure-bazelon.

64. A superb exploration of the penetration of the common law by social views is Melvin Aron Eisenberg, *The Nature of the Common Law* (Cambridge, Mass.: Harvard Univ. Press 1988).

65. Karl Llewellyn, *The Common Law Tradition: Deciding Appeals* (Boston: Little Brown 1961) 19.

66. See Lawrence Baum, *Judges and Their Audiences* (Princeton: Princeton Univ. Press 2006) chap. 4, especially 53–57.

67. See Benjamin N. Cardozo, *The Nature of the Judicial Process* (New Haven: Yale Univ. Press 1921) 177–78; Harry T. Edwards, "The Effects of Collegiality on Judicial Decision Making,"151 *U. Pa. L. Rev.* 1369 (2002).

68. See Tamanaha, *Realistic Socio-Legal Theory,* chap. 8.

69. See Lawrence B. Solum, "Equity and the Rule of Law," in Ian Shapiro, ed., *The Rule of Law* (New York: NYU Press 1994) 120–47.

70. See Posner, *How Judges Think,* 270–72, 299.

71. See Pitman B. Potter, "The Chinese Legal System: Continuing Commitment to the Primacy of State Power,"159 *China Law Quarterly.* 673–83 (Sept. 1999).

72. See generally Rafael La Porta, Florencio Lopez-de-Silanes, Cristian Pop-Eleches, and Andrei Shleifer, "Judicial Checks and Balances,"112 *J. of Pol. Econ.* 445 (2004).

73. For a candid account, see Stephen Breyer, *Active Liberty: Interpreting Our Democratic Constitution* (New York: Knopf 2005).

74. Posner, *How Judges Think,* 50.

75. See Michael A. Bailey and Forrest Matlzman, "Does Legal Doctrine Matter? Unpacking Law and Policy Preferences on the U.S. Supreme Court,"102 *Am. Pol. Sci. Rev.* 369 (2008); Mark Richards and Herbert Kritzer, "Jurisprudential Regimes in Supreme Court Decision Making," 96 *Am. Pol. Sci. Rev.* 305 (2002).

AFTERWORD

1. The classic account of this set forth in Thomas Kuhn, *Structure of Scientific Revolutions* (Chicago: University of Chicago Press 1962).

INDEX

○ ○ ● ● ●